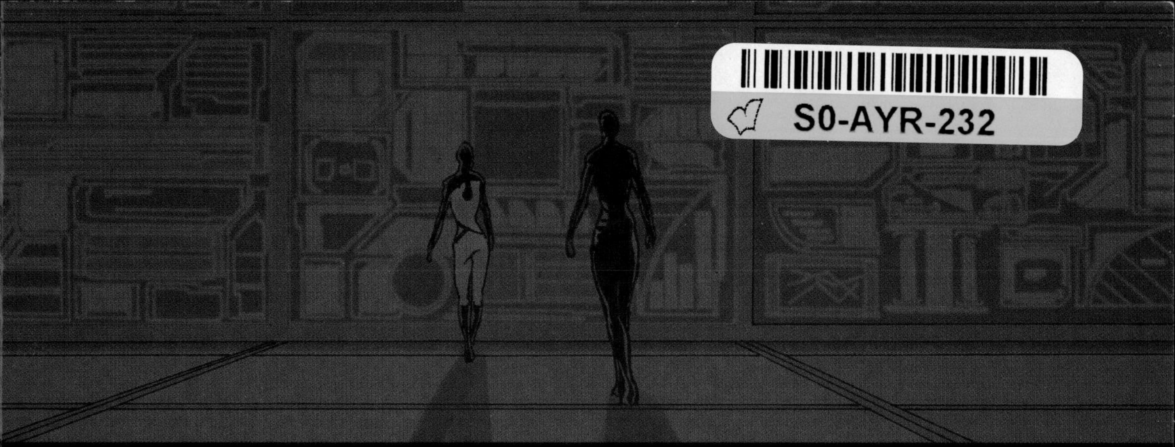

MASS EFFECT™

FOUNDATION

VOLUME 2

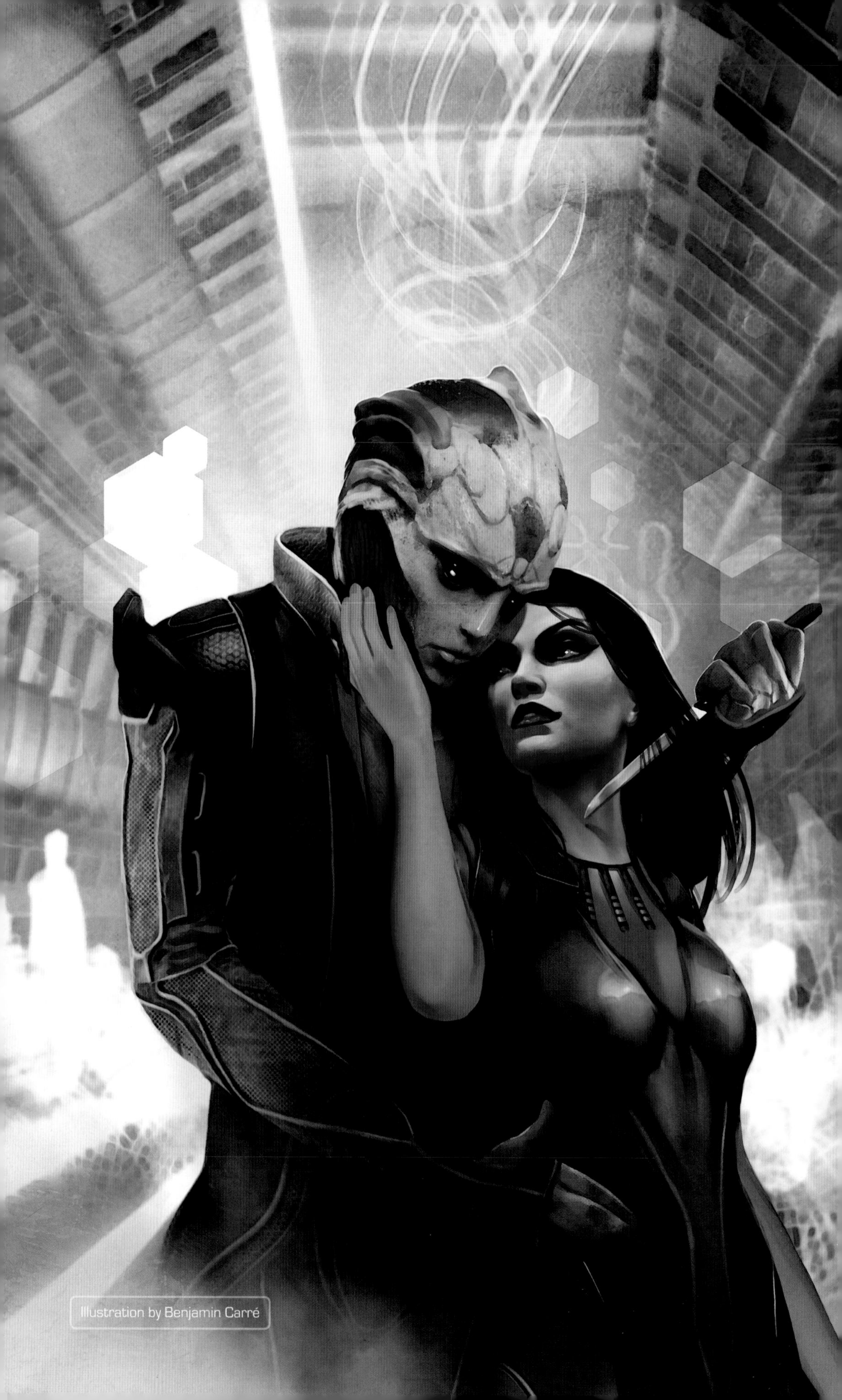
Illustration by Benjamin Carré

MASS EFFECT
FOUNDATION

VOLUME 2

STORY
MAC WALTERS

PENCILS
MATTHEW CLARK   **GARRY BROWN**   **TONY PARKER**
(pages 7–50)   (pages 51–72)   (pages 73–94)

INKS
DREW GERACI   **SEAN PARSONS**   **GARRY BROWN**   **TONY PARKER**
(pages 7–28)   (pages 29–50)   (pages 51–72)   (pages 73–94)

COLORS   LETTERING
MICHAEL ATIYEH   **MICHAEL HEISLER**

DARK HORSE BOOKS

PUBLISHER
MIKE RICHARDSON

COLLECTION DESIGNER
SANDY TANAKA

ASSISTANT EDITORS
SHANTEL LaROCQUE, ROXY POLK, IAN TUCKER, AND **AARON WALKER**

EDITOR
DAVE MARSHALL

MASS EFFECT: FOUNDATION Volume 2

This volume collects issues #5–#8 of the Dark Horse comic-book series *Mass Effect: Foundation*, a short story from
Free Comic Book Day 2013, and the one-shot *Mass Effect: Blasto—Eternity Is Forever.*

Special thanks to BioWare, including:
Derek Watts, Art Director • Casey Hudson, Executive Producer • Aaryn Flynn, Studio GM,
BioWare Edmonton • Ray Muzyka and Greg Zeschuk, BioWare Co-Founders

Published by Dark Horse Books
A division of Dark Horse Comics, Inc.
10956 SE Main Street, Milwaukie, OR 97222

DarkHorse.com MassEffect.com

International Licensing: (503) 905-2377
To find a comics shop in your area, call the Comic Shop Locator Service toll-free at 1-888-266-4226.

First edition: June 2014
ISBN 978-1-61655-349-4
10 9 8 7 6 5 4 3 2 1
Printed in China

NEIL HANKERSON Executive Vice President TOM WEDDLE Chief Financial Officer RANDY STRADLEY Vice President
of Publishing MICHAEL MARTENS Vice President of Book Trade Sales ANITA NELSON Vice President of Business
Affairs SCOTT ALLIE Editor in Chief MATT PARKINSON Vice President of Marketing DAVID SCROGGY Vice President
of Product Development DALE LaFOUNTAIN Vice President of Information Technology DARLENE VOGEL Senior Director
of Print, Design, and Production KEN LIZZI General Counsel DAVEY ESTRADA Editorial Director CHRIS WARNER
Senior Books Editor DIANA SCHUTZ Executive Editor CARY GRAZZINI Director of Print and Development LIA
RIBACCHI Art Director CARA NIECE Director of Scheduling TIM WIESCH Director of International Licensing MARK
BERNARDI Director of Digital Publishing

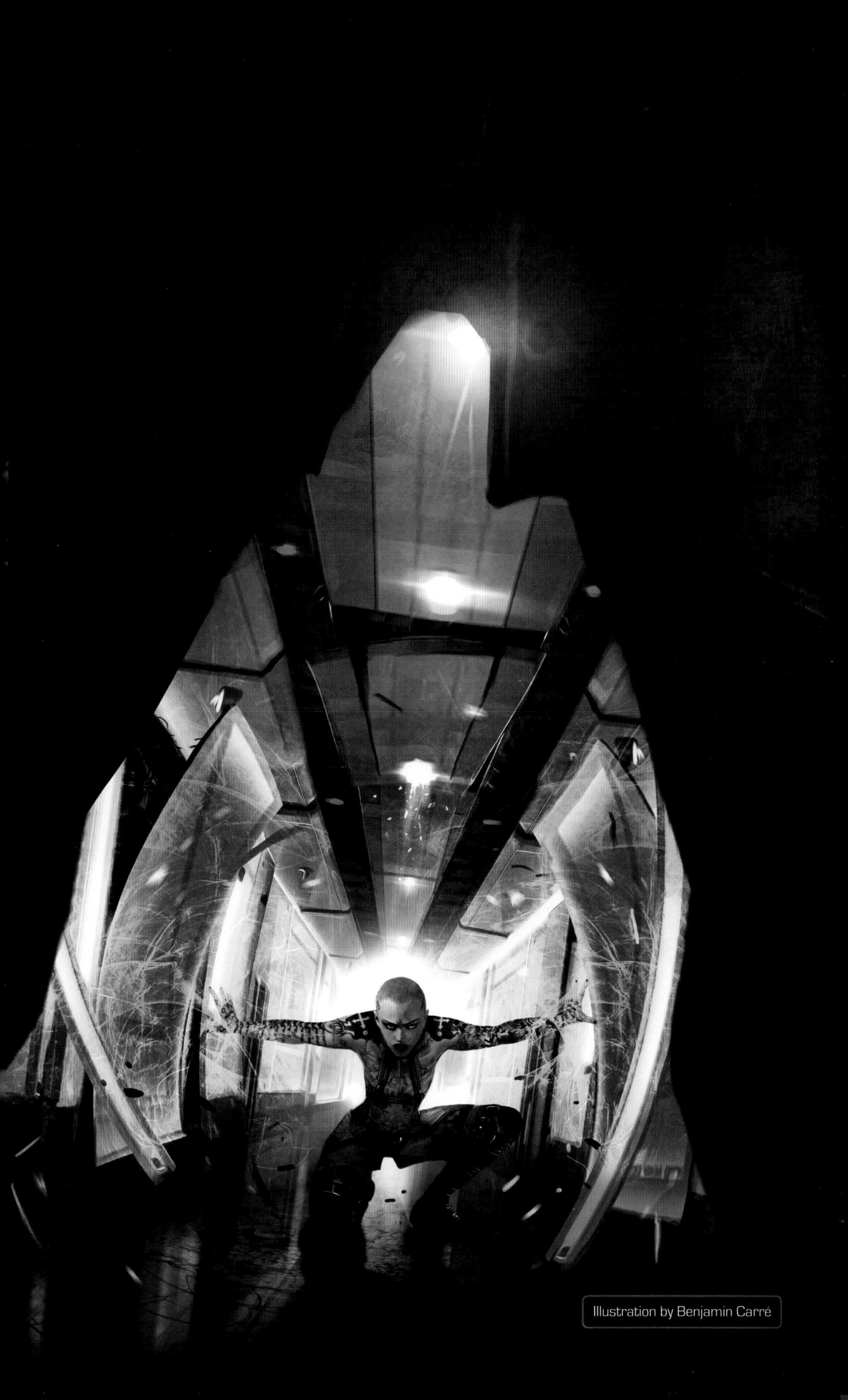

Illustration by Benjamin Carré

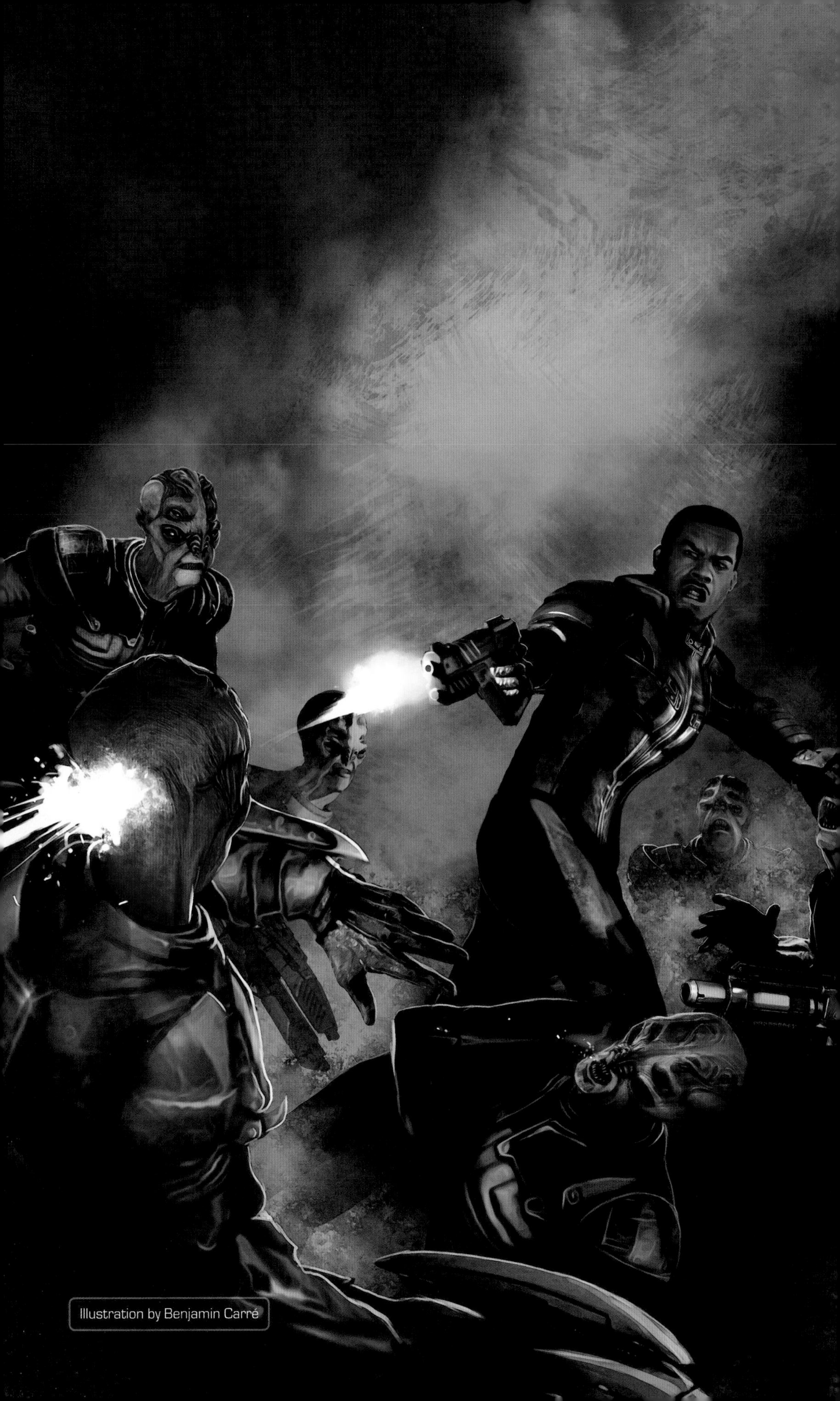

Illustration by Benjamin Carré

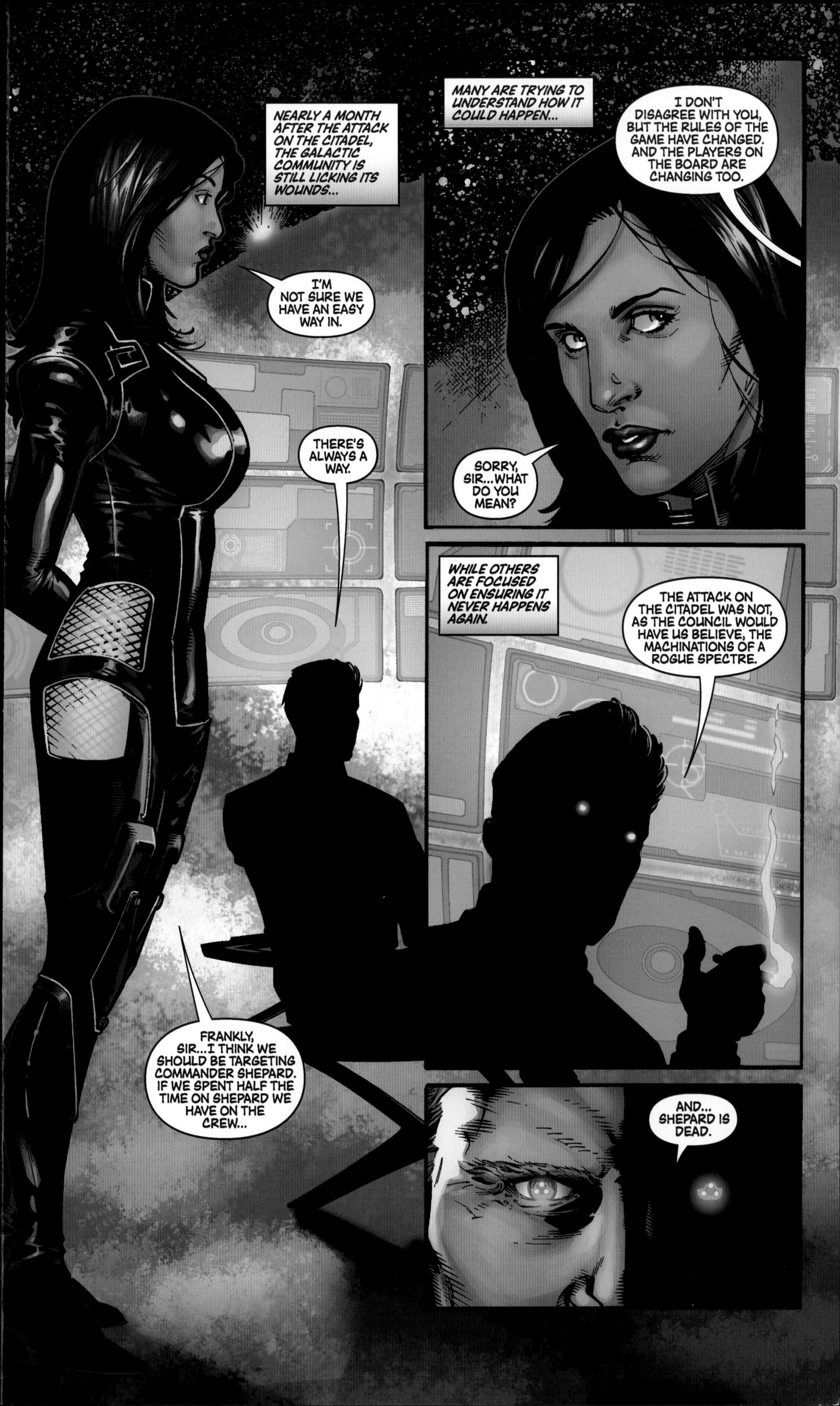

NEARLY A MONTH AFTER THE ATTACK ON THE CITADEL, THE GALACTIC COMMUNITY IS STILL LICKING ITS WOUNDS...
I'M NOT SURE WE HAVE AN EASY WAY IN.
THERE'S ALWAYS A WAY.
MANY ARE TRYING TO UNDERSTAND HOW IT COULD HAPPEN...
I DON'T DISAGREE WITH YOU, BUT THE RULES OF THE GAME HAVE CHANGED. AND THE PLAYERS ON THE BOARD ARE CHANGING TOO.
SORRY, SIR...WHAT DO YOU MEAN?
WHILE OTHERS ARE FOCUSED ON ENSURING IT NEVER HAPPENS AGAIN.
THE ATTACK ON THE CITADEL WAS NOT, AS THE COUNCIL WOULD HAVE US BELIEVE, THE MACHINATIONS OF A ROGUE SPECTRE.
FRANKLY, SIR...I THINK WE SHOULD BE TARGETING COMMANDER SHEPARD. IF WE SPENT HALF THE TIME ON SHEPARD WE HAVE ON THE CREW...
AND... SHEPARD IS DEAD.

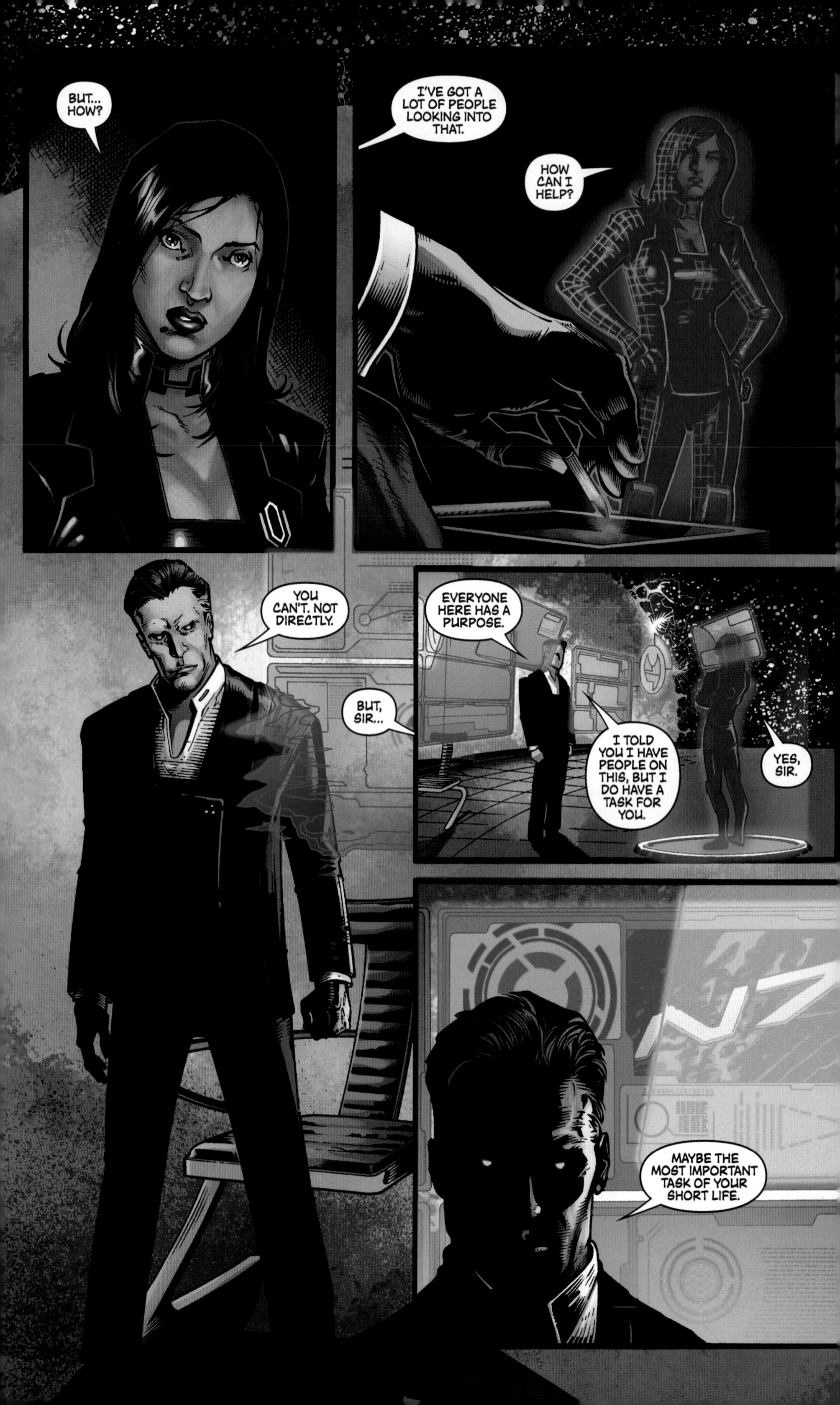
BUT... HOW?
I'VE GOT A LOT OF PEOPLE LOOKING INTO THAT.
HOW CAN I HELP?
YOU CAN'T. NOT DIRECTLY.
BUT, SIR...
EVERYONE HERE HAS A PURPOSE.
I TOLD YOU I HAVE PEOPLE ON THIS, BUT I DO HAVE A TASK FOR YOU.
YES, SIR.
MAYBE THE MOST IMPORTANT TASK OF YOUR SHORT LIFE.

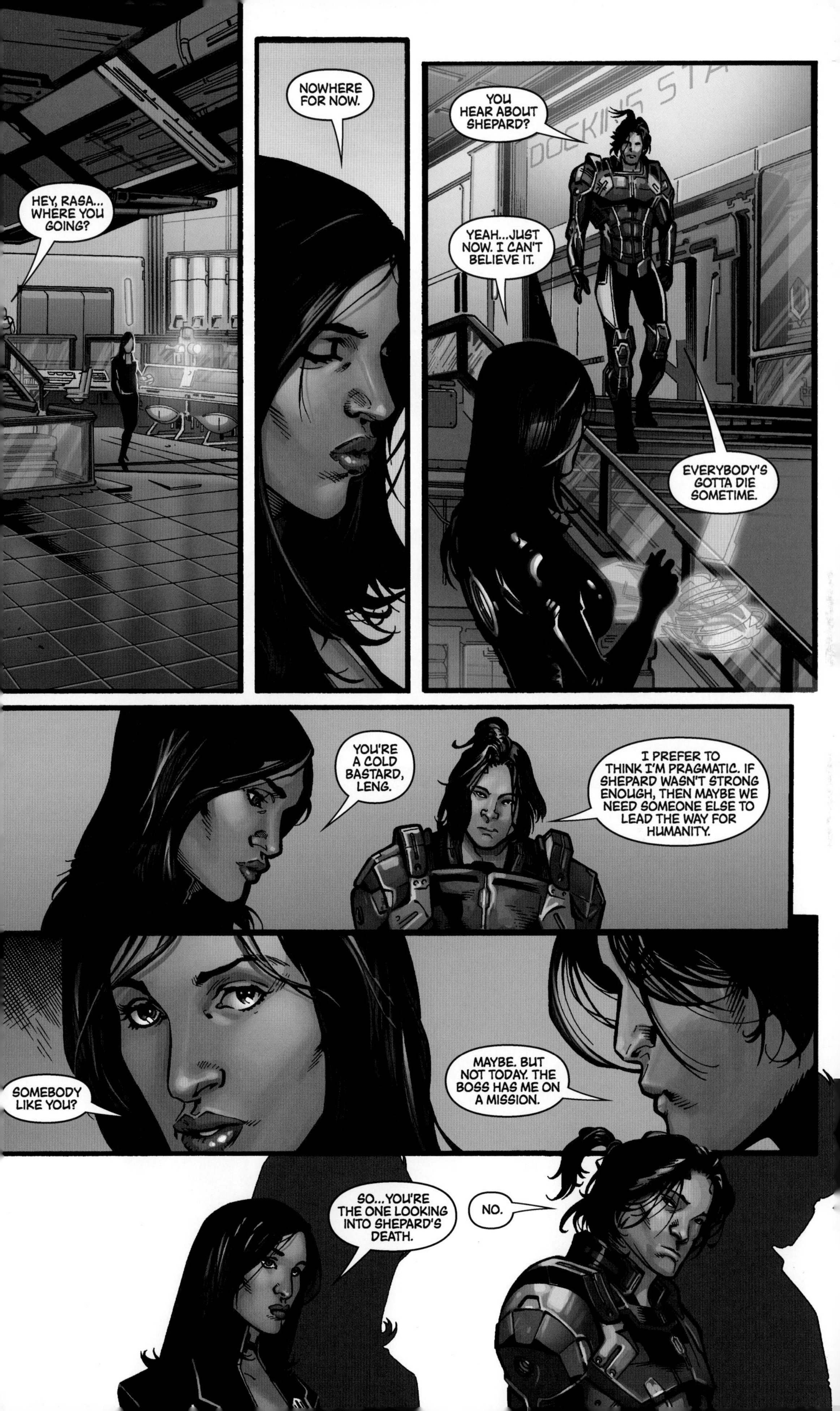
HEY, RASA... WHERE YOU GOING?
NOWHERE FOR NOW.
YOU HEAR ABOUT SHEPARD?
DOCKING STA
YEAH...JUST NOW. I CAN'T BELIEVE IT.
EVERYBODY'S GOTTA DIE SOMETIME.
YOU'RE A COLD BASTARD, LENG.
I PREFER TO THINK I'M PRAGMATIC. IF SHEPARD WASN'T STRONG ENOUGH, THEN MAYBE WE NEED SOMEONE ELSE TO LEAD THE WAY FOR HUMANITY.
SOMEBODY LIKE YOU?
MAYBE. BUT NOT TODAY. THE BOSS HAS ME ON A MISSION.
SO...YOU'RE THE ONE LOOKING INTO SHEPARD'S DEATH.
NO.

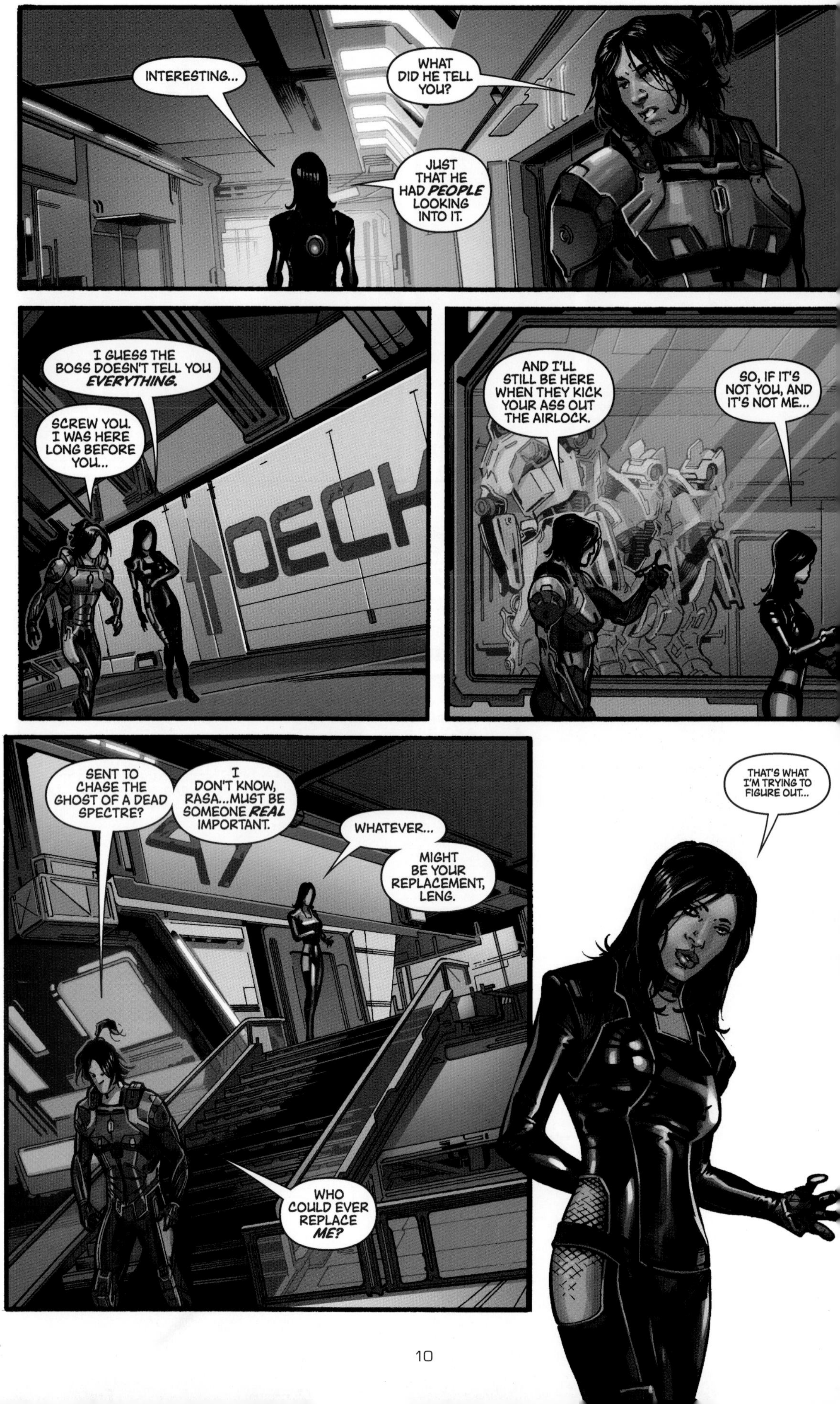
INTERESTING...
WHAT DID HE TELL YOU?
JUST THAT HE HAD *PEOPLE* LOOKING INTO IT.
I GUESS THE BOSS DOESN'T TELL YOU *EVERYTHING.*
SCREW YOU. I WAS HERE LONG BEFORE YOU...
DECK
AND I'LL STILL BE HERE WHEN THEY KICK YOUR ASS OUT THE AIRLOCK.
SO, IF IT'S NOT YOU, AND IT'S NOT ME...
SENT TO CHASE THE GHOST OF A DEAD SPECTRE?
I DON'T KNOW, RASA...MUST BE SOMEONE *REAL* IMPORTANT.
WHATEVER...
MIGHT BE YOUR REPLACEMENT, LENG.
WHO COULD EVER REPLACE *ME?*
THAT'S WHAT I'M TRYING TO FIGURE OUT...

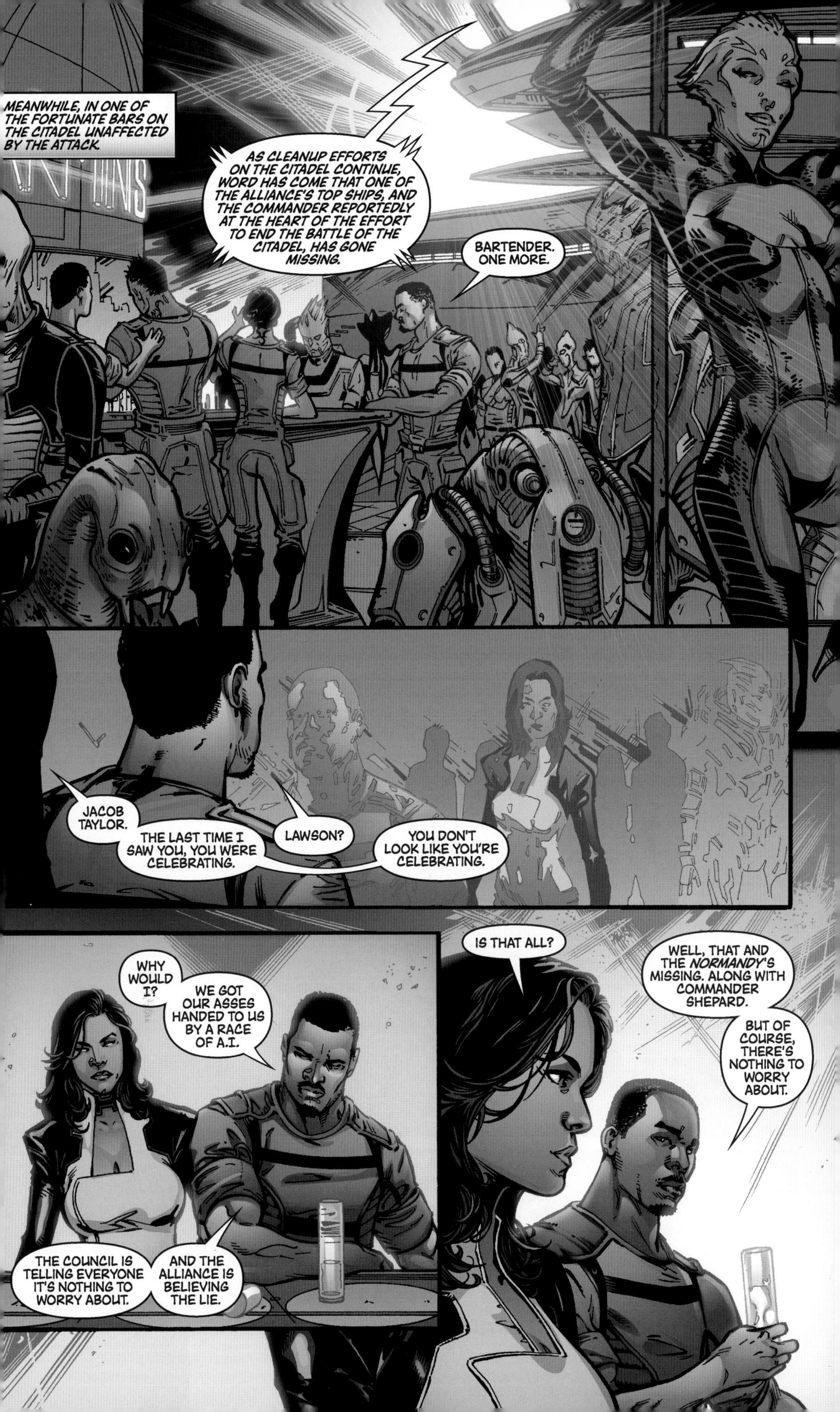

MEANWHILE, IN ONE OF THE FORTUNATE BARS ON THE CITADEL UNAFFECTED BY THE ATTACK.
AS CLEANUP EFFORTS ON THE CITADEL CONTINUE, WORD HAS COME THAT ONE OF THE ALLIANCE'S TOP SHIPS, AND THE COMMANDER REPORTEDLY AT THE HEART OF THE EFFORT TO END THE BATTLE OF THE CITADEL, HAS GONE MISSING.
BARTENDER. ONE MORE.
JACOB TAYLOR.
THE LAST TIME I SAW YOU, YOU WERE CELEBRATING.
LAWSON?
YOU DON'T LOOK LIKE YOU'RE CELEBRATING.
WHY WOULD I?
WE GOT OUR ASSES HANDED TO US BY A RACE OF A.I.
THE COUNCIL IS TELLING EVERYONE IT'S NOTHING TO WORRY ABOUT.
AND THE ALLIANCE IS BELIEVING THE LIE.
IS THAT ALL?
WELL, THAT AND THE *NORMANDY*'S MISSING. ALONG WITH COMMANDER SHEPARD.
BUT OF COURSE, THERE'S NOTHING TO WORRY ABOUT.

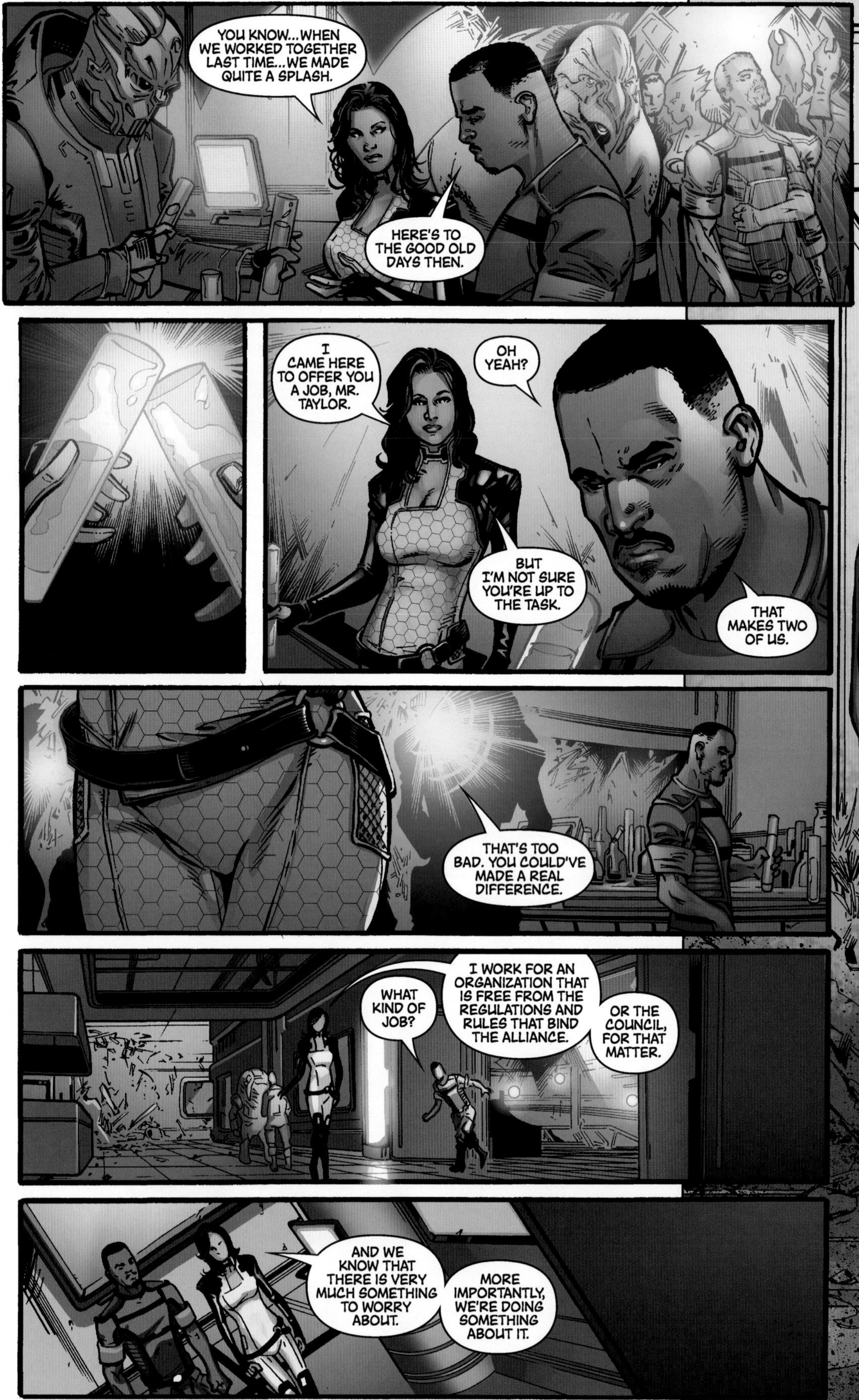
YOU KNOW...WHEN WE WORKED TOGETHER LAST TIME...WE MADE QUITE A SPLASH.
HERE'S TO THE GOOD OLD DAYS THEN.
I CAME HERE TO OFFER YOU A JOB, MR. TAYLOR.
OH YEAH?
BUT I'M NOT SURE YOU'RE UP TO THE TASK.
THAT MAKES TWO OF US.
THAT'S TOO BAD. YOU COULD'VE MADE A REAL DIFFERENCE.
WHAT KIND OF JOB?
I WORK FOR AN ORGANIZATION THAT IS FREE FROM THE REGULATIONS AND RULES THAT BIND THE ALLIANCE.
OR THE COUNCIL, FOR THAT MATTER.
AND WE KNOW THAT THERE IS VERY MUCH SOMETHING TO WORRY ABOUT.
MORE IMPORTANTLY, WE'RE DOING SOMETHING ABOUT IT.

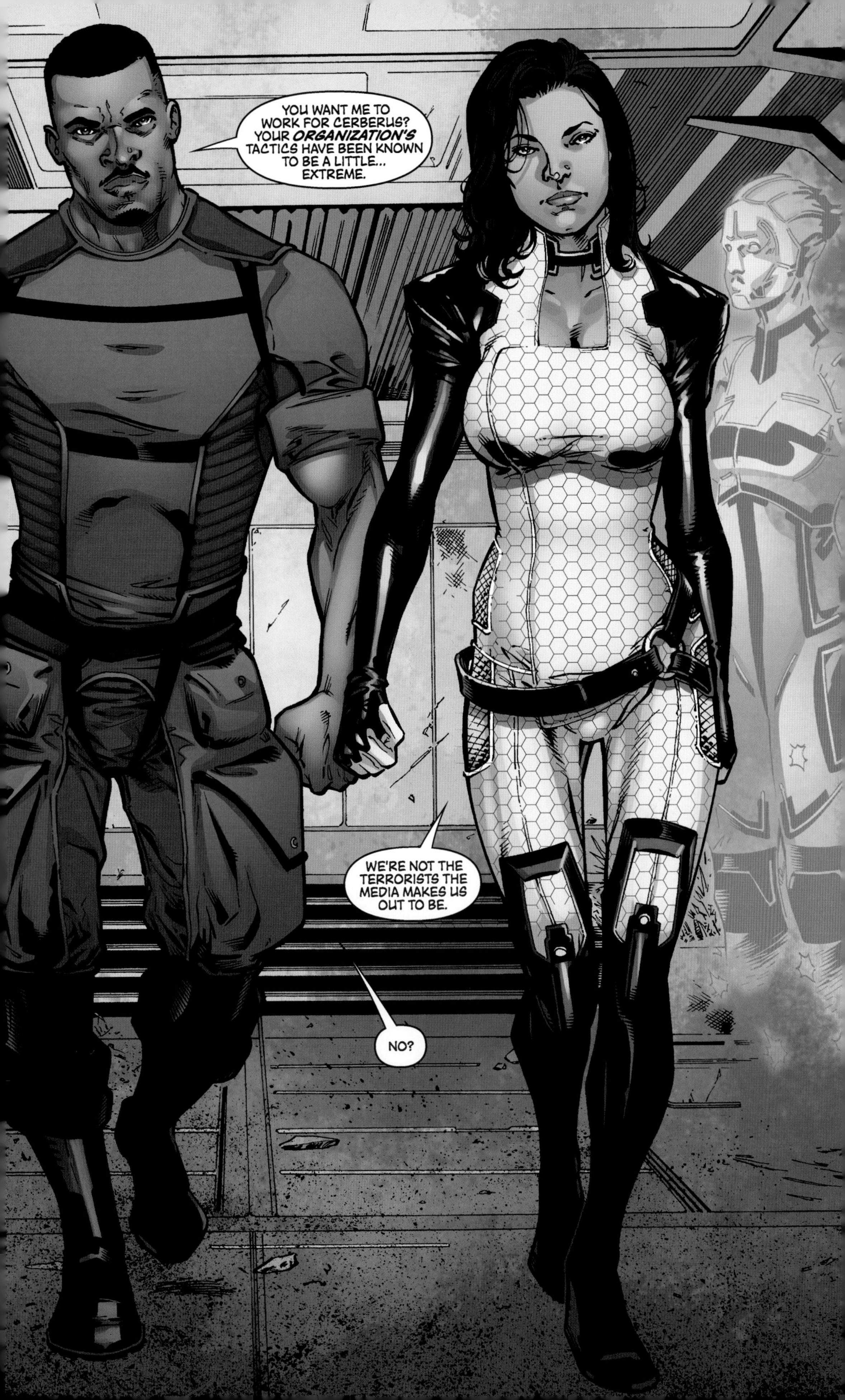
YOU WANT ME TO WORK FOR CERBERUS? YOUR ORGANIZATION'S TACTICS HAVE BEEN KNOWN TO BE A LITTLE... EXTREME.
WE'RE NOT THE TERRORISTS THE MEDIA MAKES US OUT TO BE.
NO?

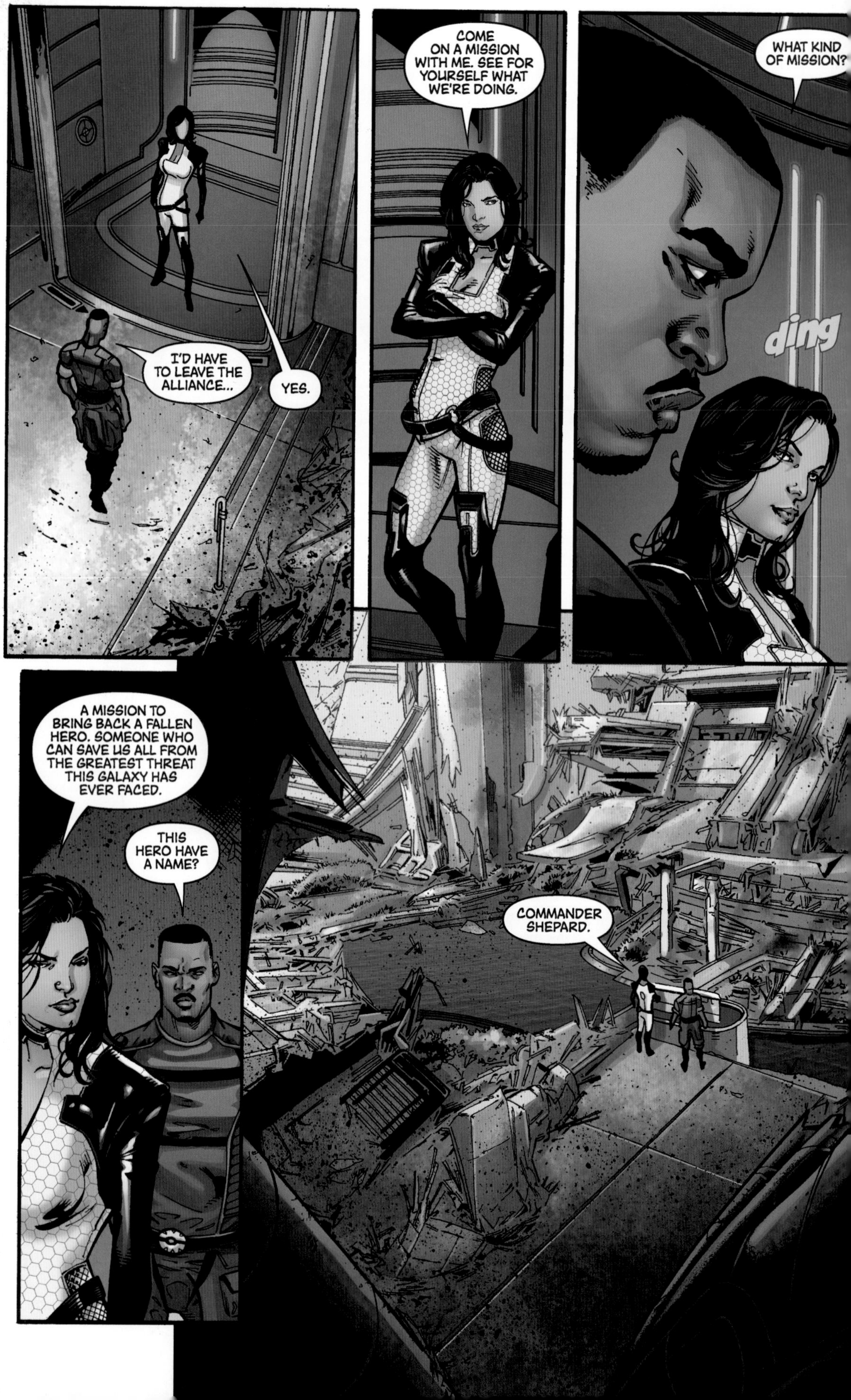
I'D HAVE TO LEAVE THE ALLIANCE...
YES.
COME ON A MISSION WITH ME. SEE FOR YOURSELF WHAT WE'RE DOING.
WHAT KIND OF MISSION?
ding
A MISSION TO BRING BACK A FALLEN HERO. SOMEONE WHO CAN SAVE US ALL FROM THE GREATEST THREAT THIS GALAXY HAS EVER FACED.
THIS HERO HAVE A NAME?
COMMANDER SHEPARD.

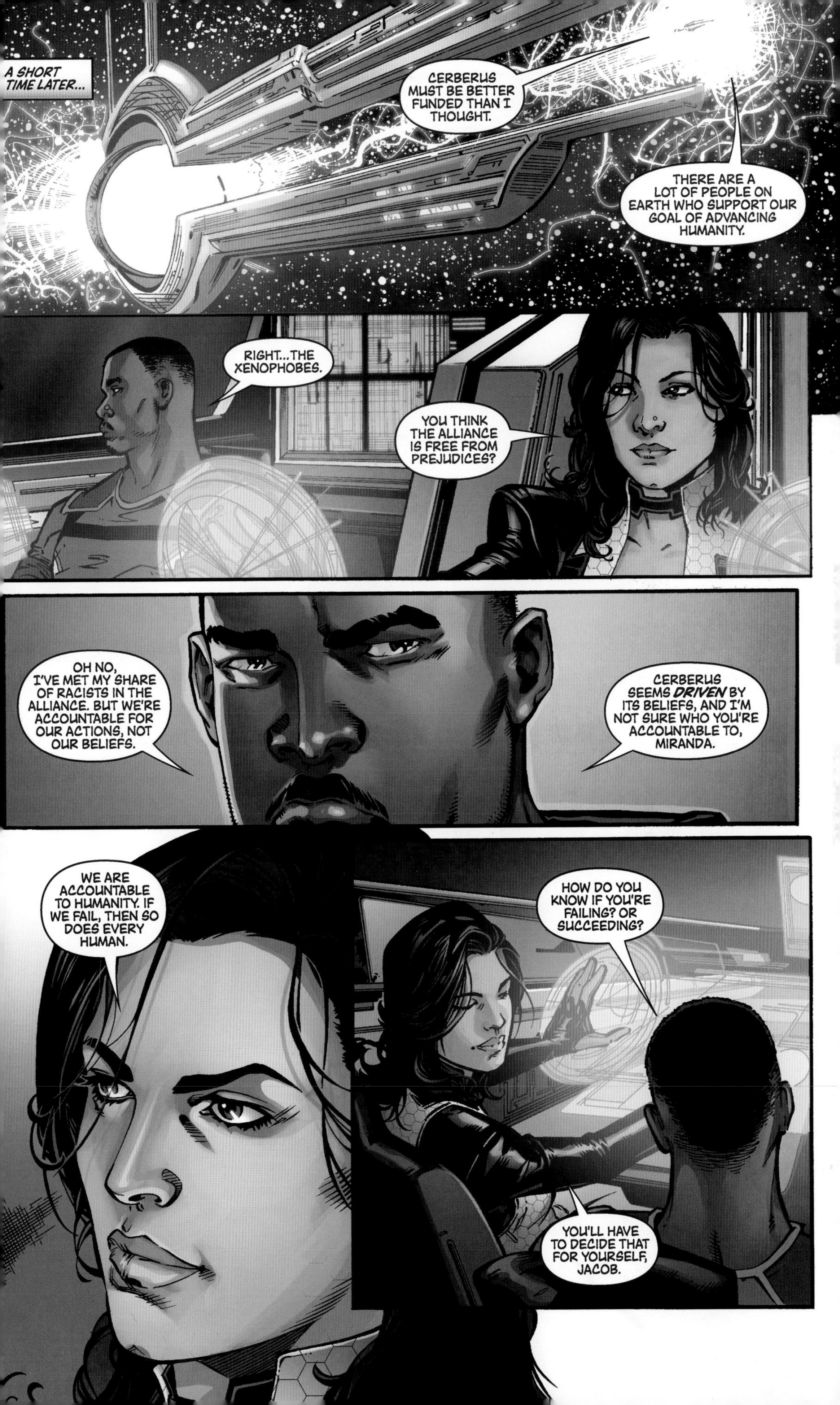
A SHORT TIME LATER...
CERBERUS MUST BE BETTER FUNDED THAN I THOUGHT.
THERE ARE A LOT OF PEOPLE ON EARTH WHO SUPPORT OUR GOAL OF ADVANCING HUMANITY.
RIGHT...THE XENOPHOBES.
YOU THINK THE ALLIANCE IS FREE FROM PREJUDICES?
OH NO, I'VE MET MY SHARE OF RACISTS IN THE ALLIANCE. BUT WE'RE ACCOUNTABLE FOR OUR ACTIONS, NOT OUR BELIEFS.
CERBERUS SEEMS DRIVEN BY ITS BELIEFS, AND I'M NOT SURE WHO YOU'RE ACCOUNTABLE TO, MIRANDA.
WE ARE ACCOUNTABLE TO HUMANITY. IF WE FAIL, THEN SO DOES EVERY HUMAN.
HOW DO YOU KNOW IF YOU'RE FAILING? OR SUCCEEDING?
YOU'LL HAVE TO DECIDE THAT FOR YOURSELF, JACOB.

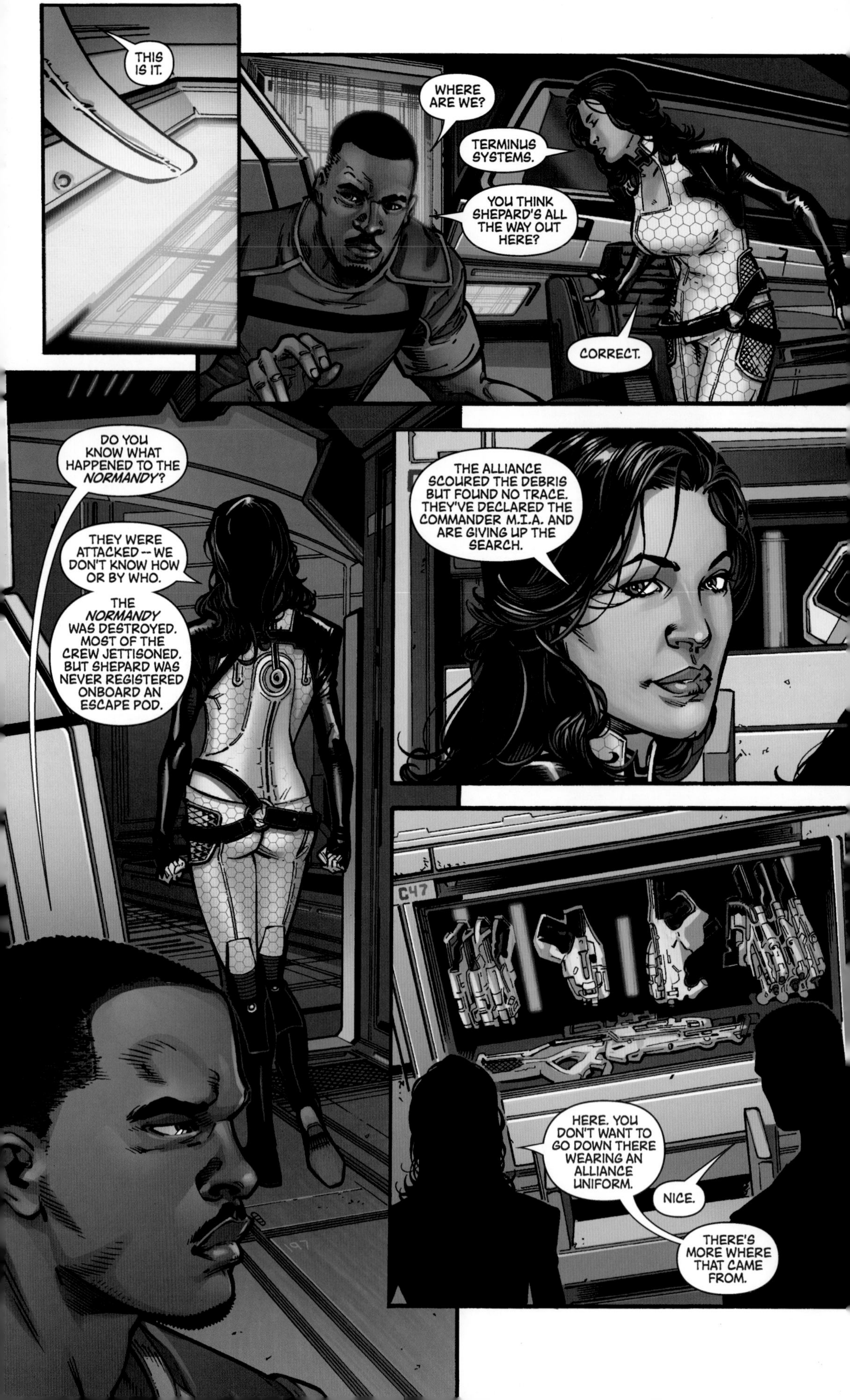
THIS IS IT.
WHERE ARE WE?
TERMINUS SYSTEMS.
YOU THINK SHEPARD'S ALL THE WAY OUT HERE?
CORRECT.
DO YOU KNOW WHAT HAPPENED TO THE *NORMANDY*?
THEY WERE ATTACKED -- WE DON'T KNOW HOW OR BY WHO.
THE *NORMANDY* WAS DESTROYED. MOST OF THE CREW JETTISONED. BUT SHEPARD WAS NEVER REGISTERED ONBOARD AN ESCAPE POD.
THE ALLIANCE SCOURED THE DEBRIS BUT FOUND NO TRACE. THEY'VE DECLARED THE COMMANDER M.I.A. AND ARE GIVING UP THE SEARCH.
C47
HERE. YOU DON'T WANT TO GO DOWN THERE WEARING AN ALLIANCE UNIFORM.
NICE.
THERE'S MORE WHERE THAT CAME FROM.

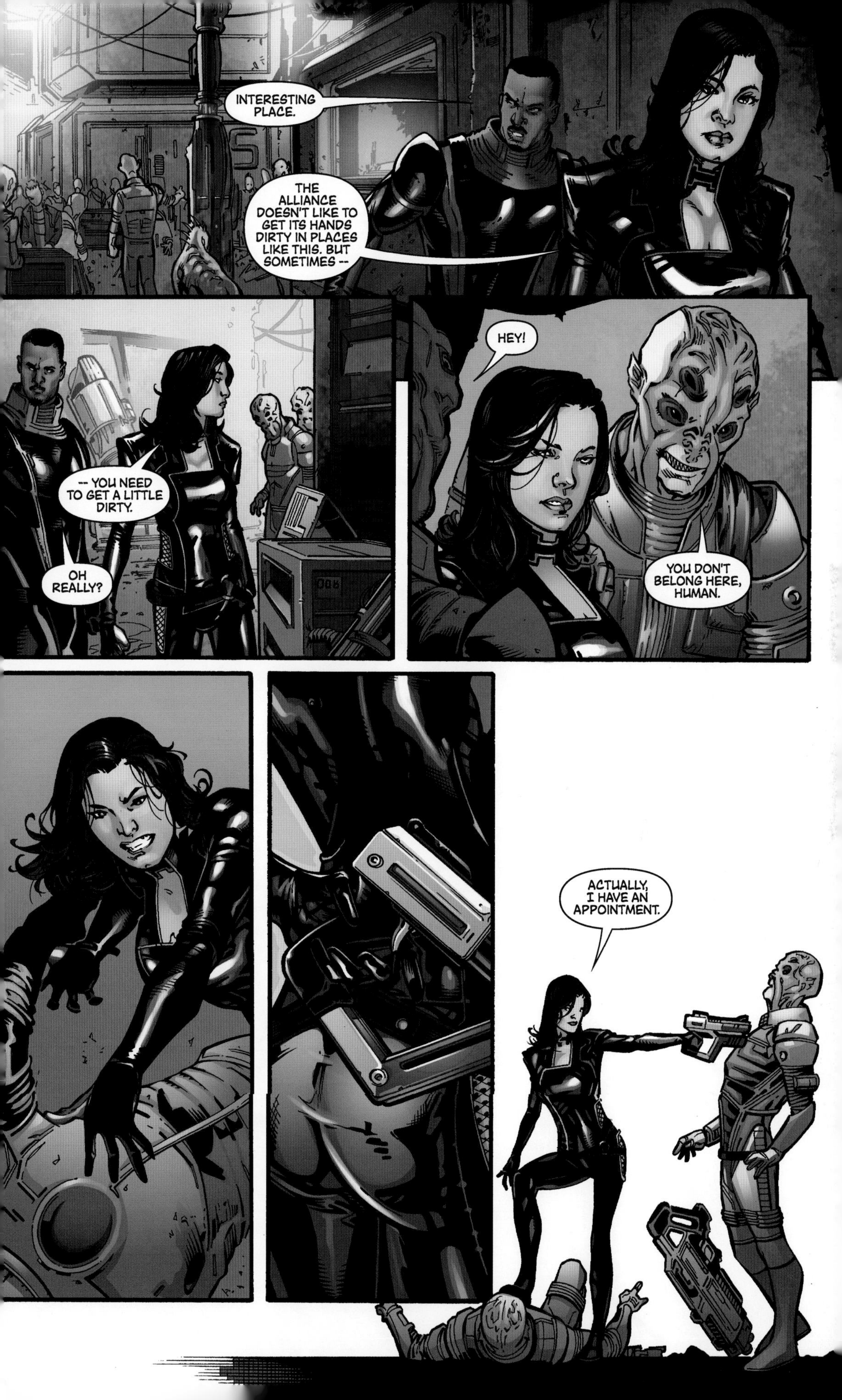
INTERESTING PLACE.
THE ALLIANCE DOESN'T LIKE TO GET ITS HANDS DIRTY IN PLACES LIKE THIS. BUT SOMETIMES --
-- YOU NEED TO GET A LITTLE DIRTY.
OH REALLY?
HEY!
YOU DON'T BELONG HERE, HUMAN.
ACTUALLY, I HAVE AN APPOINTMENT.

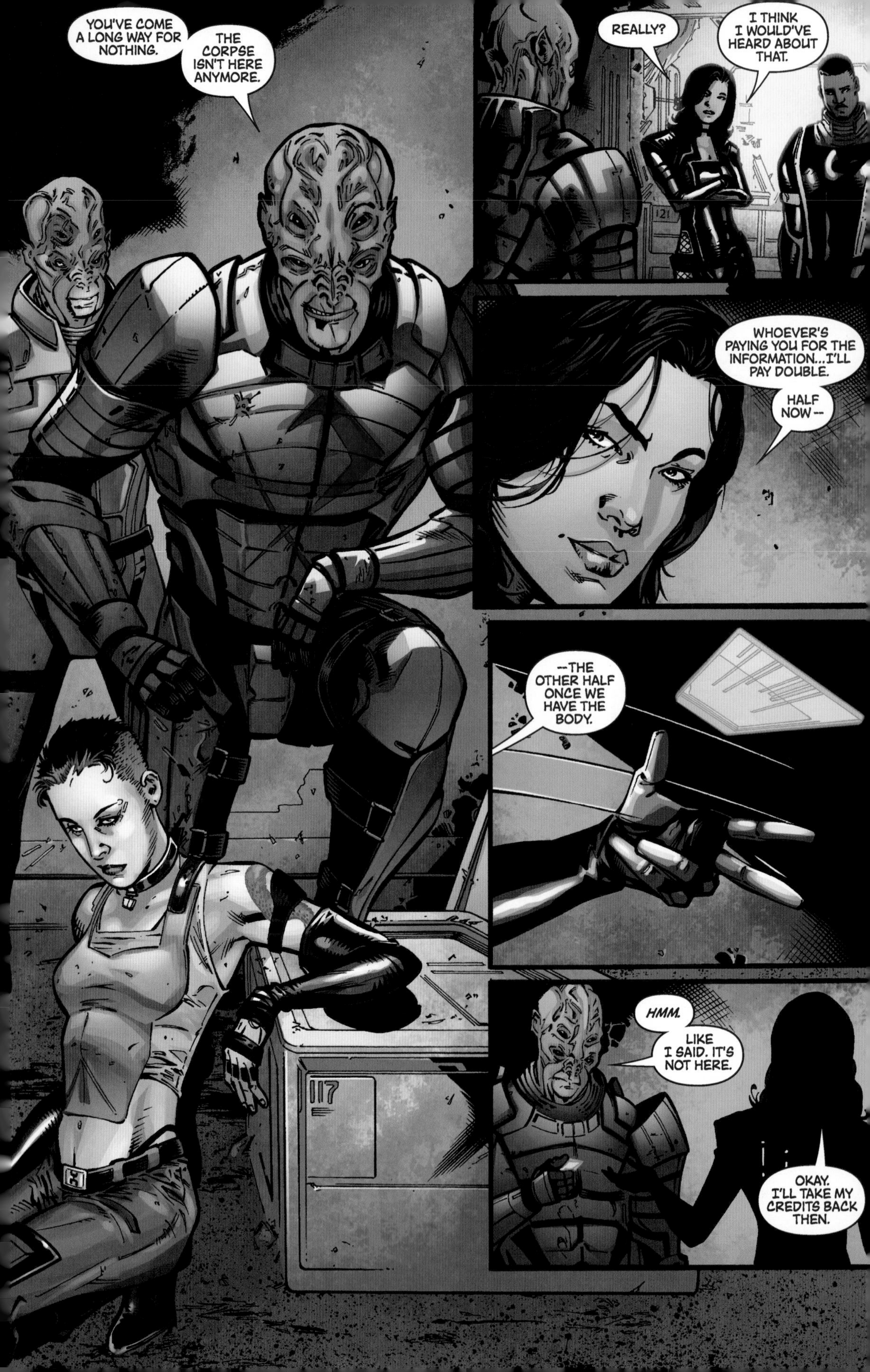
YOU'VE COME A LONG WAY FOR NOTHING.
THE CORPSE ISN'T HERE ANYMORE.
REALLY?
I THINK I WOULD'VE HEARD ABOUT THAT.
WHOEVER'S PAYING YOU FOR THE INFORMATION...I'LL PAY DOUBLE.
HALF NOW --
--THE OTHER HALF ONCE WE HAVE THE BODY.
HMM.
LIKE I SAID. IT'S NOT HERE.
OKAY. I'LL TAKE MY CREDITS BACK THEN.

HOW'D YOU KNOW HE'D TAKE THE CREDITS?

I DIDN'T.

BUT IT'S A LOT HARDER TO TURN THEM DOWN ONCE YOU'RE HOLDING THEM.

AND WHY'D HE REFER TO SHEPARD AS A CORPSE?

BECAUSE THAT'S ALL THAT MIGHT BE LEFT.

IT'S THIS WAY. LET'S GO.

SERIOUSLY?

THEN WHAT THE HELL ARE WE DOING HERE?

SHANKS FOR TWENTY CREDITS!

KNUCKLES FOR TEN!

MAKING SURE.

YOU COULD'VE TOLD ME THAT BEFORE.

WOULD YOU HAVE COME?

MAYBE.

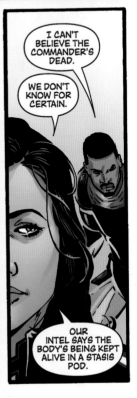

I CAN'T BELIEVE THE COMMANDER'S DEAD.

WE DON'T KNOW FOR CERTAIN.

OUR INTEL SAYS THE BODY'S BEING KEPT ALIVE IN A STASIS POD.

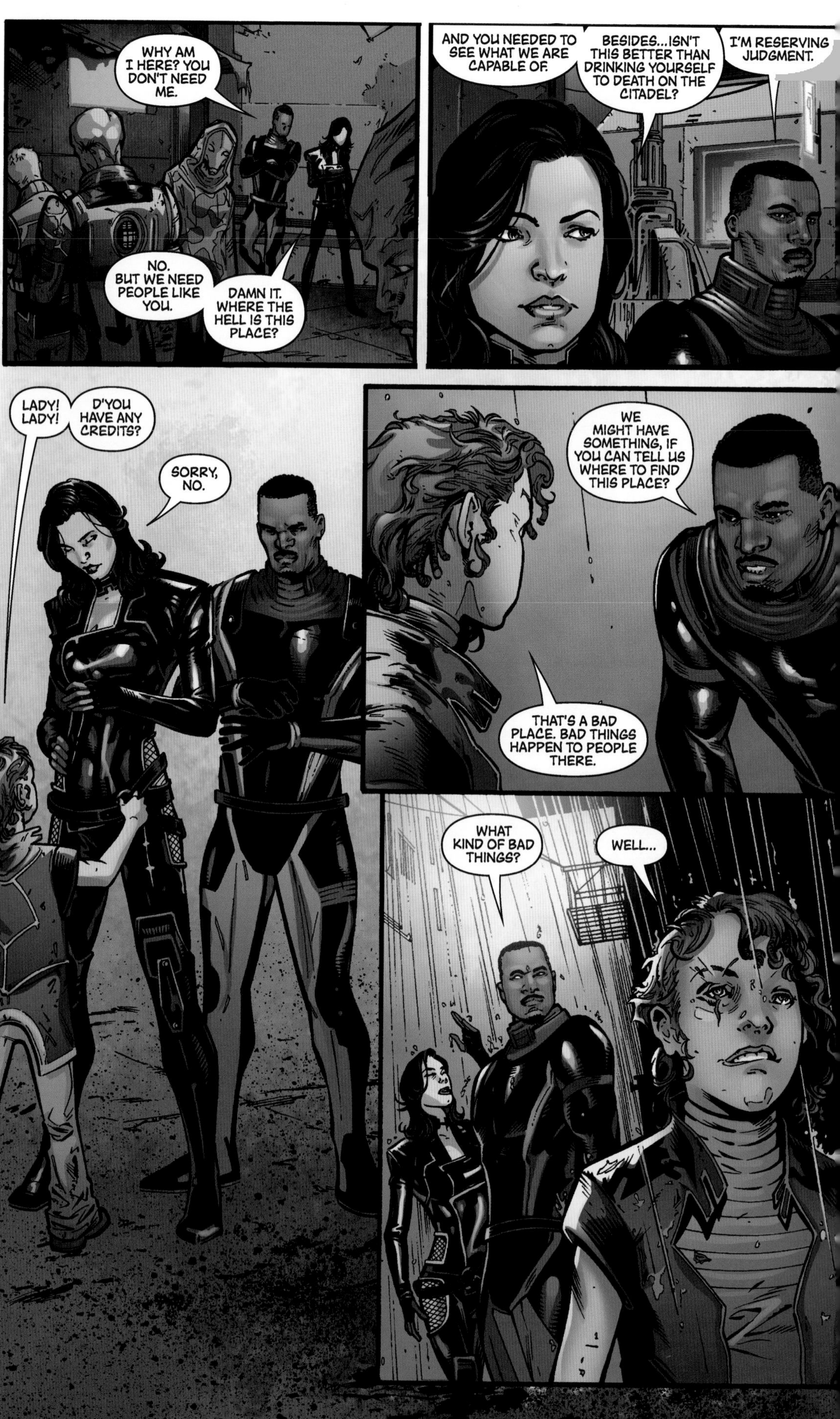
WHY AM I HERE? YOU DON'T NEED ME.
NO. BUT WE NEED PEOPLE LIKE YOU.
DAMN IT. WHERE THE HELL IS THIS PLACE?
AND YOU NEEDED TO SEE WHAT WE ARE CAPABLE OF.
BESIDES...ISN'T THIS BETTER THAN DRINKING YOURSELF TO DEATH ON THE CITADEL?
I'M RESERVING JUDGMENT.
LADY! LADY!
D'YOU HAVE ANY CREDITS?
SORRY, NO.
WE MIGHT HAVE SOMETHING, IF YOU CAN TELL US WHERE TO FIND THIS PLACE?
THAT'S A BAD PLACE. BAD THINGS HAPPEN TO PEOPLE THERE.
WHAT KIND OF BAD THINGS?
WELL...

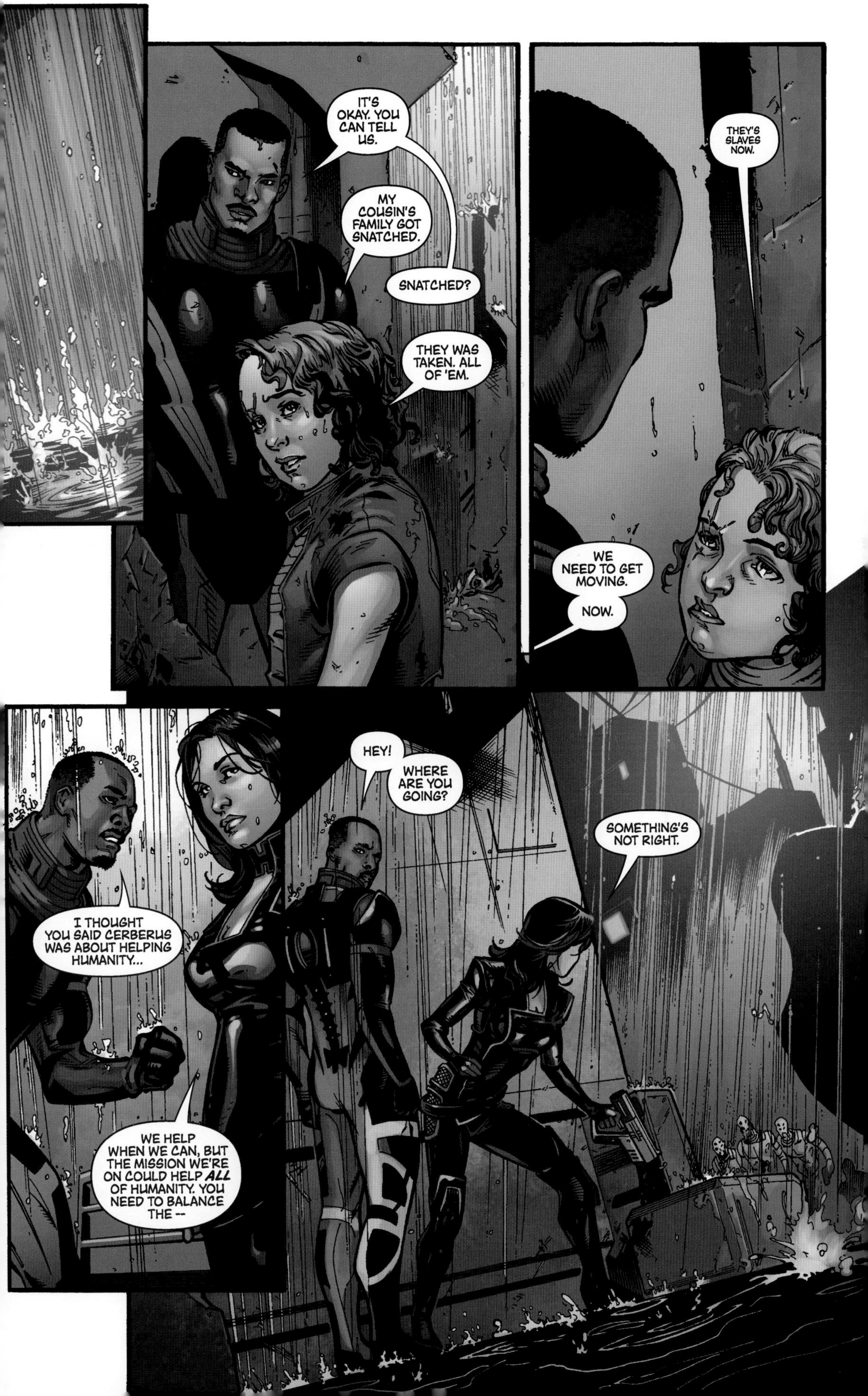
IT'S OKAY. YOU CAN TELL US.
MY COUSIN'S FAMILY GOT SNATCHED.
SNATCHED?
THEY WAS TAKEN. ALL OF 'EM.
THEY'S SLAVES NOW.
WE NEED TO GET MOVING.
NOW.
HEY!
WHERE ARE YOU GOING?
SOMETHING'S NOT RIGHT.
I THOUGHT YOU SAID CERBERUS WAS ABOUT HELPING HUMANITY...
WE HELP WHEN WE CAN, BUT THE MISSION WE'RE ON COULD HELP ALL OF HUMANITY. YOU NEED TO BALANCE THE --

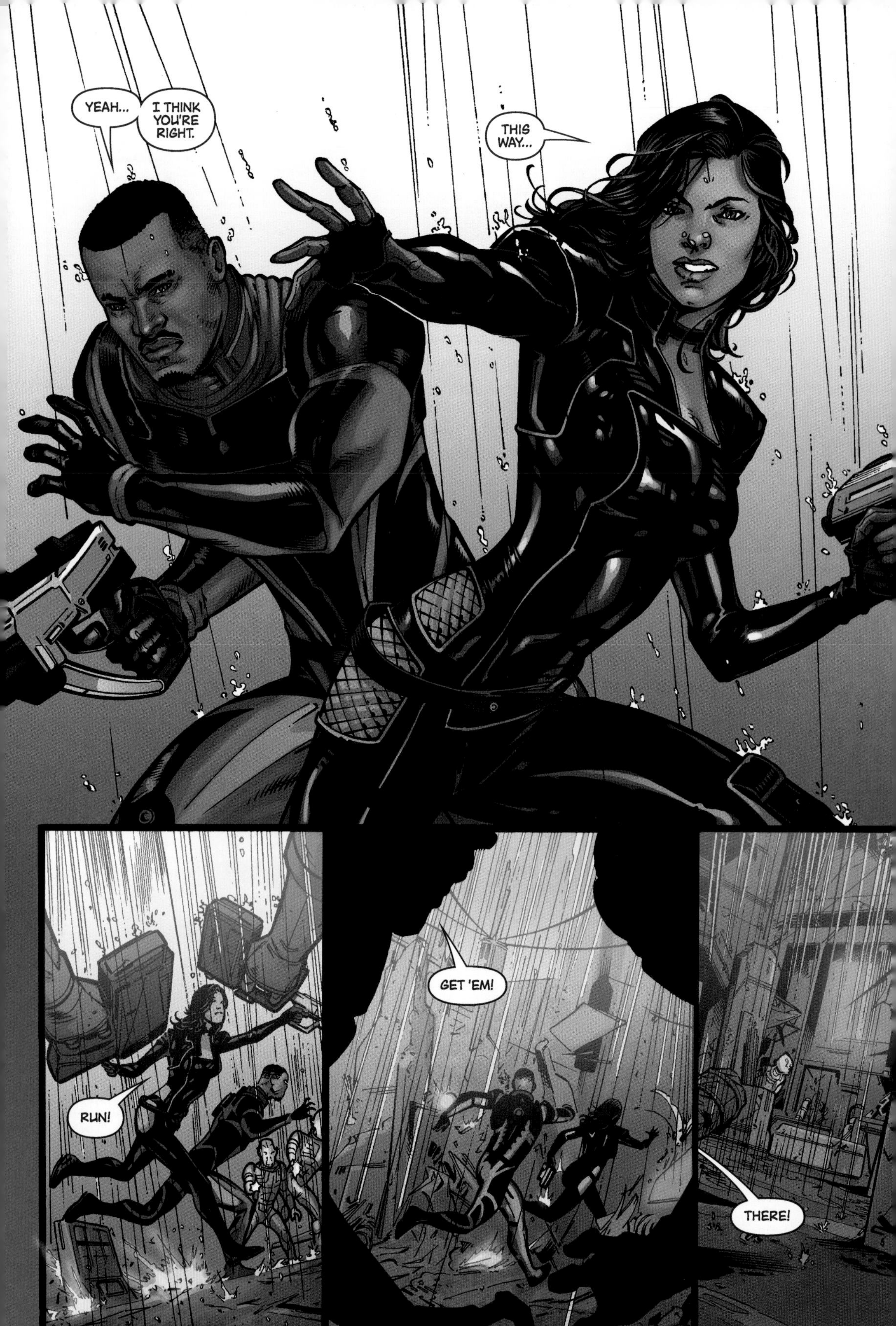
YEAH...
I THINK YOU'RE RIGHT.
THIS WAY...
RUN!
GET 'EM!
THERE!

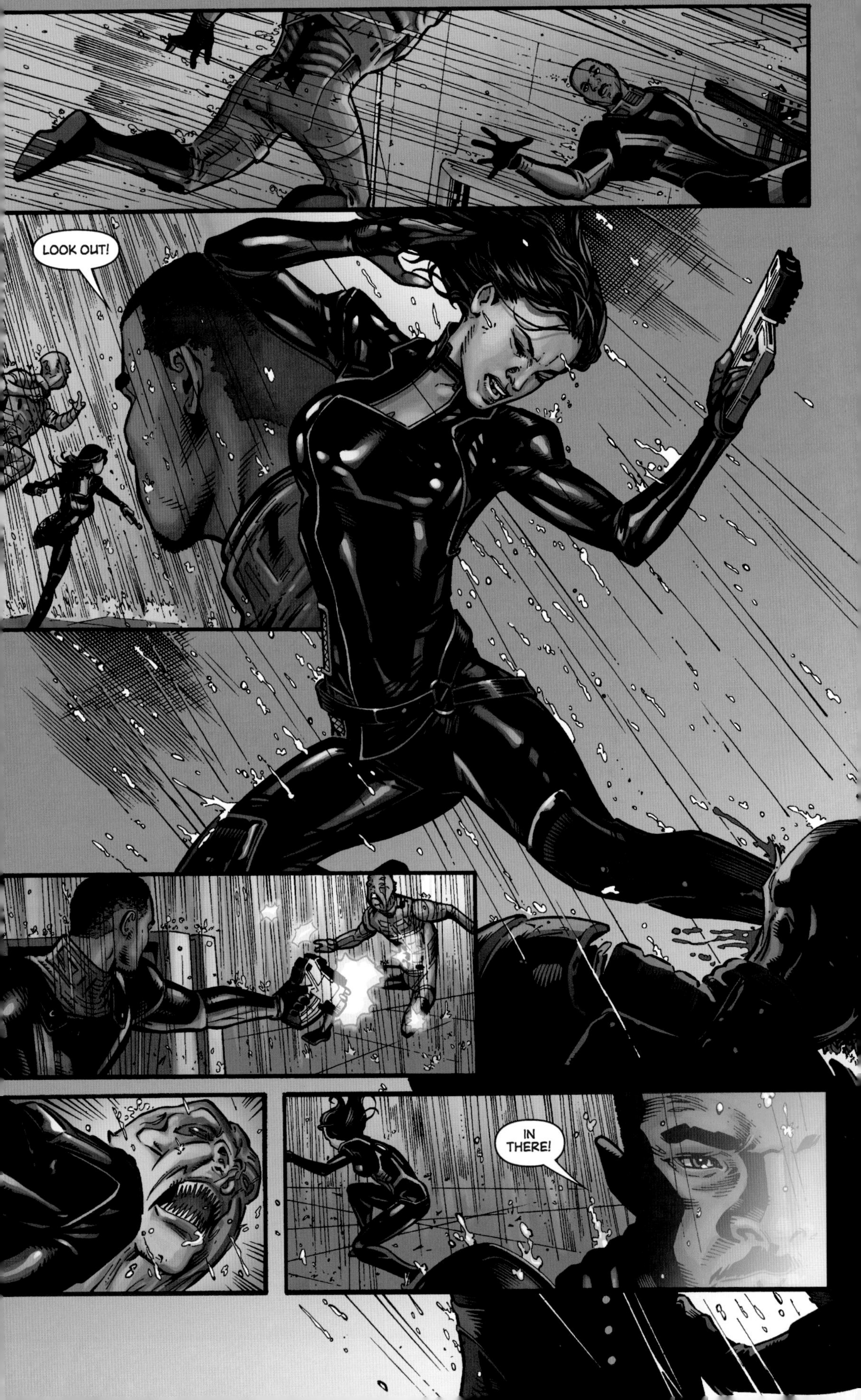
LOOK OUT!
IN THERE!

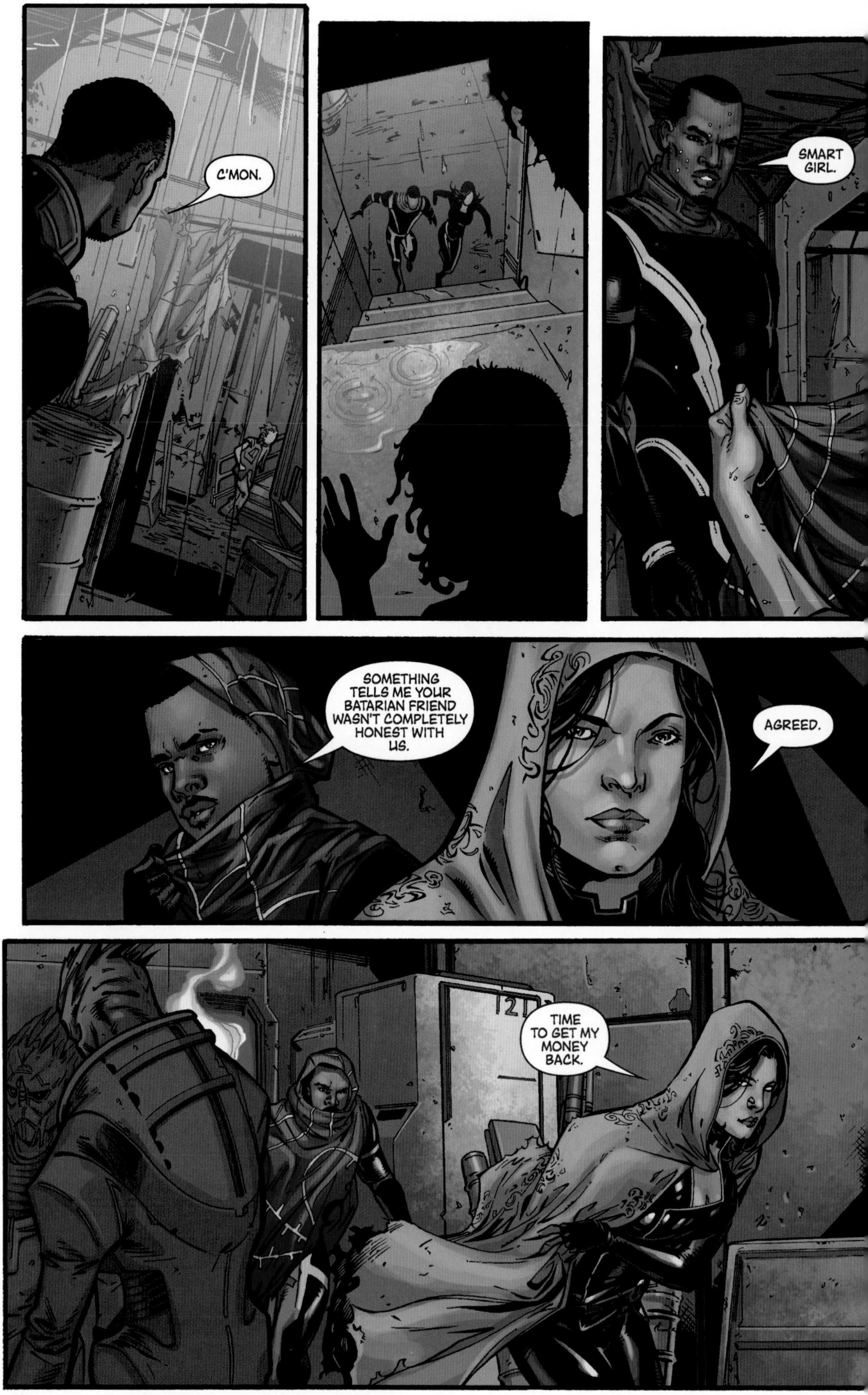
C'MON.
SMART GIRL.
SOMETHING TELLS ME YOUR BATARIAN FRIEND WASN'T COMPLETELY HONEST WITH US.
AGREED.
TIME TO GET MY MONEY BACK.

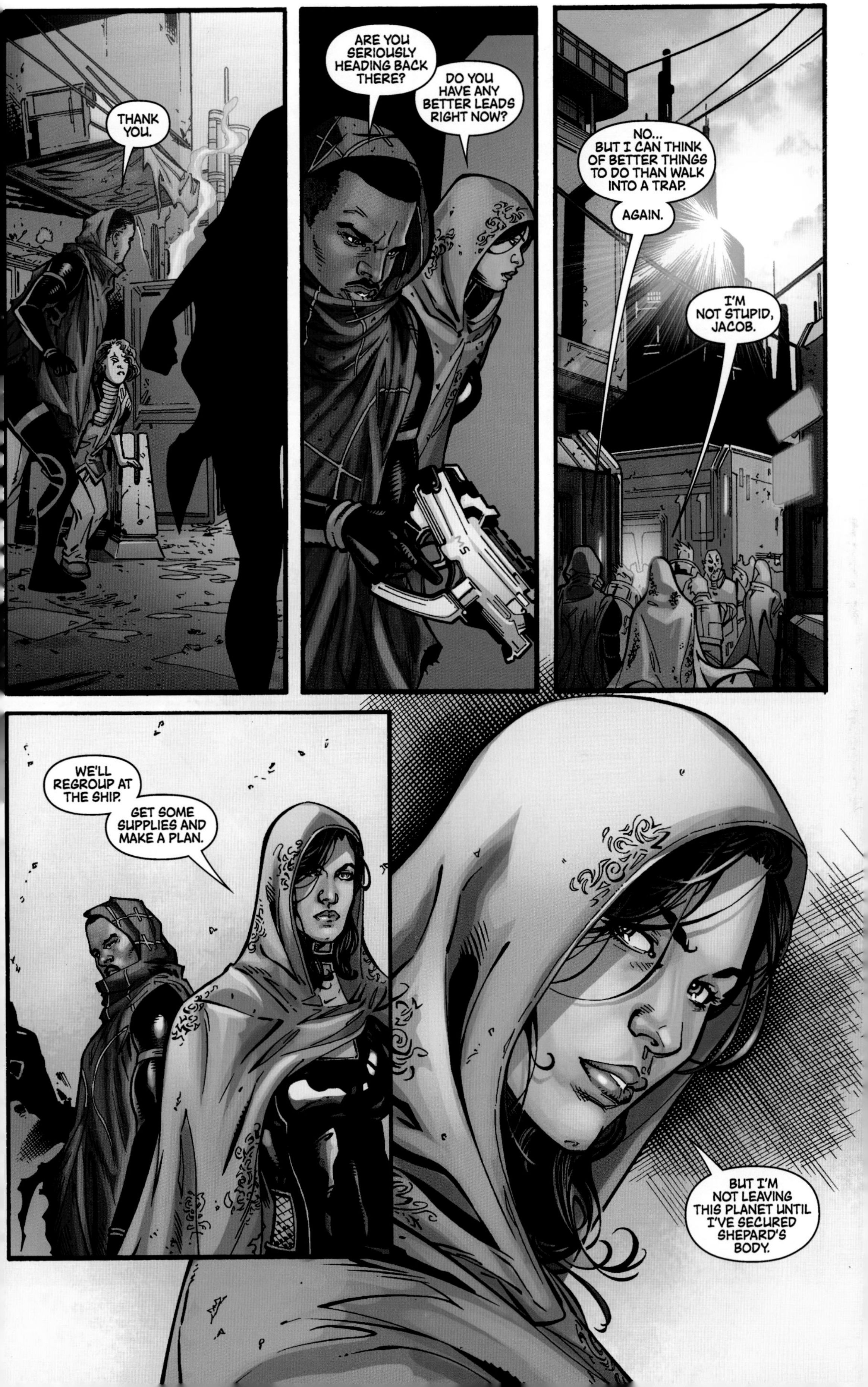

THANK YOU.
ARE YOU SERIOUSLY HEADING BACK THERE?
DO YOU HAVE ANY BETTER LEADS RIGHT NOW?
NO... BUT I CAN THINK OF BETTER THINGS TO DO THAN WALK INTO A TRAP.
AGAIN.
I'M NOT STUPID, JACOB.
WE'LL REGROUP AT THE SHIP.
GET SOME SUPPLIES AND MAKE A PLAN.
BUT I'M NOT LEAVING THIS PLANET UNTIL I'VE SECURED SHEPARD'S BODY.

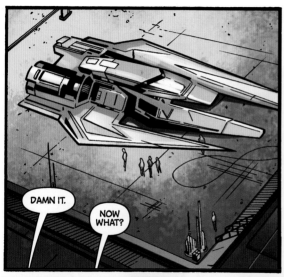

DAMN IT.

NOW WHAT?

MOVE IT. LET'S BLOW THIS THING.

I'M NOT LETTING MY SHIP GET DESTROYED, FOR STARTERS!

MOVE IT!

TELL THEM TO REMOVE THE EXPLOSIVES.

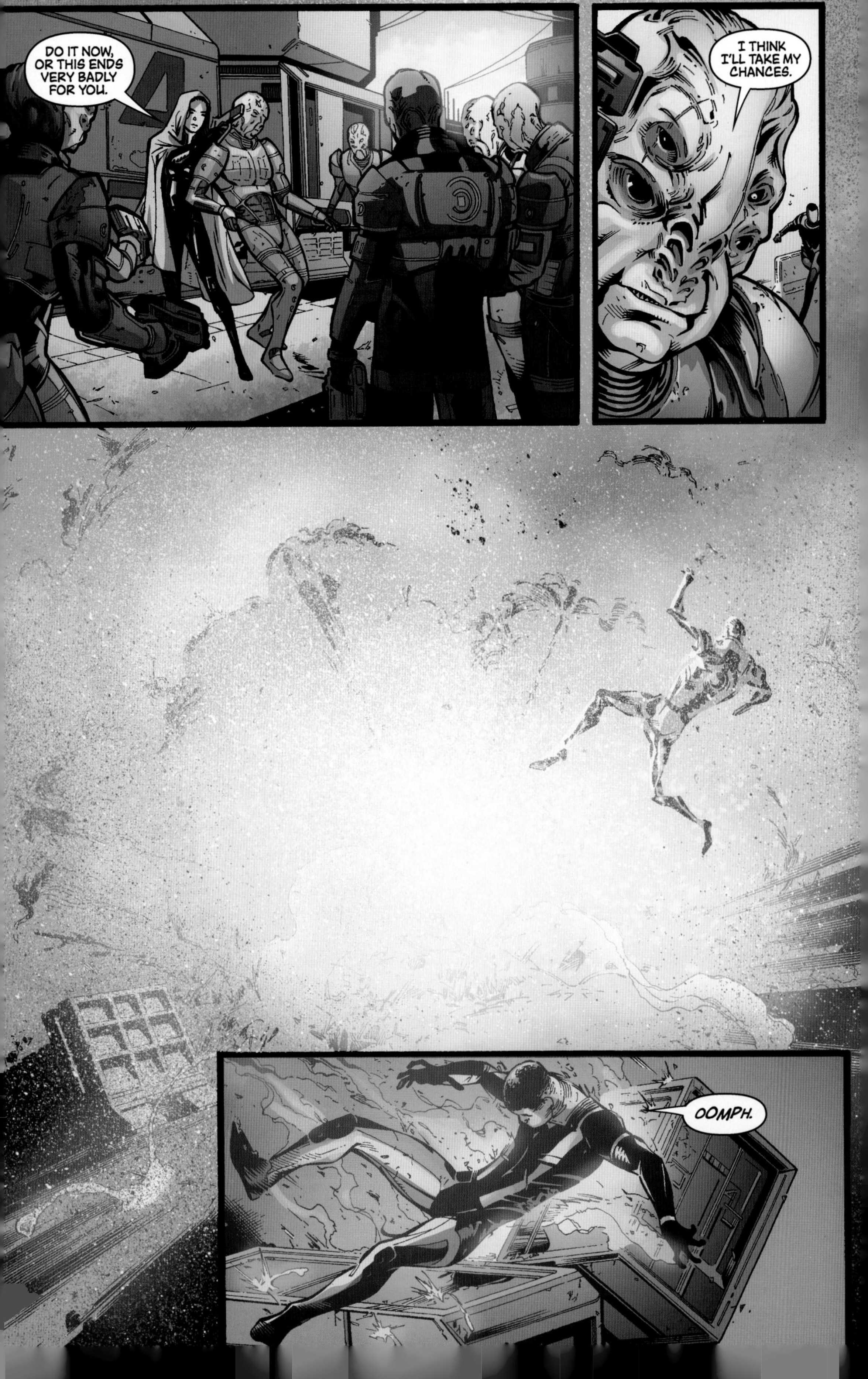
DO IT NOW, OR THIS ENDS VERY BADLY FOR YOU.
I THINK I'LL TAKE MY CHANCES.
OOMPH.

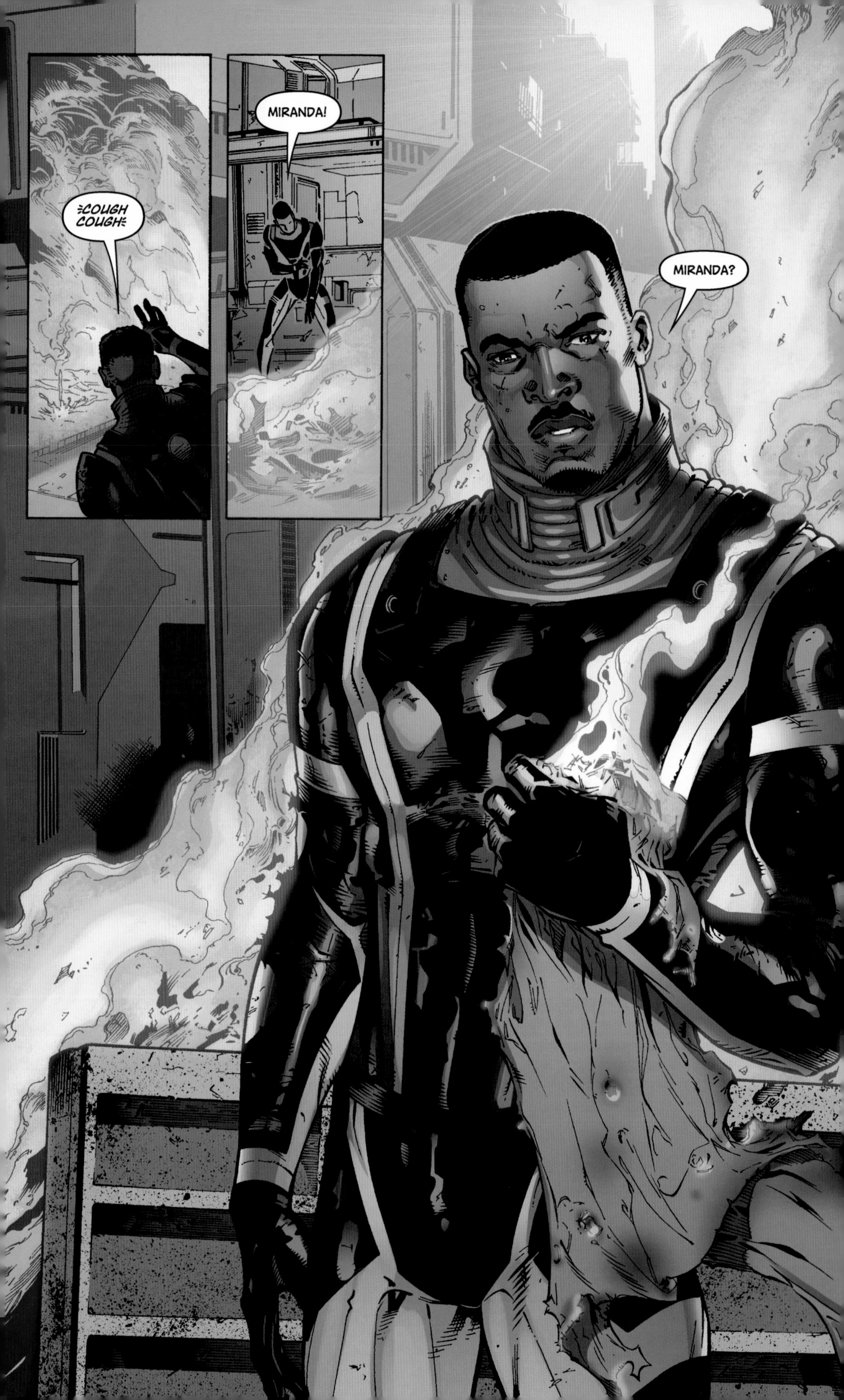
COUGH COUGH
MIRANDA!
MIRANDA?

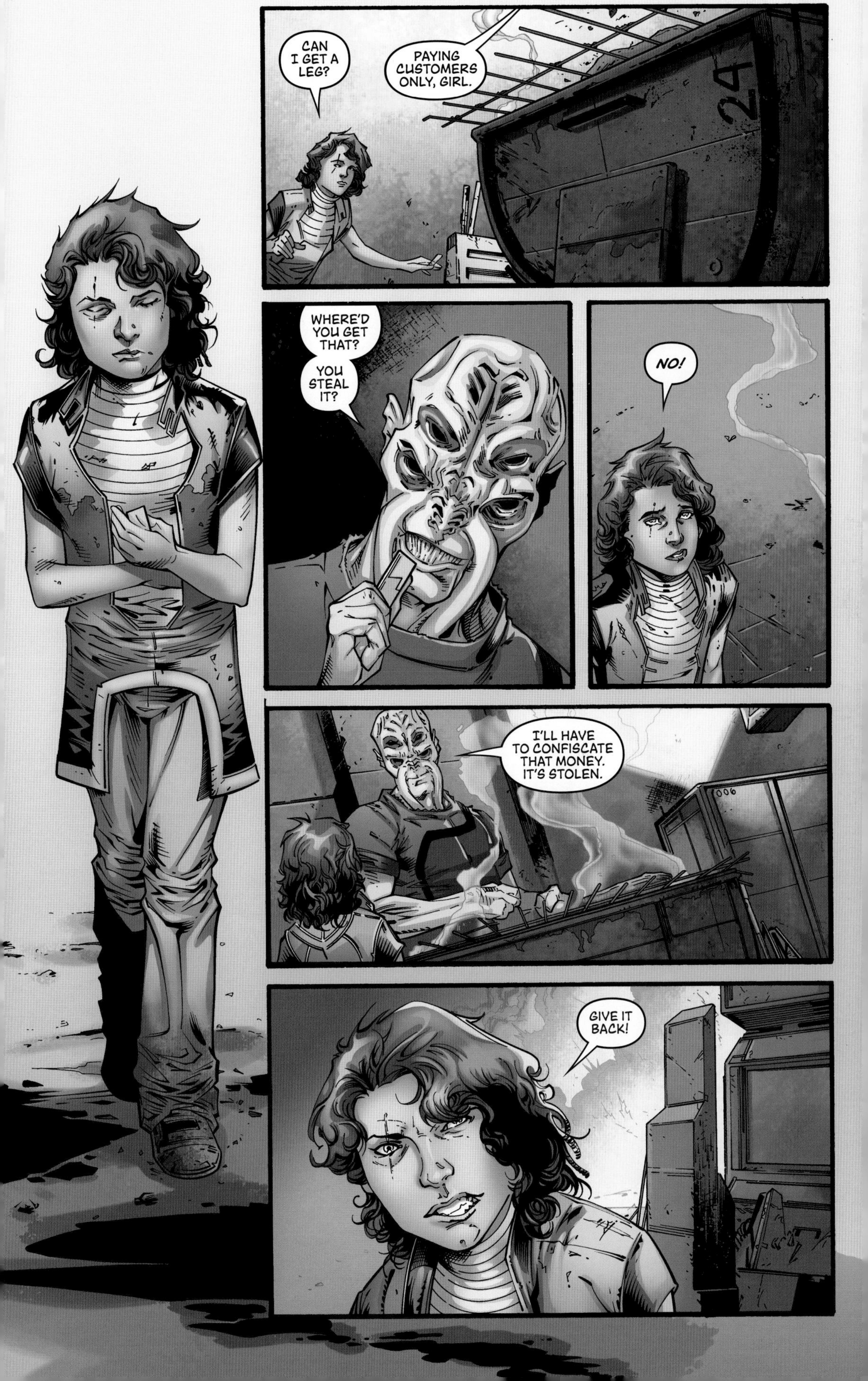
CAN I GET A LEG?
PAYING CUSTOMERS ONLY, GIRL.
WHERE'D YOU GET THAT?
YOU STEAL IT?
NO!
I'LL HAVE TO CONFISCATE THAT MONEY. IT'S STOLEN.
GIVE IT BACK!

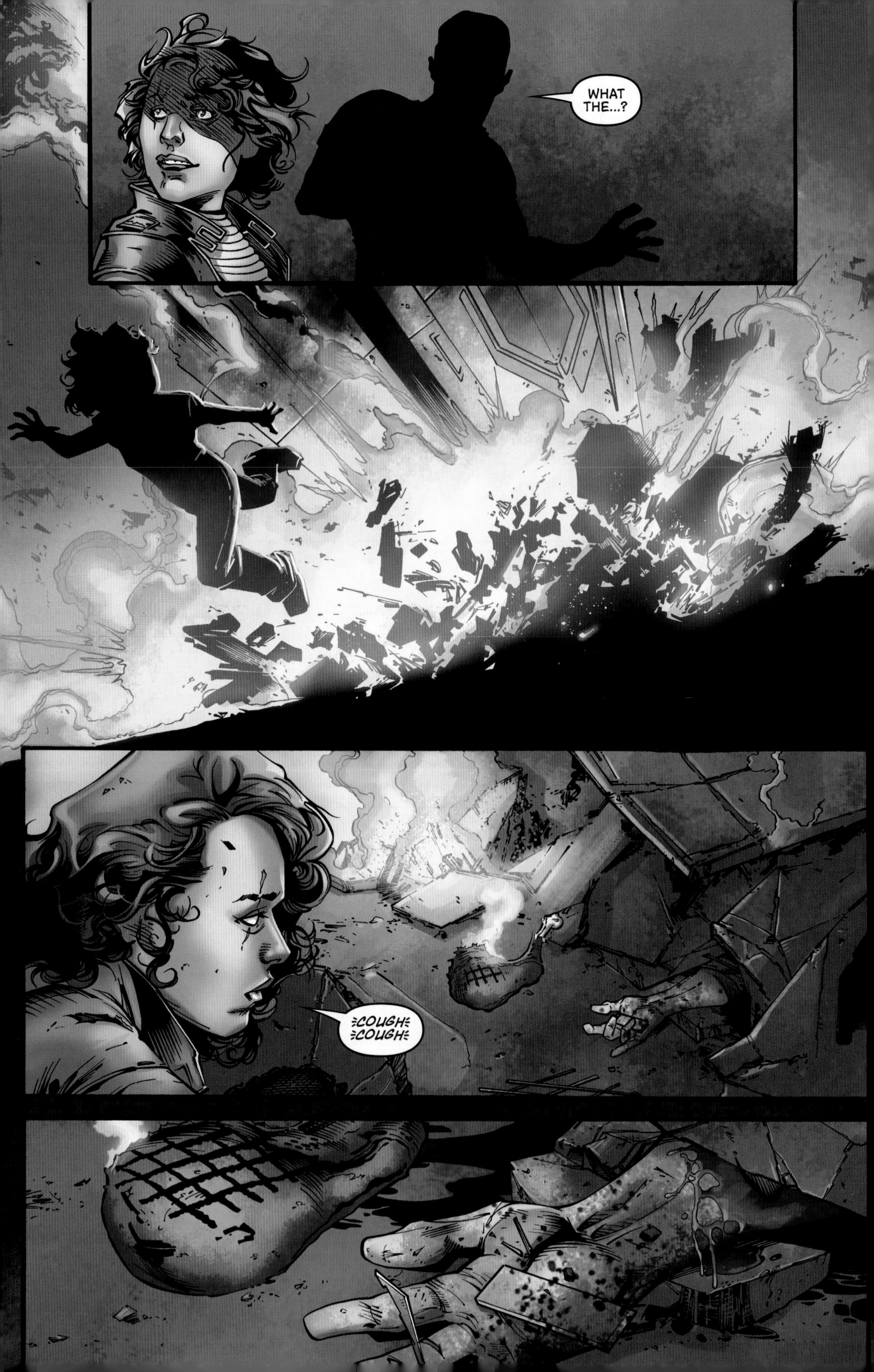
WHAT THE...?
COUGH COUGH

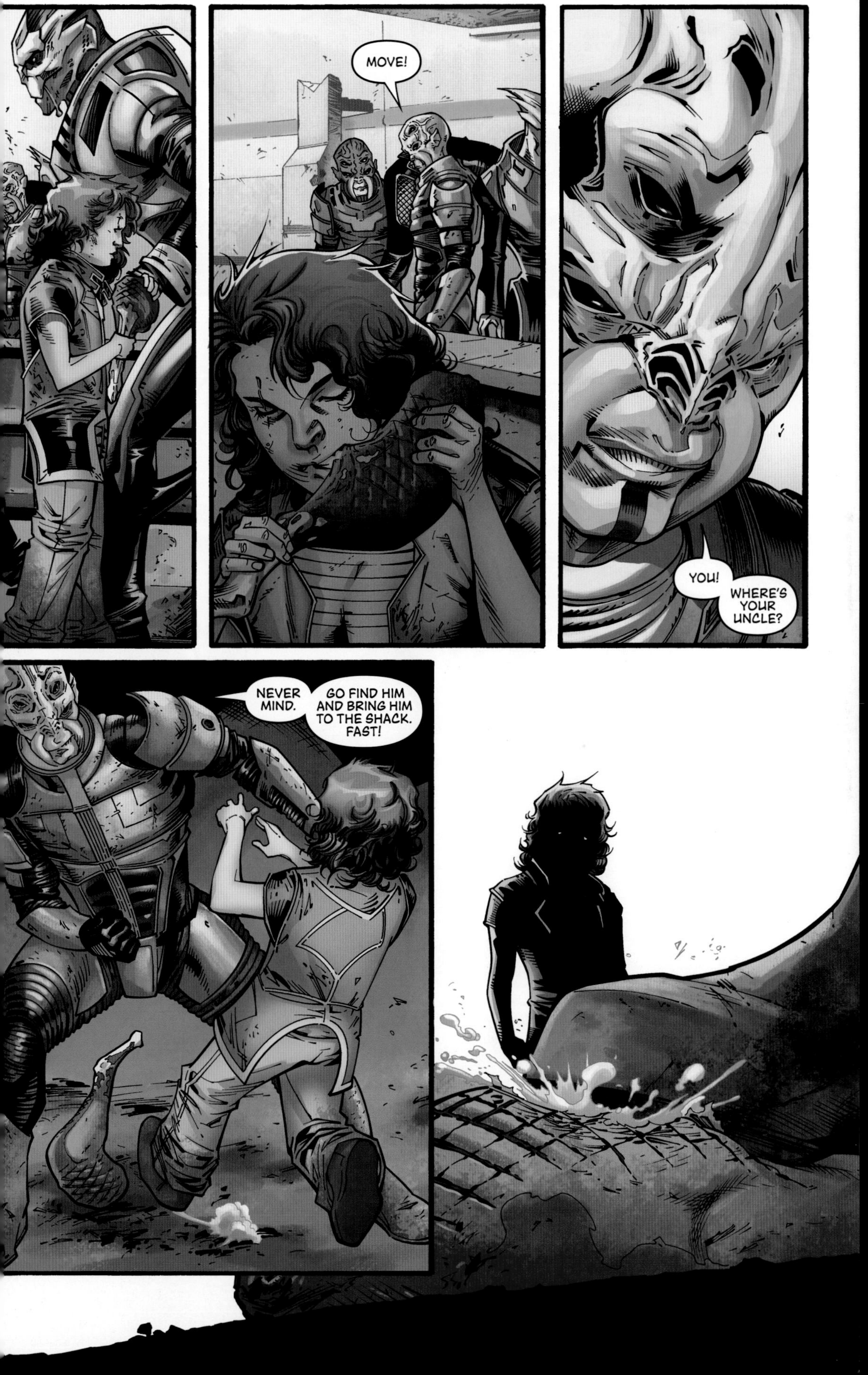
MOVE!
YOU!
WHERE'S YOUR UNCLE?
NEVER MIND.
GO FIND HIM AND BRING HIM TO THE SHACK. FAST!

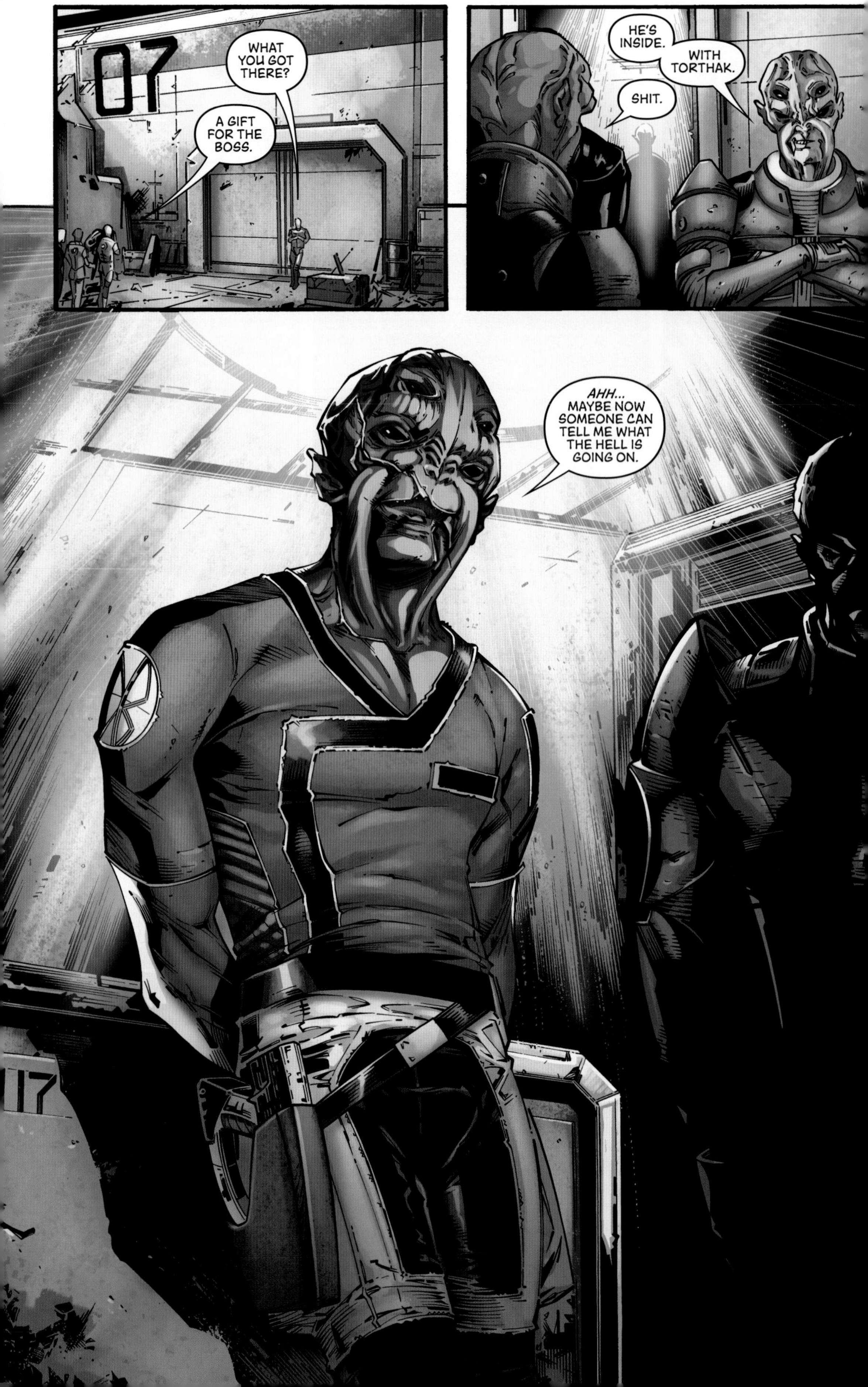
WHAT YOU GOT THERE?
A GIFT FOR THE BOSS.
HE'S INSIDE.
WITH TORTHAK.
SHIT.
AHH... MAYBE NOW SOMEONE CAN TELL ME WHAT THE HELL IS GOING ON.

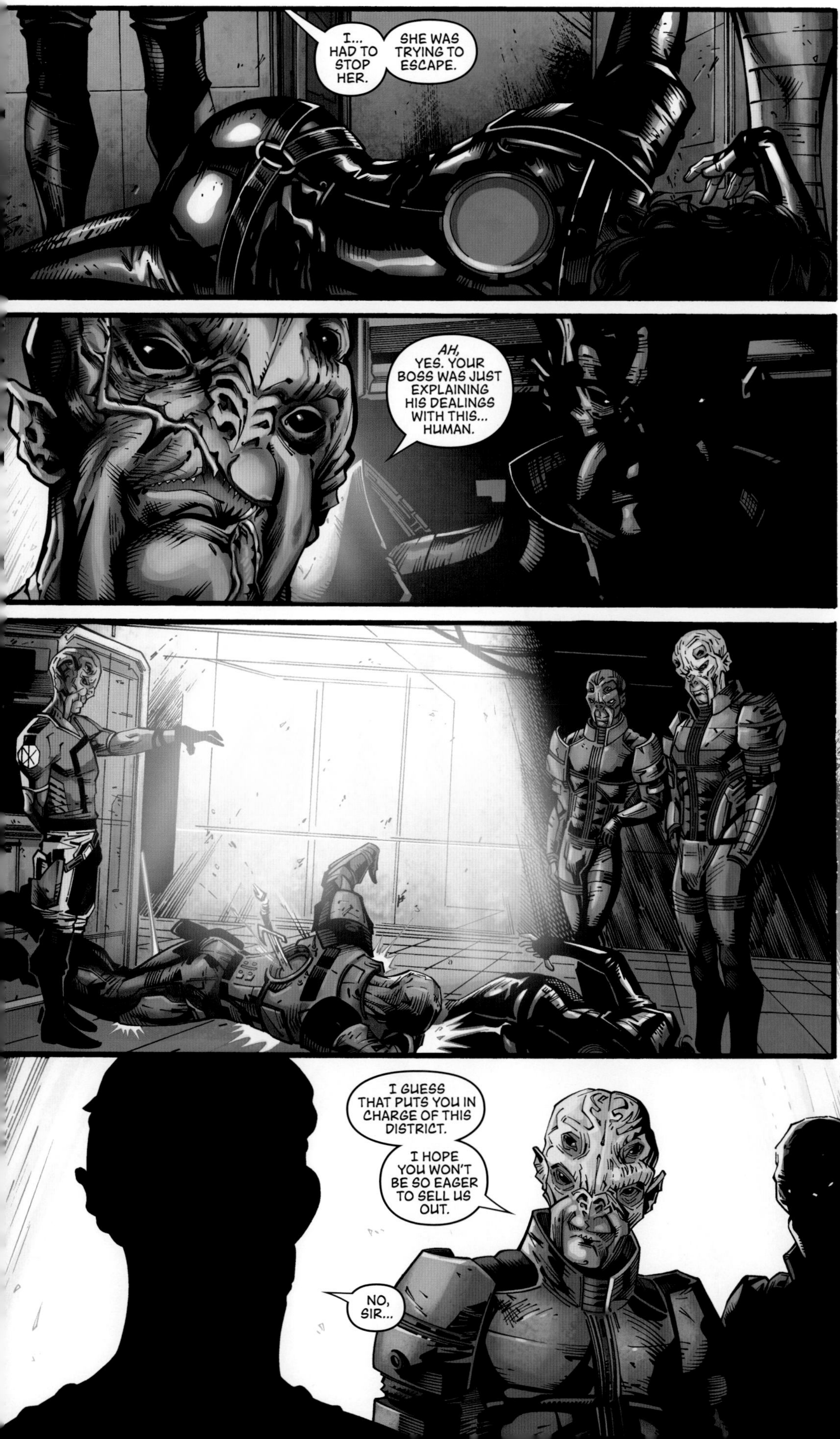

I... HAD TO STOP HER.
SHE WAS TRYING TO ESCAPE.
AH, YES. YOUR BOSS WAS JUST EXPLAINING HIS DEALINGS WITH THIS... HUMAN.
I GUESS THAT PUTS YOU IN CHARGE OF THIS DISTRICT.
I HOPE YOU WON'T BE SO EAGER TO SELL US OUT.
NO, SIR...

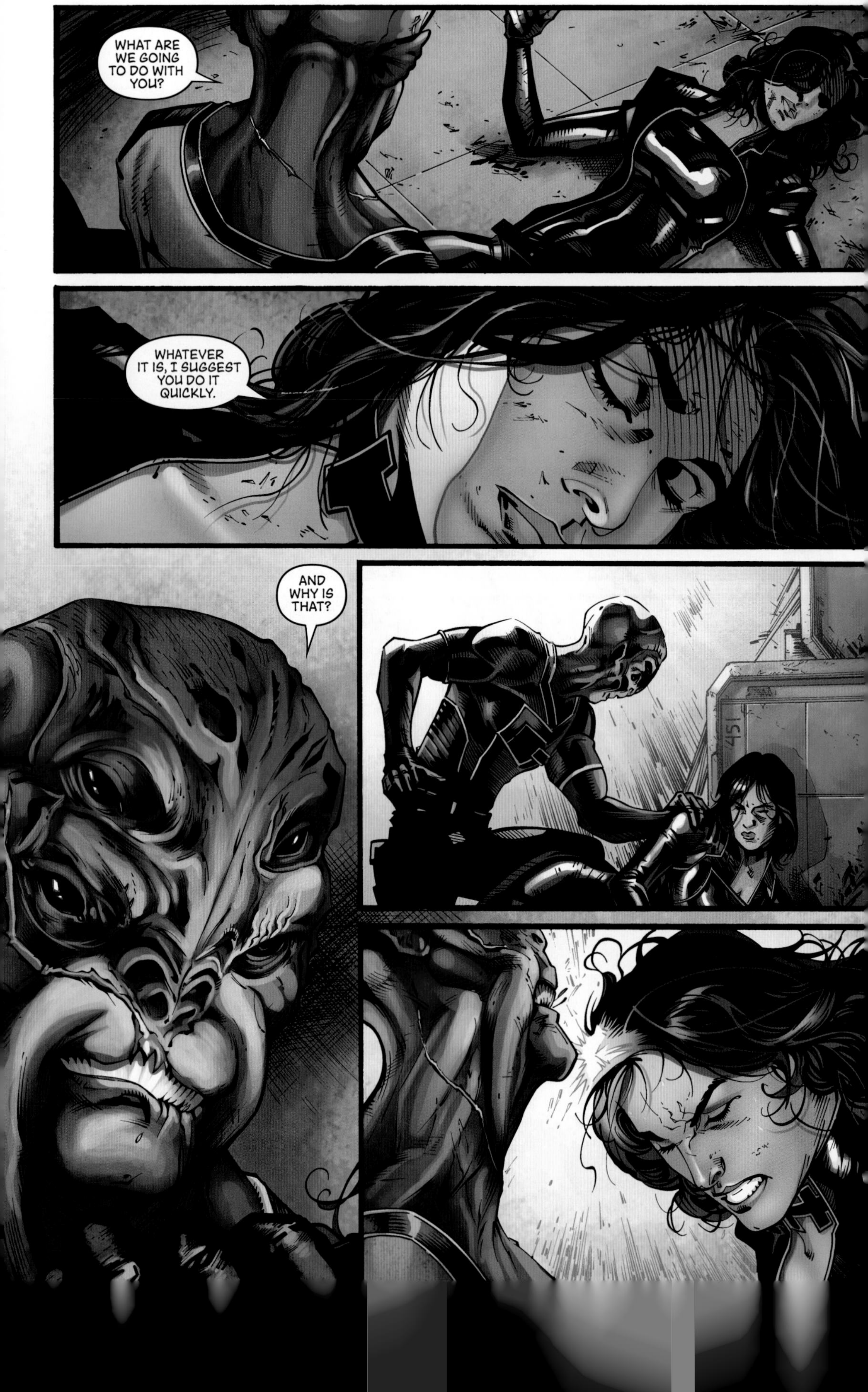
WHAT ARE WE GOING TO DO WITH YOU?
WHATEVER IT IS, I SUGGEST YOU DO IT QUICKLY.
AND WHY IS THAT?
451

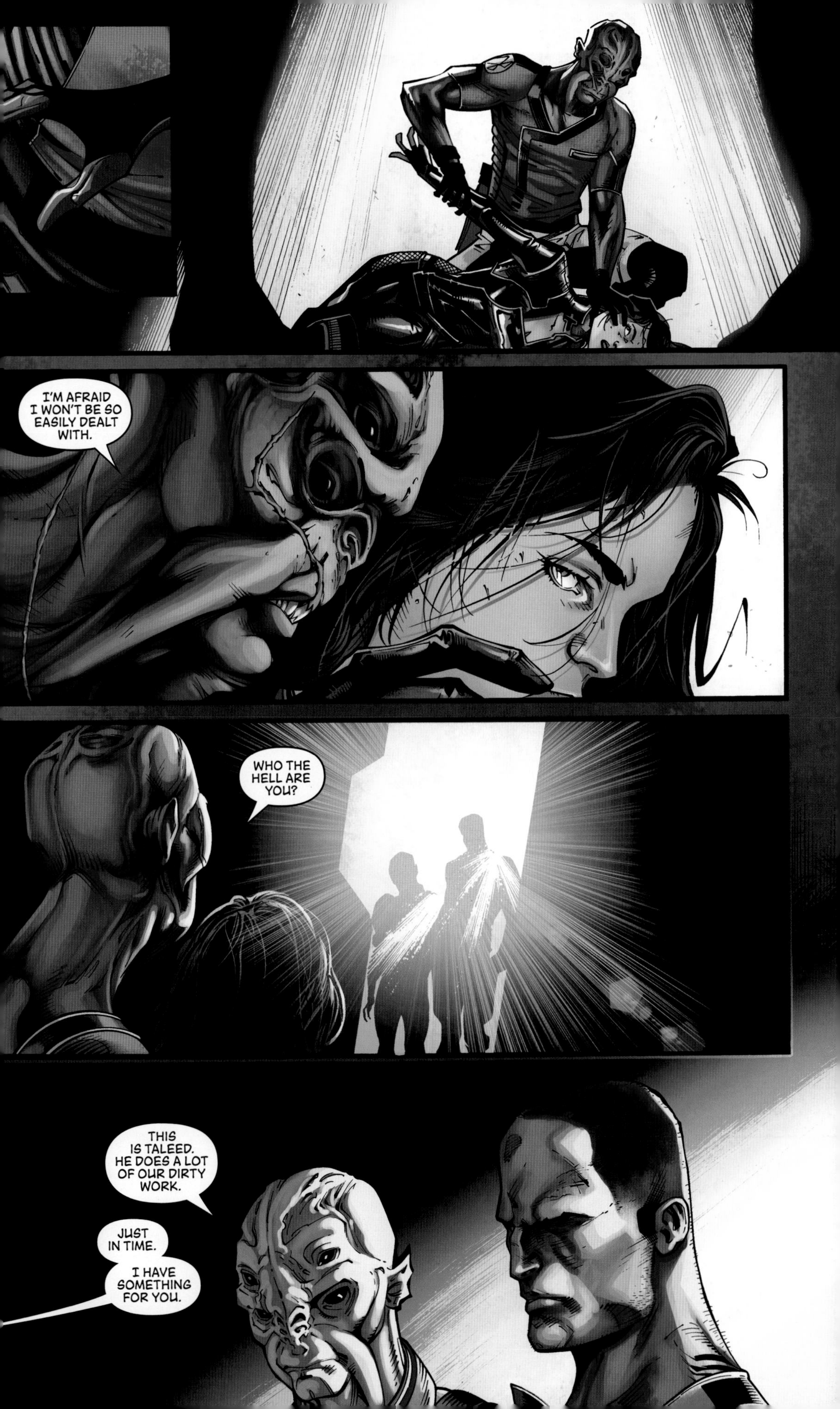
I'M AFRAID I WON'T BE SO EASILY DEALT WITH.
WHO THE HELL ARE YOU?
THIS IS TALEED. HE DOES A LOT OF OUR DIRTY WORK.
JUST IN TIME.
I HAVE SOMETHING FOR YOU.

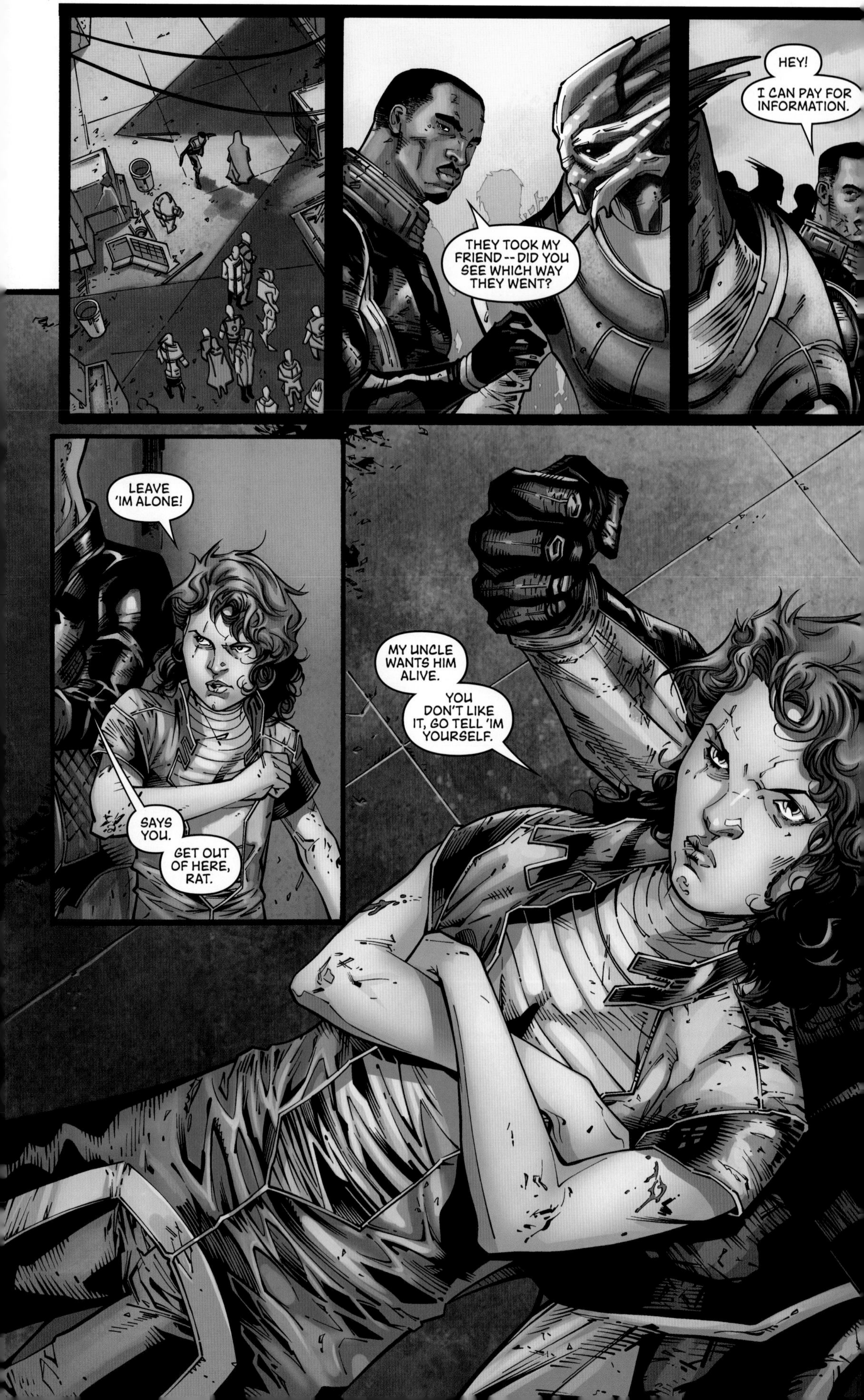
THEY TOOK MY FRIEND -- DID YOU SEE WHICH WAY THEY WENT?
HEY!
I CAN PAY FOR INFORMATION.
LEAVE 'IM ALONE!
SAYS YOU.
GET OUT OF HERE, RAT.
MY UNCLE WANTS HIM ALIVE.
YOU DON'T LIKE IT, GO TELL 'IM YOURSELF.

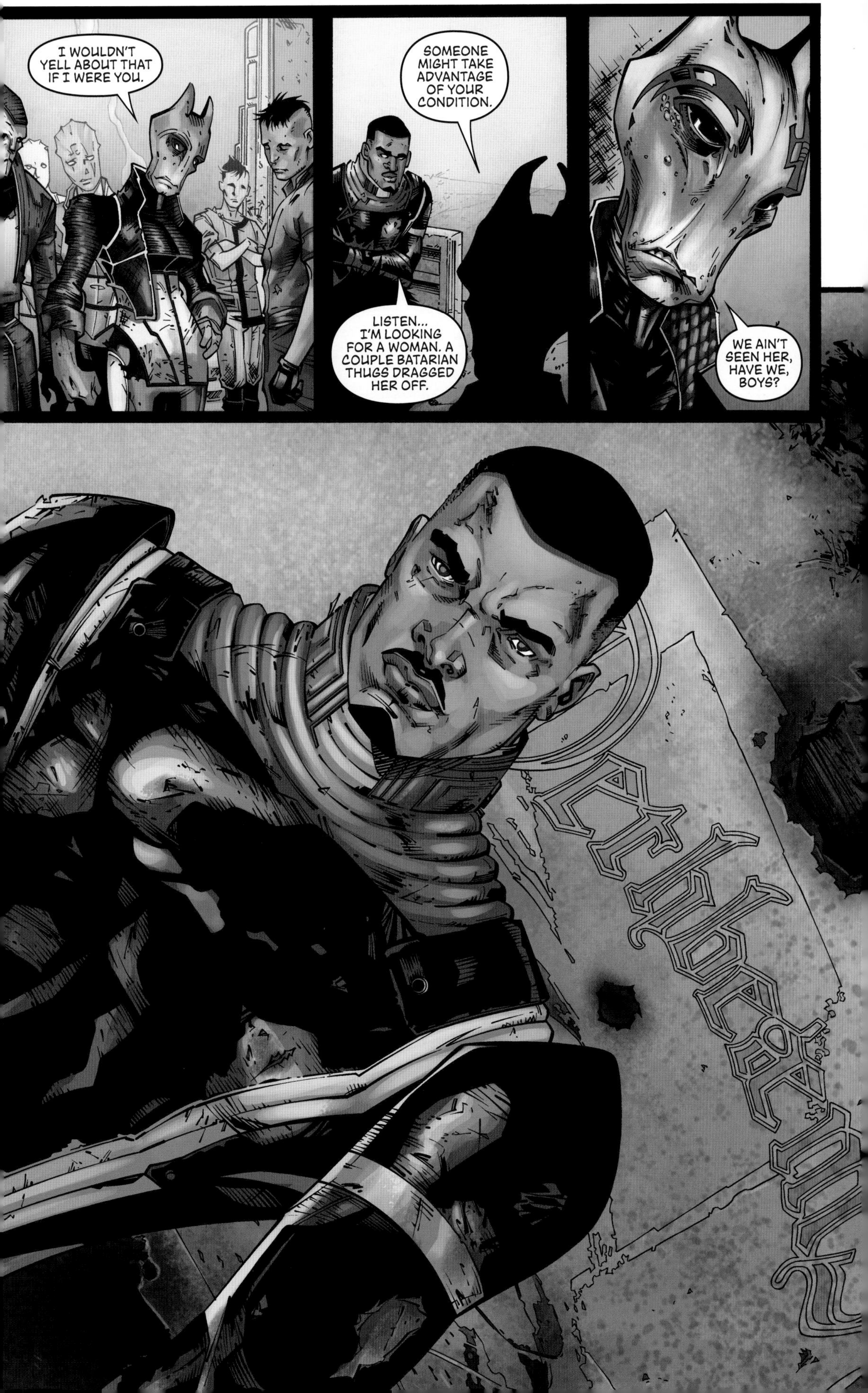
I WOULDN'T YELL ABOUT THAT IF I WERE YOU.
SOMEONE MIGHT TAKE ADVANTAGE OF YOUR CONDITION.
LISTEN... I'M LOOKING FOR A WOMAN. A COUPLE BATARIAN THUGS DRAGGED HER OFF.
WE AIN'T SEEN HER, HAVE WE, BOYS?

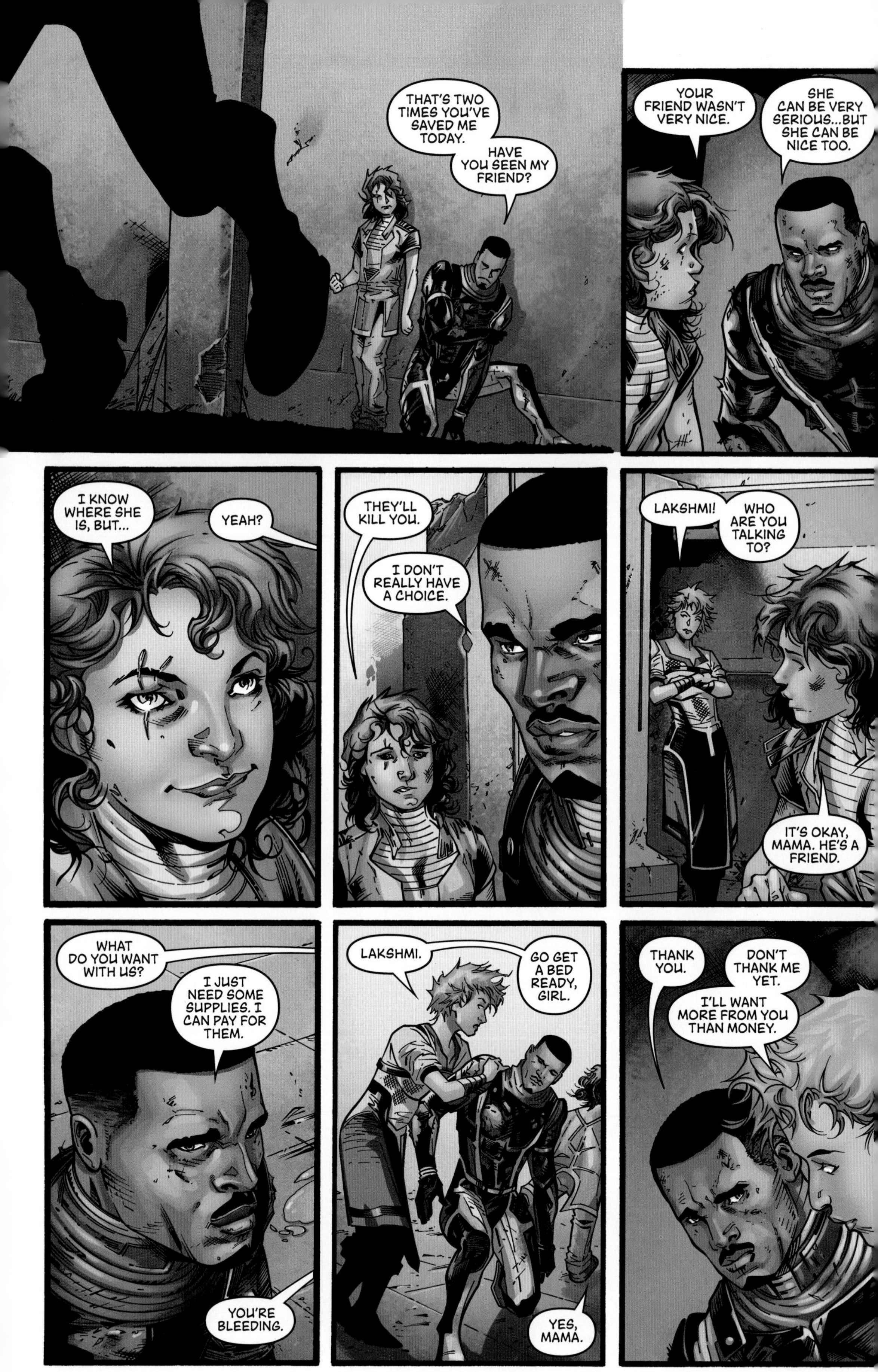

THAT'S TWO TIMES YOU'VE SAVED ME TODAY.
HAVE YOU SEEN MY FRIEND?
YOUR FRIEND WASN'T VERY NICE.
SHE CAN BE VERY SERIOUS...BUT SHE CAN BE NICE TOO.
I KNOW WHERE SHE IS, BUT...
YEAH?
THEY'LL KILL YOU.
I DON'T REALLY HAVE A CHOICE.
LAKSHMI!
WHO ARE YOU TALKING TO?
IT'S OKAY, MAMA. HE'S A FRIEND.
WHAT DO YOU WANT WITH US?
I JUST NEED SOME SUPPLIES. I CAN PAY FOR THEM.
YOU'RE BLEEDING.
LAKSHMI.
GO GET A BED READY, GIRL.
YES, MAMA.
THANK YOU.
DON'T THANK ME YET.
I'LL WANT MORE FROM YOU THAN MONEY.

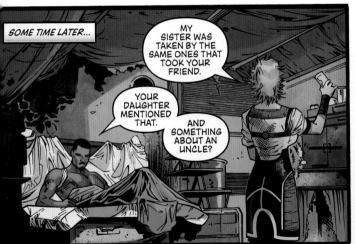

SOME TIME LATER...

MY SISTER WAS TAKEN BY THE SAME ONES THAT TOOK YOUR FRIEND.

YOUR DAUGHTER MENTIONED THAT.

AND SOMETHING ABOUT AN UNCLE?

HE'S THE PROBLEM! STARTED WORKING WITH THOSE THUGS.

TRADED HIS KIDS AND MY SISTER AS PAYMENT TO ENTER INTO THEIR GANG.

I'LL GET THEM BACK FOR YOU.

BUT I NEED SOME SUPPLIES.

LAKSHMI.

DID YOU FIND WHAT I TOLD YOU?

I BROUGHT EVERYTHING I COULD FIND.

I KNOW WHERE MY UNCLE HIDES HIS THINGS.

WILL THIS DO?

I THINK SO.

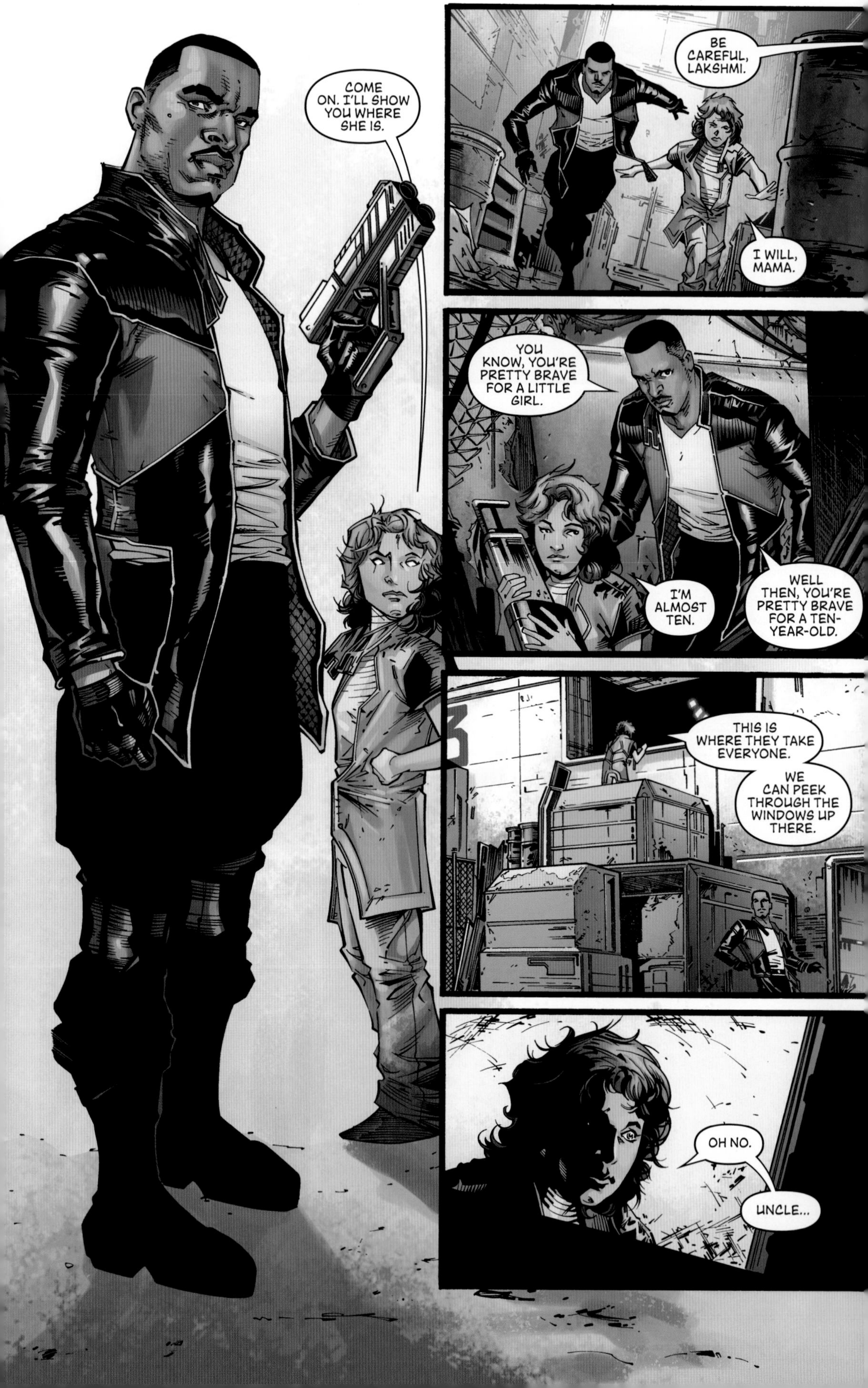
COME ON. I'LL SHOW YOU WHERE SHE IS.
BE CAREFUL, LAKSHMI.
I WILL, MAMA.
YOU KNOW, YOU'RE PRETTY BRAVE FOR A LITTLE GIRL.
I'M ALMOST TEN.
WELL THEN, YOU'RE PRETTY BRAVE FOR A TEN-YEAR-OLD.
THIS IS WHERE THEY TAKE EVERYONE.
WE CAN PEEK THROUGH THE WINDOWS UP THERE.
OH NO.
UNCLE...

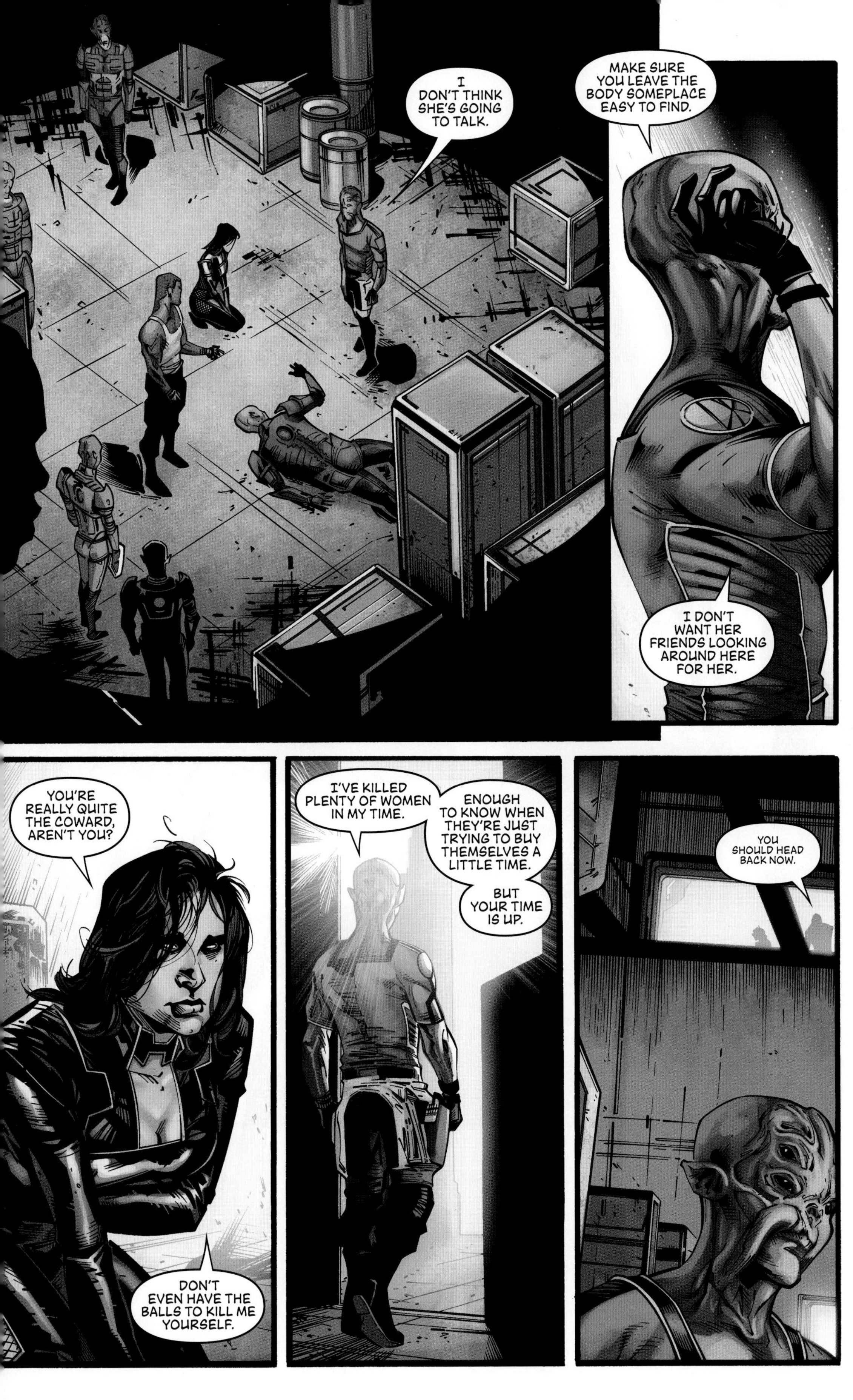
I DON'T THINK SHE'S GOING TO TALK.
MAKE SURE YOU LEAVE THE BODY SOMEPLACE EASY TO FIND.
I DON'T WANT HER FRIENDS LOOKING AROUND HERE FOR HER.
YOU'RE REALLY QUITE THE COWARD, AREN'T YOU?
DON'T EVEN HAVE THE BALLS TO KILL ME YOURSELF.
I'VE KILLED PLENTY OF WOMEN IN MY TIME.
ENOUGH TO KNOW WHEN THEY'RE JUST TRYING TO BUY THEMSELVES A LITTLE TIME.
BUT YOUR TIME IS UP.
YOU SHOULD HEAD BACK NOW.

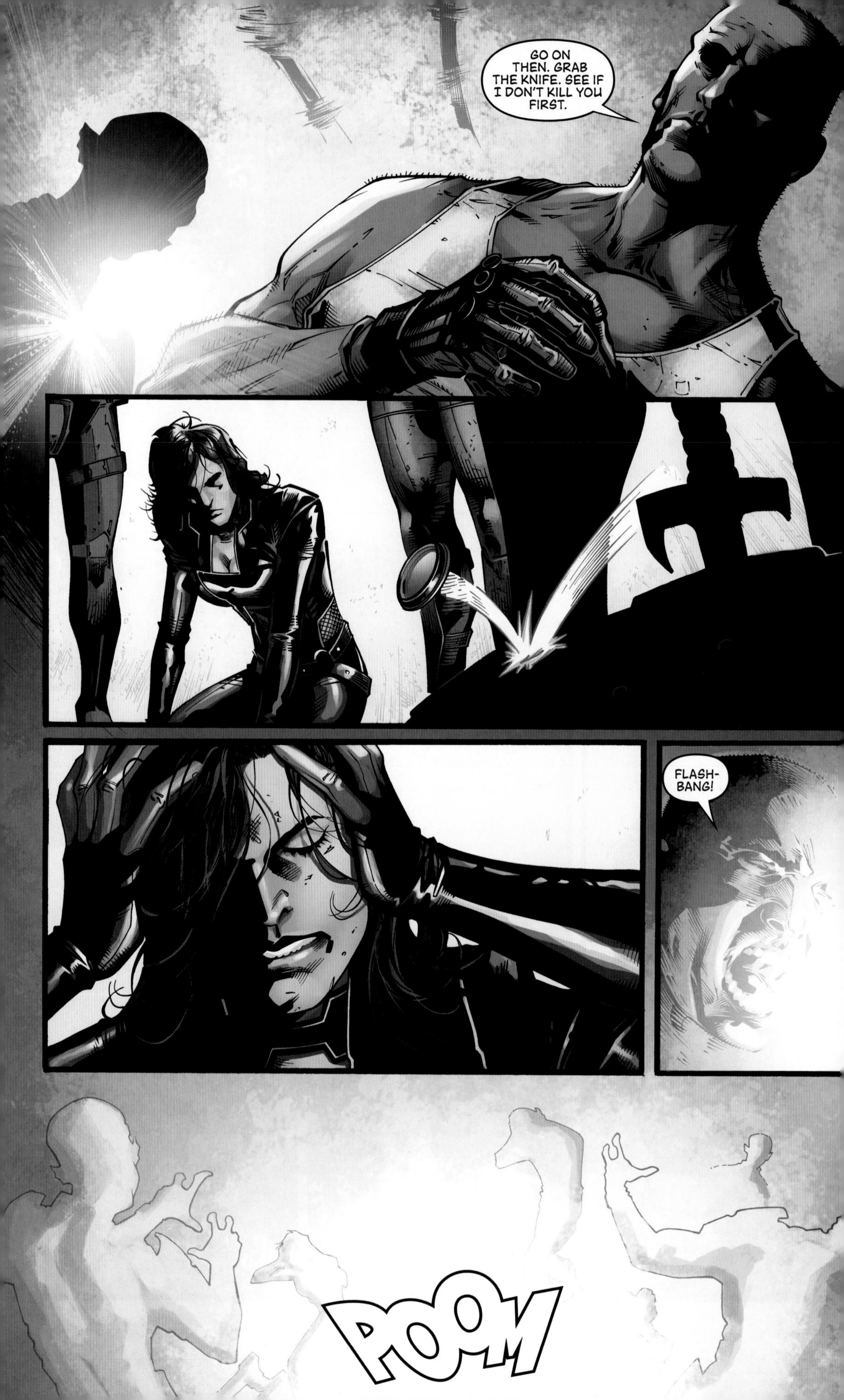
GO ON THEN. GRAB THE KNIFE. SEE IF I DON'T KILL YOU FIRST.
FLASH-BANG!
POOM

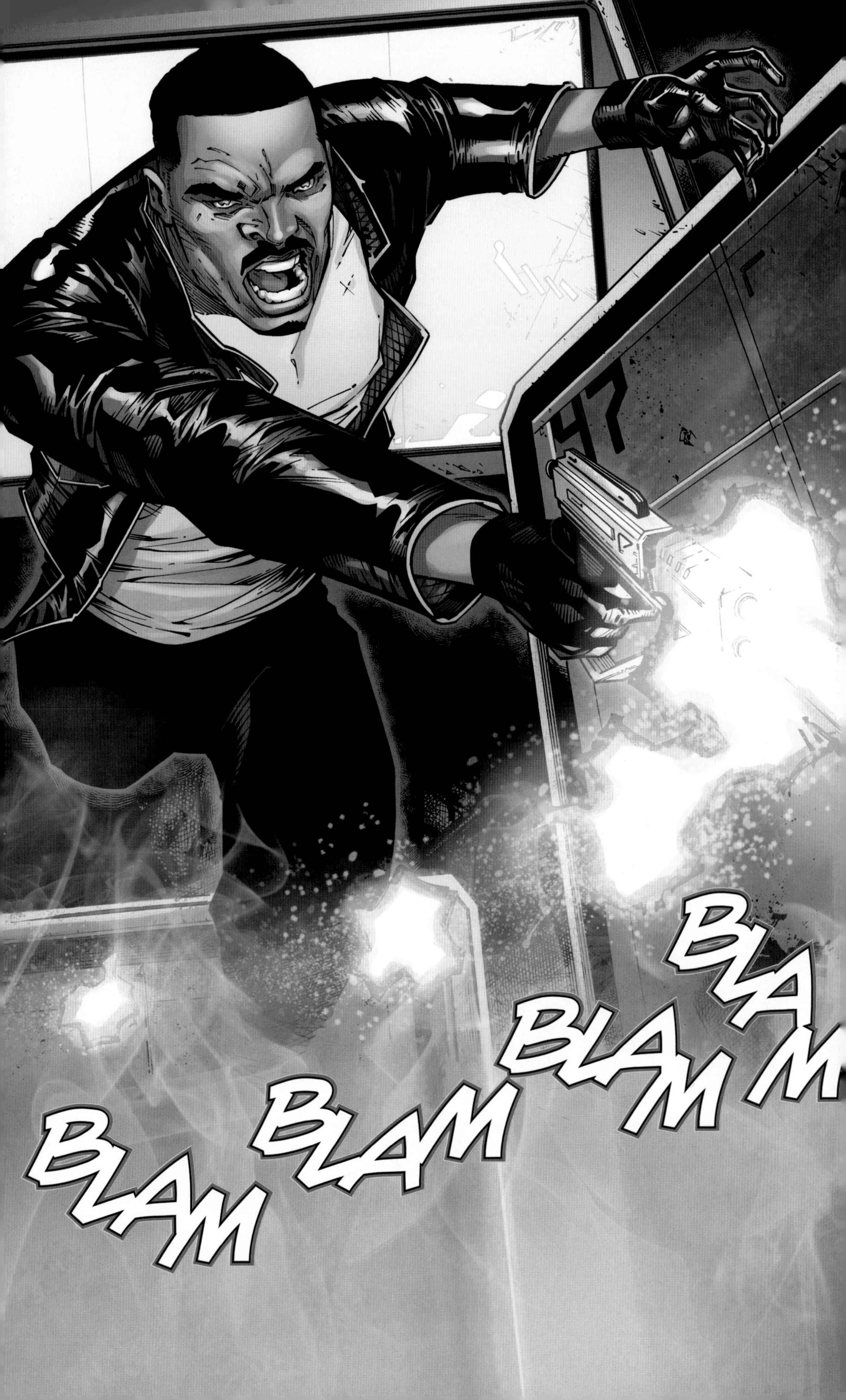
BLAM
BLAM
BLAM
BLAM

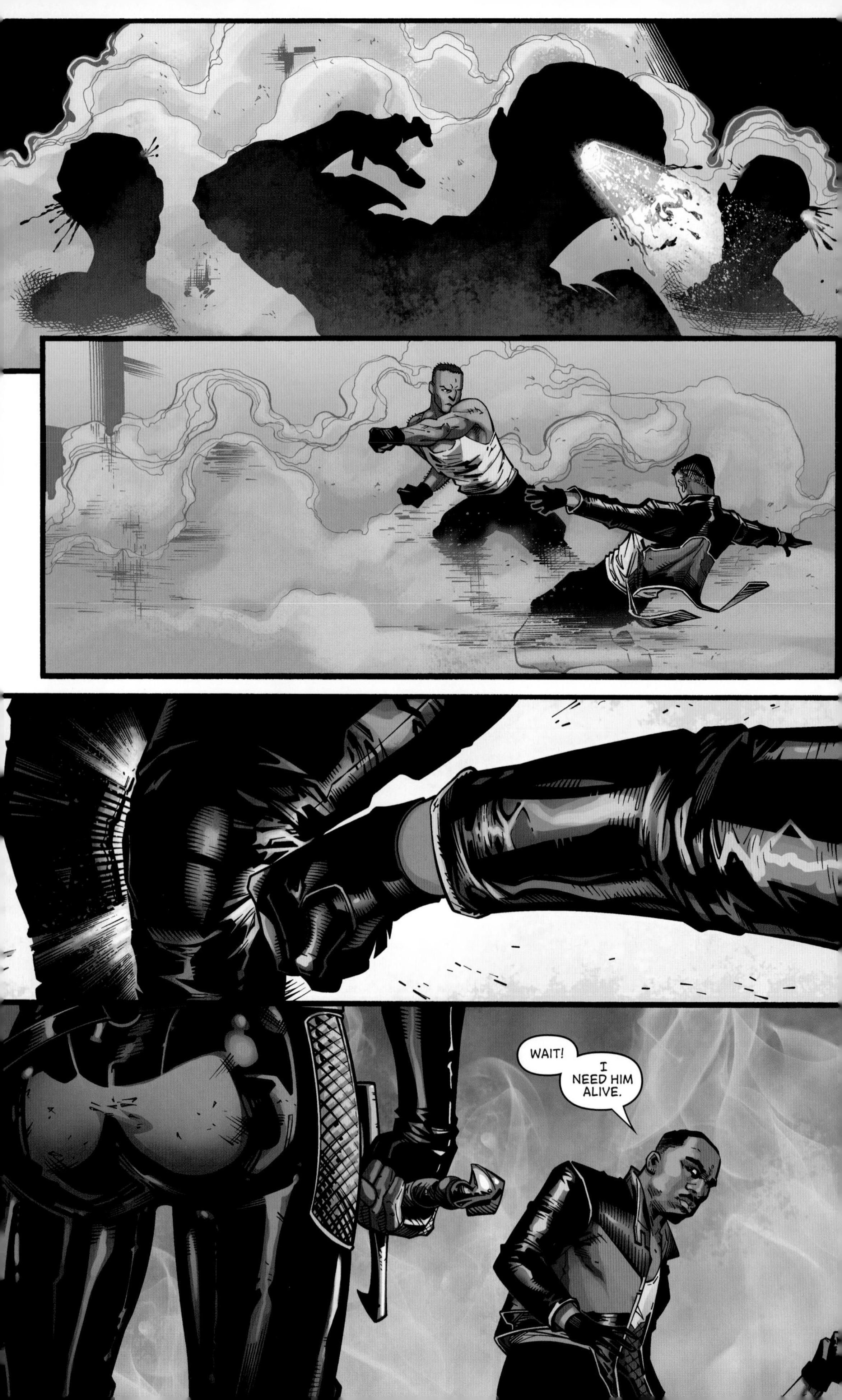
WAIT!
I NEED HIM ALIVE.

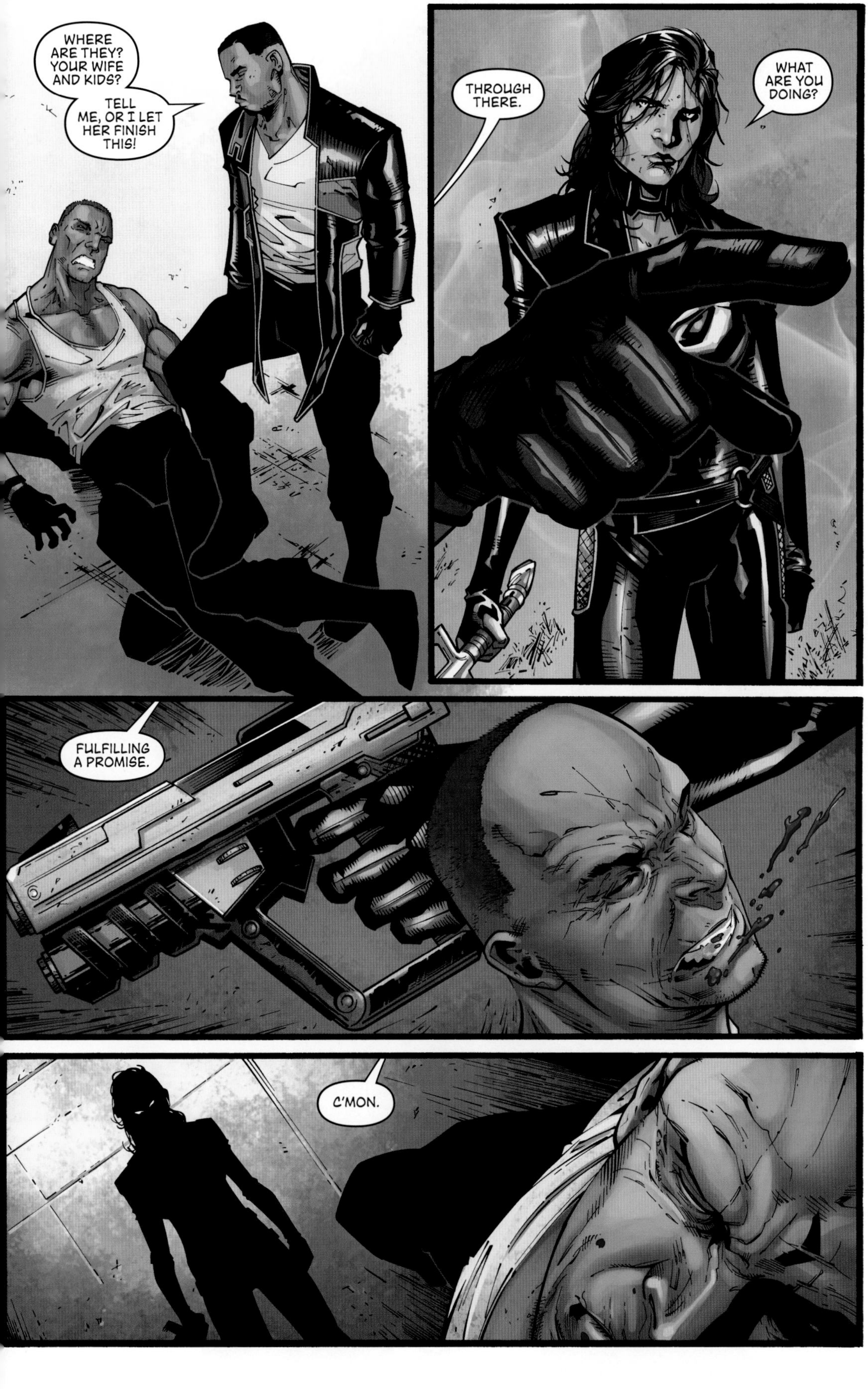
WHERE ARE THEY? YOUR WIFE AND KIDS?
TELL ME, OR I LET HER FINISH THIS!
THROUGH THERE.
WHAT ARE YOU DOING?
FULFILLING A PROMISE.
C'MON.

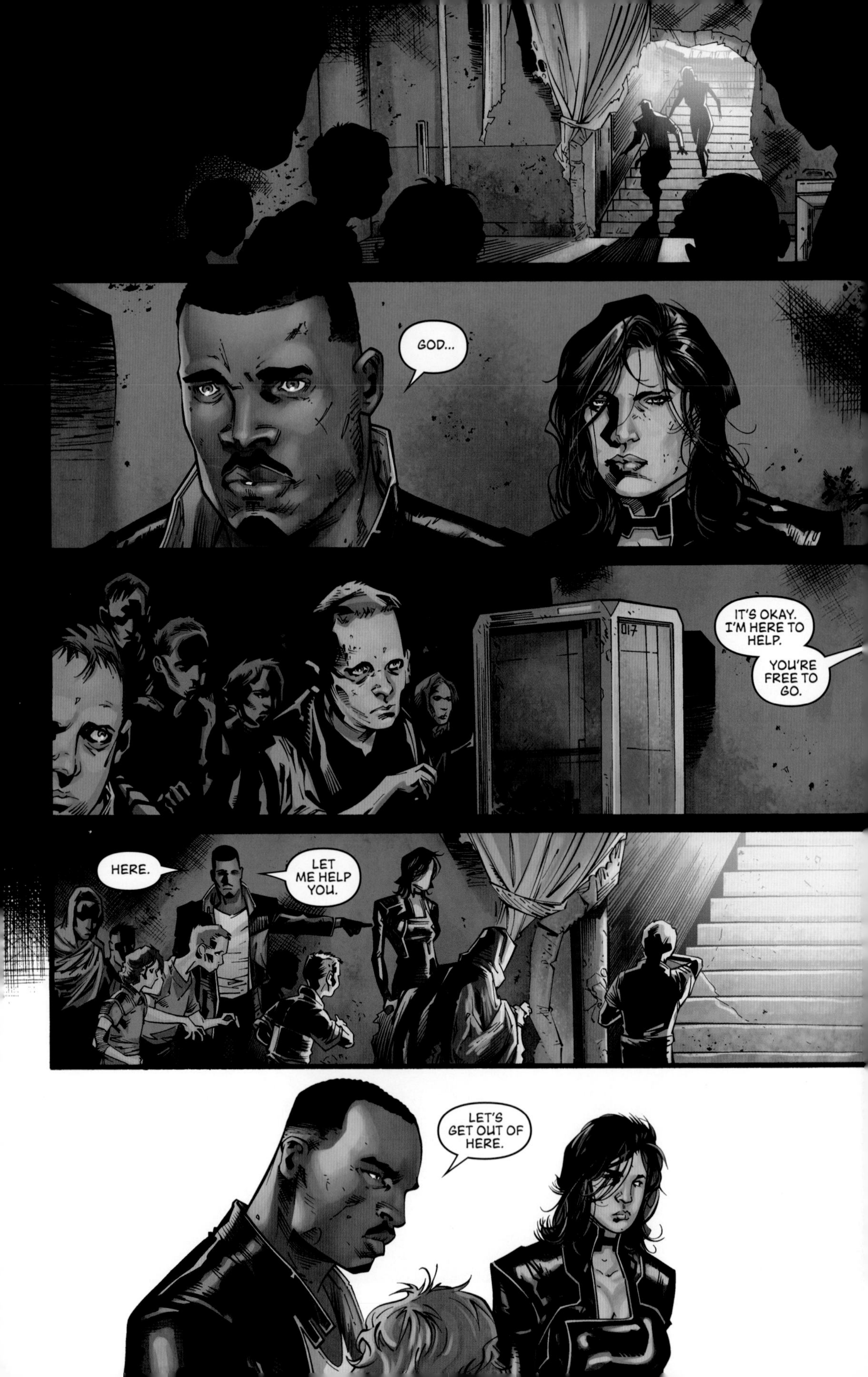
GOD...
IT'S OKAY. I'M HERE TO HELP.
YOU'RE FREE TO GO.
HERE.
LET ME HELP YOU.
LET'S GET OUT OF HERE.

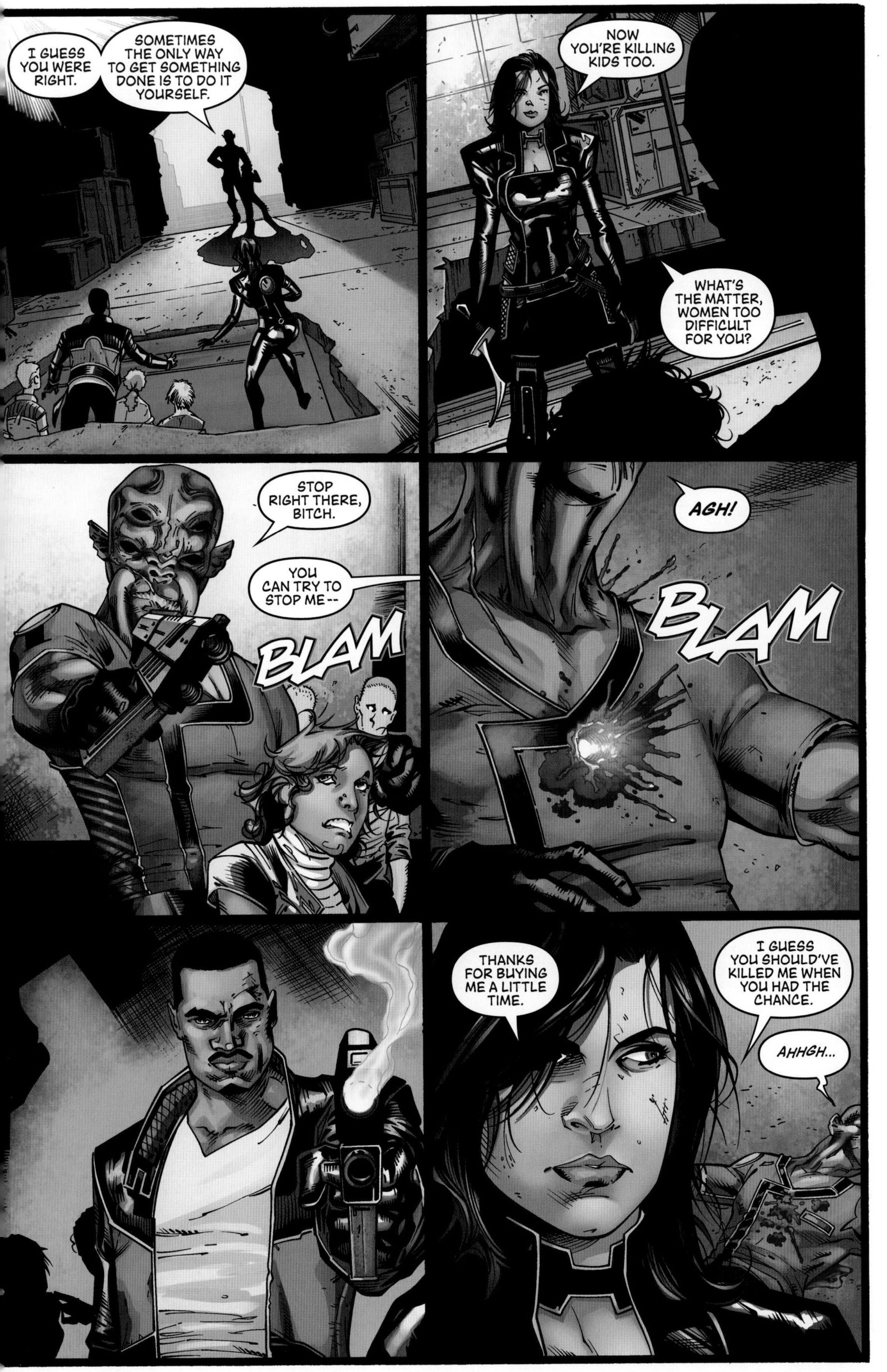

I GUESS YOU WERE RIGHT.
SOMETIMES THE ONLY WAY TO GET SOMETHING DONE IS TO DO IT YOURSELF.
NOW YOU'RE KILLING KIDS TOO.
WHAT'S THE MATTER, WOMEN TOO DIFFICULT FOR YOU?
STOP RIGHT THERE, BITCH.
YOU CAN TRY TO STOP ME--
BLAM
AGH!
BLAM
THANKS FOR BUYING ME A LITTLE TIME.
I GUESS YOU SHOULD'VE KILLED ME WHEN YOU HAD THE CHANCE.
AHHGH...

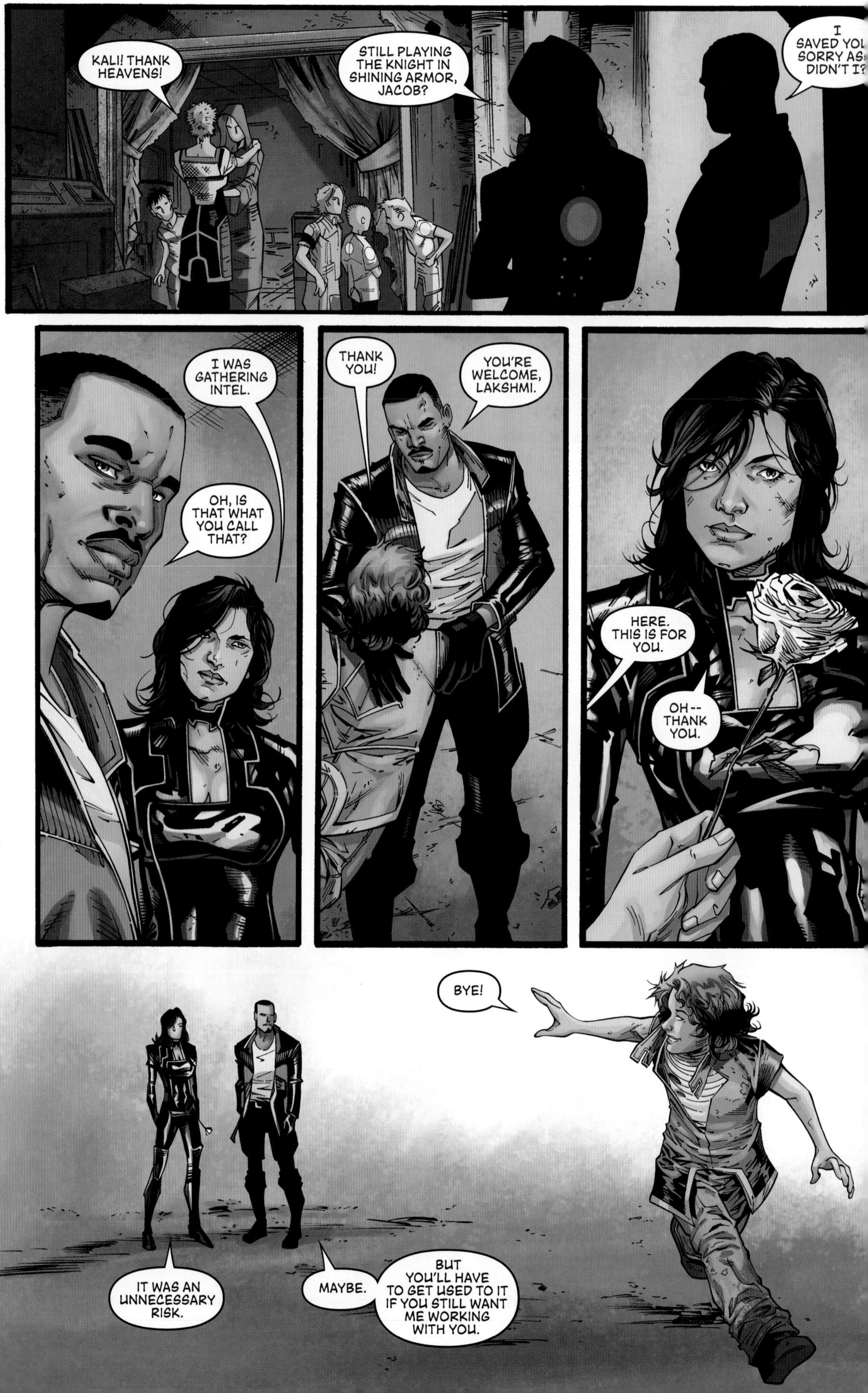
KALI! THANK HEAVENS!
STILL PLAYING THE KNIGHT IN SHINING ARMOR, JACOB?
I SAVED YOU SORRY AS DIDN'T I?
I WAS GATHERING INTEL.
OH, IS THAT WHAT YOU CALL THAT?
THANK YOU!
YOU'RE WELCOME, LAKSHMI.
HERE. THIS IS FOR YOU.
OH-- THANK YOU.
BYE!
IT WAS AN UNNECESSARY RISK.
MAYBE.
BUT YOU'LL HAVE TO GET USED TO IT IF YOU STILL WANT ME WORKING WITH YOU.

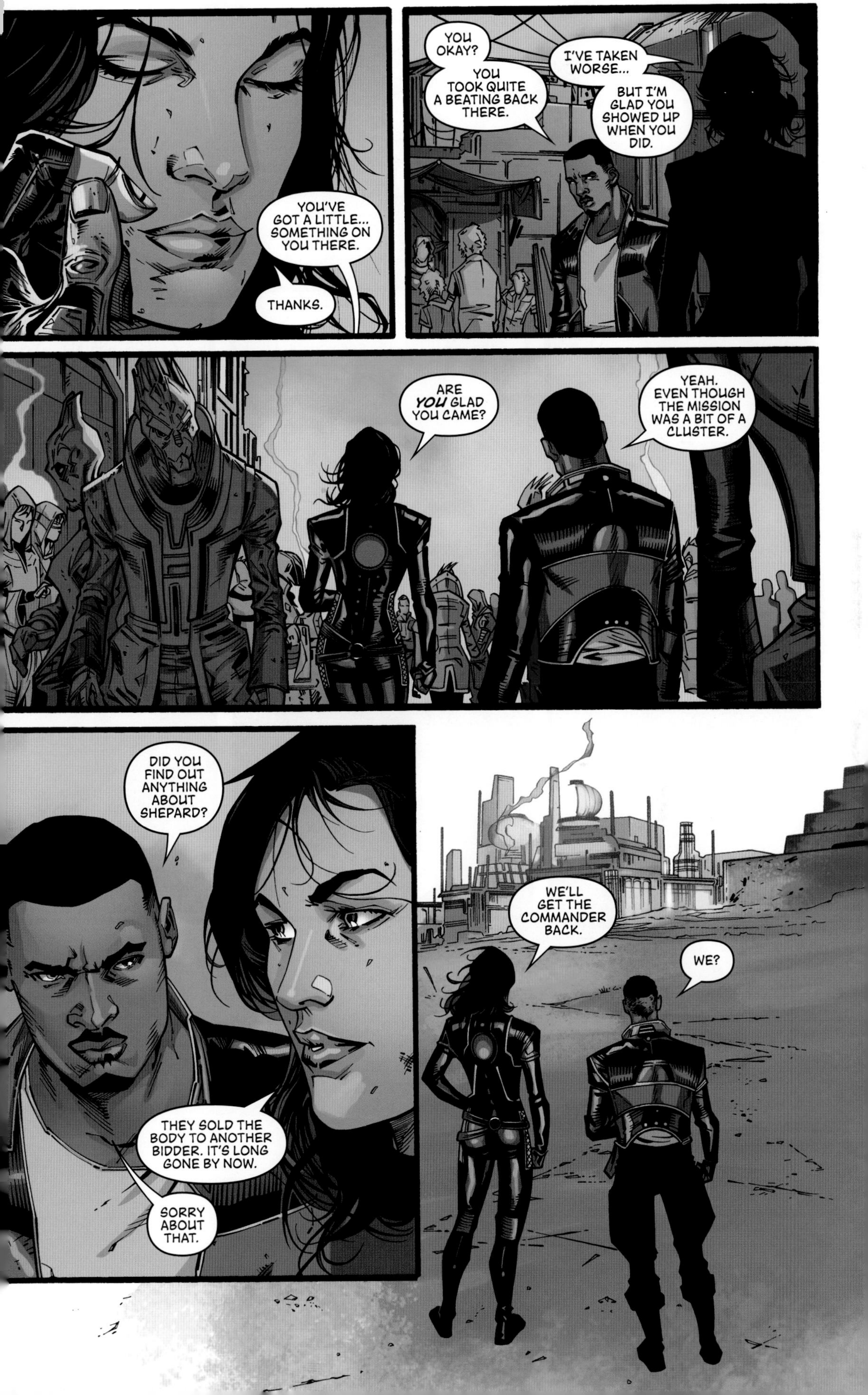
YOU'VE GOT A LITTLE... SOMETHING ON YOU THERE.
THANKS.
YOU OKAY?
YOU TOOK QUITE A BEATING BACK THERE.
I'VE TAKEN WORSE...
BUT I'M GLAD YOU SHOWED UP WHEN YOU DID.
ARE *YOU* GLAD YOU CAME?
YEAH. EVEN THOUGH THE MISSION WAS A BIT OF A CLUSTER.
DID YOU FIND OUT ANYTHING ABOUT SHEPARD?
THEY SOLD THE BODY TO ANOTHER BIDDER. IT'S LONG GONE BY NOW.
SORRY ABOUT THAT.
WE'LL GET THE COMMANDER BACK.
WE?

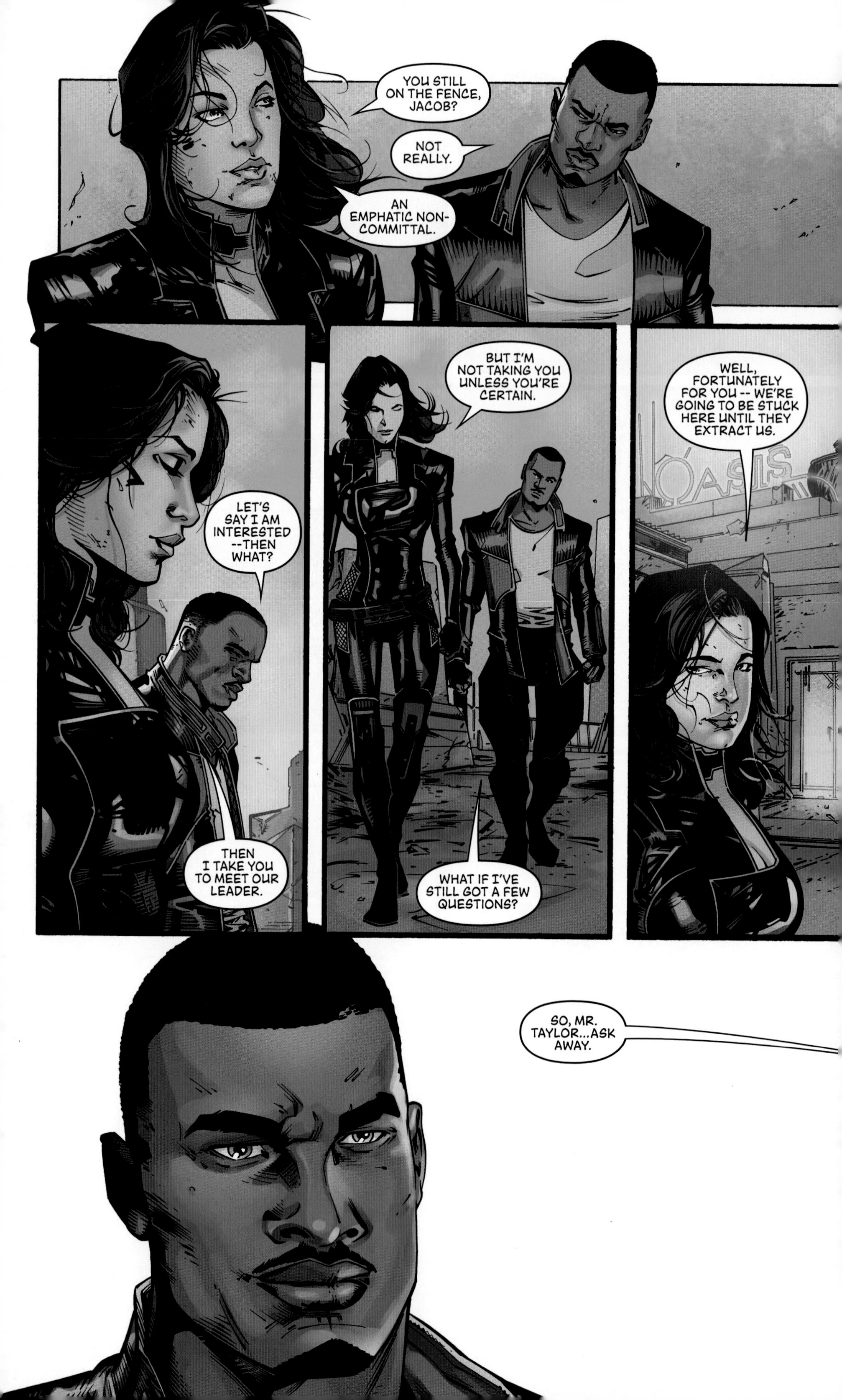

YOU STILL ON THE FENCE, JACOB?
NOT REALLY.
AN EMPHATIC NON-COMMITTAL.
LET'S SAY I AM INTERESTED --THEN WHAT?
THEN I TAKE YOU TO MEET OUR LEADER.
BUT I'M NOT TAKING YOU UNLESS YOU'RE CERTAIN.
WHAT IF I'VE STILL GOT A FEW QUESTIONS?
WELL, FORTUNATELY FOR YOU -- WE'RE GOING TO BE STUCK HERE UNTIL THEY EXTRACT US.
OASIS
SO, MR. TAYLOR...ASK AWAY.

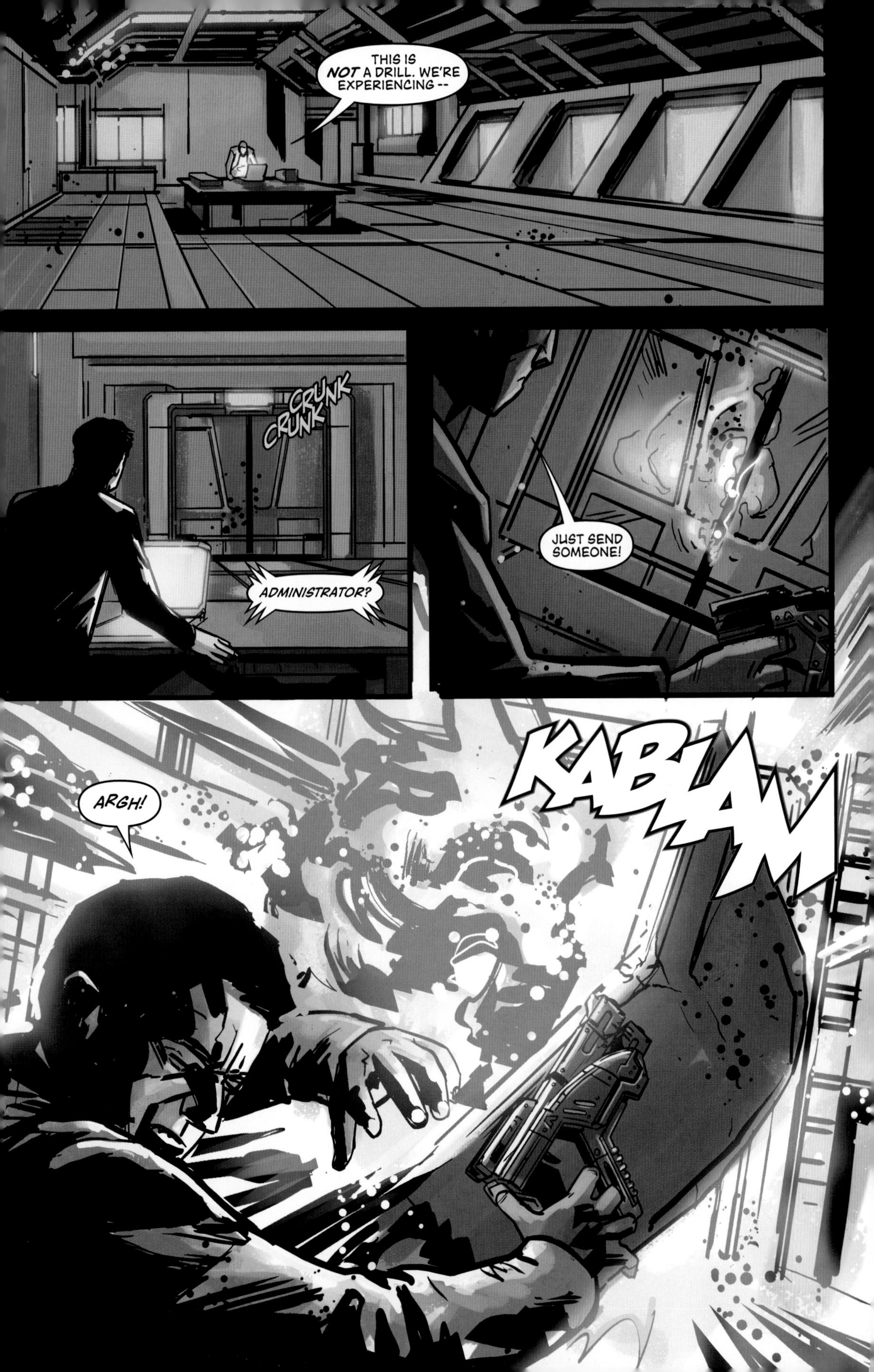
THIS IS *NOT* A DRILL. WE'RE EXPERIENCING --
CRUNK CRUNK
ADMINISTRATOR?
JUST SEND SOMEONE!
ARGH!
KABLAM

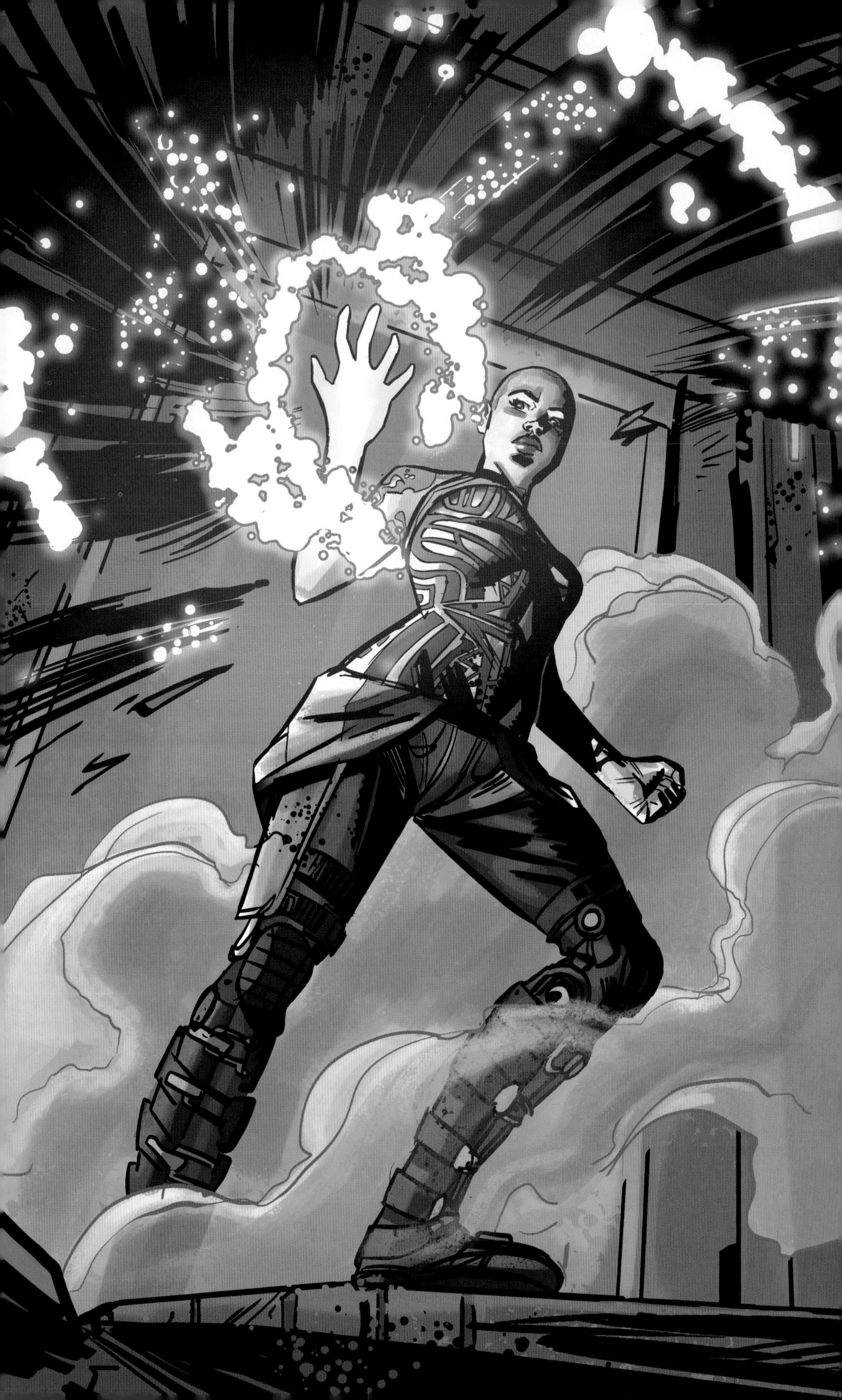

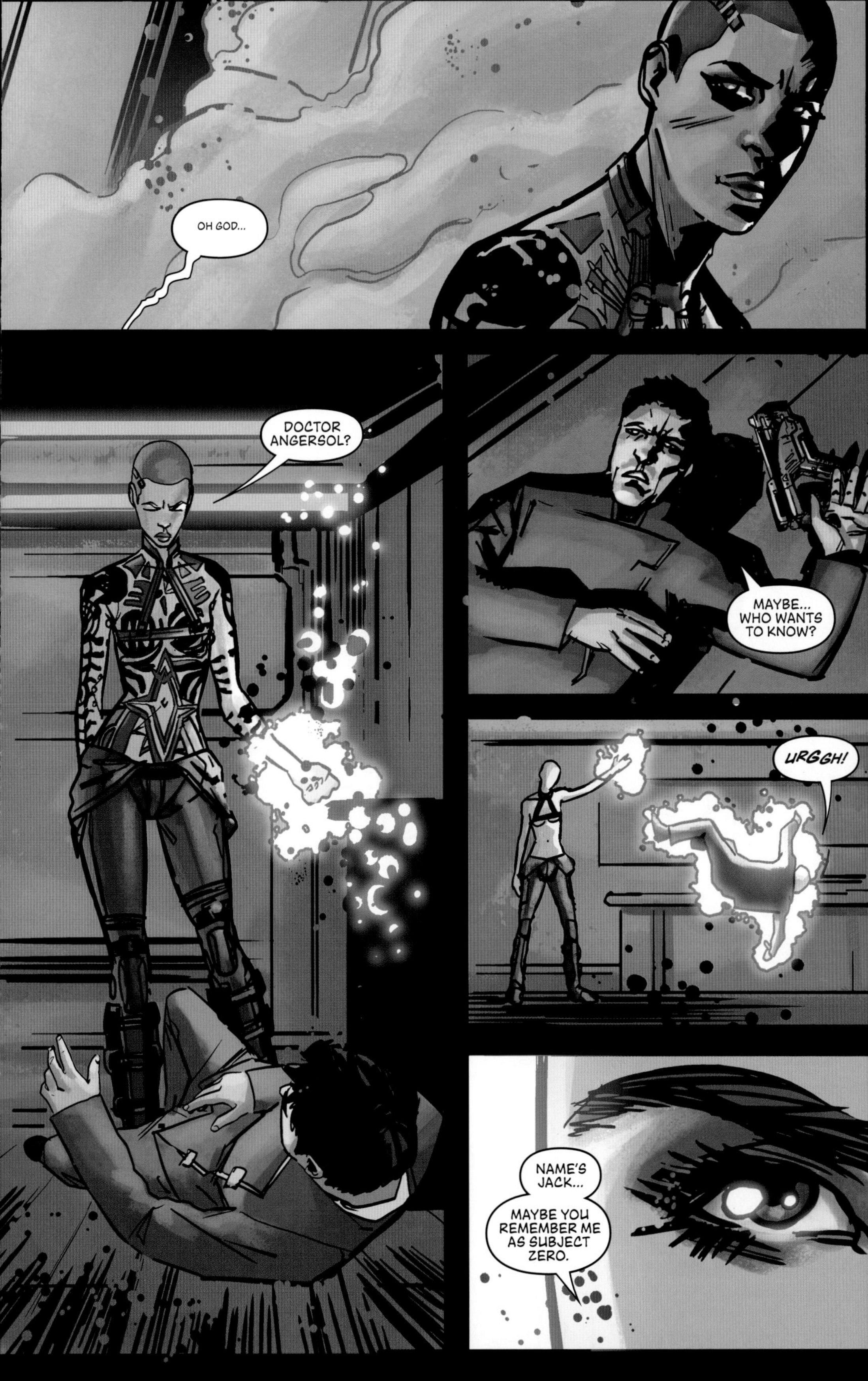
OH GOD...
DOCTOR ANGERSOL?
MAYBE... WHO WANTS TO KNOW?
URGGH!
NAME'S JACK...
MAYBE YOU REMEMBER ME AS SUBJECT ZERO.

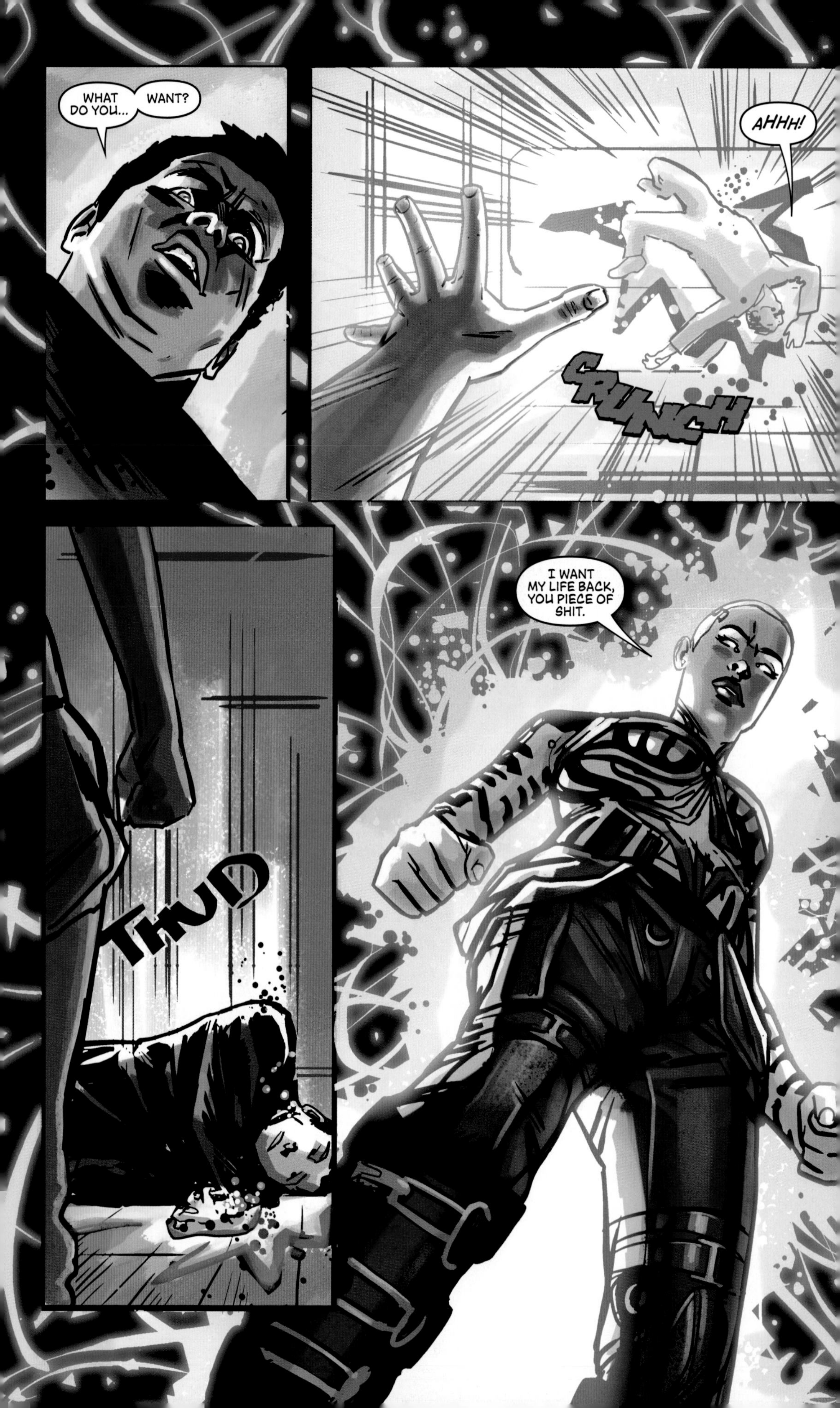
WHAT DO YOU...
WANT?
AHHH!
CRUNCH
THUD
I WANT MY LIFE BACK, YOU PIECE OF SHIT.

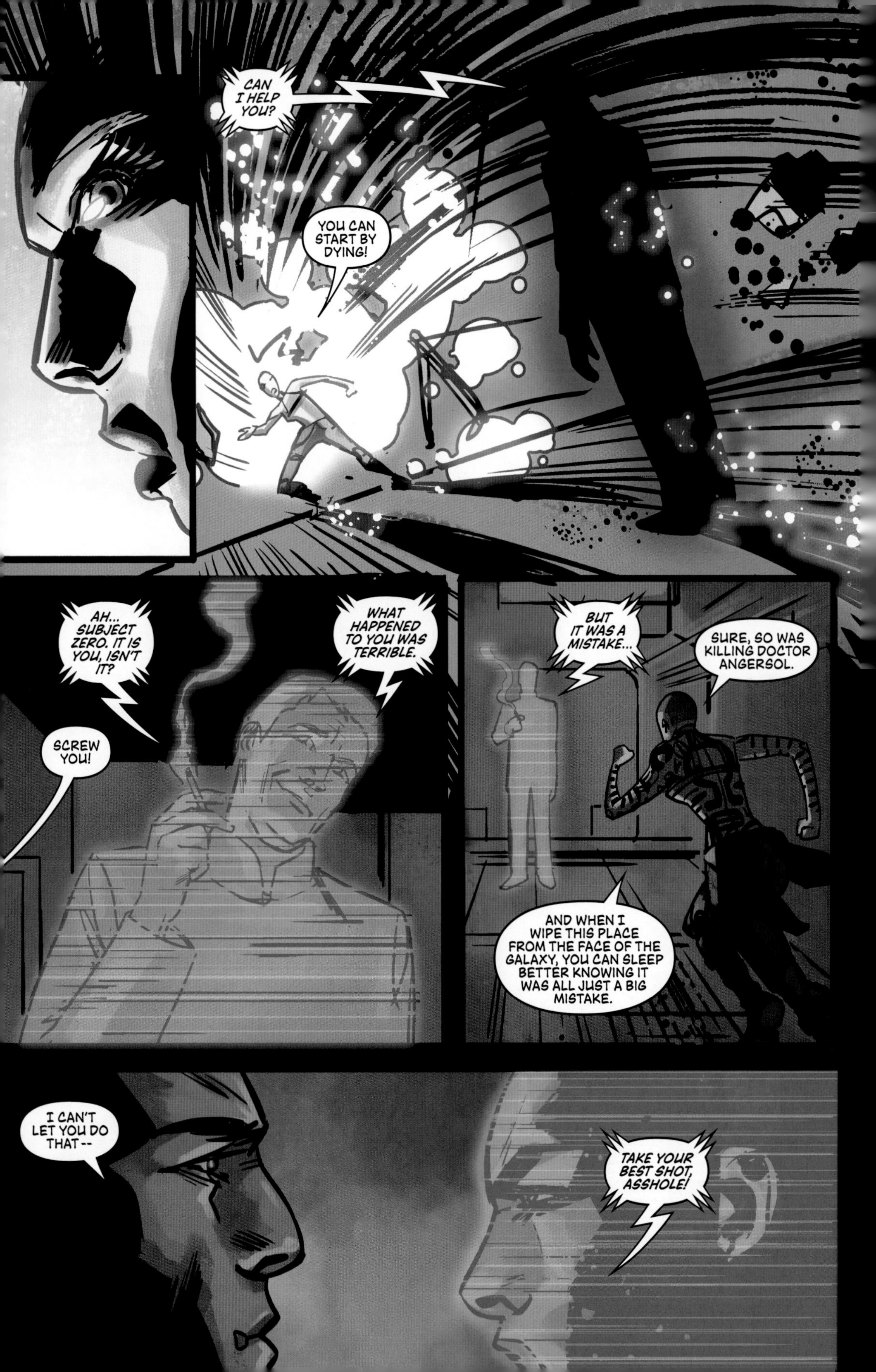
CAN I HELP YOU?
YOU CAN START BY DYING!
AH... SUBJECT ZERO. IT IS YOU, ISN'T IT?
WHAT HAPPENED TO YOU WAS TERRIBLE.
SCREW YOU!
BUT IT WAS A MISTAKE...
SURE, SO WAS KILLING DOCTOR ANGERSOL.
AND WHEN I WIPE THIS PLACE FROM THE FACE OF THE GALAXY, YOU CAN SLEEP BETTER KNOWING IT WAS ALL JUST A BIG MISTAKE.
I CAN'T LET YOU DO THAT--
TAKE YOUR BEST SHOT, ASSHOLE!

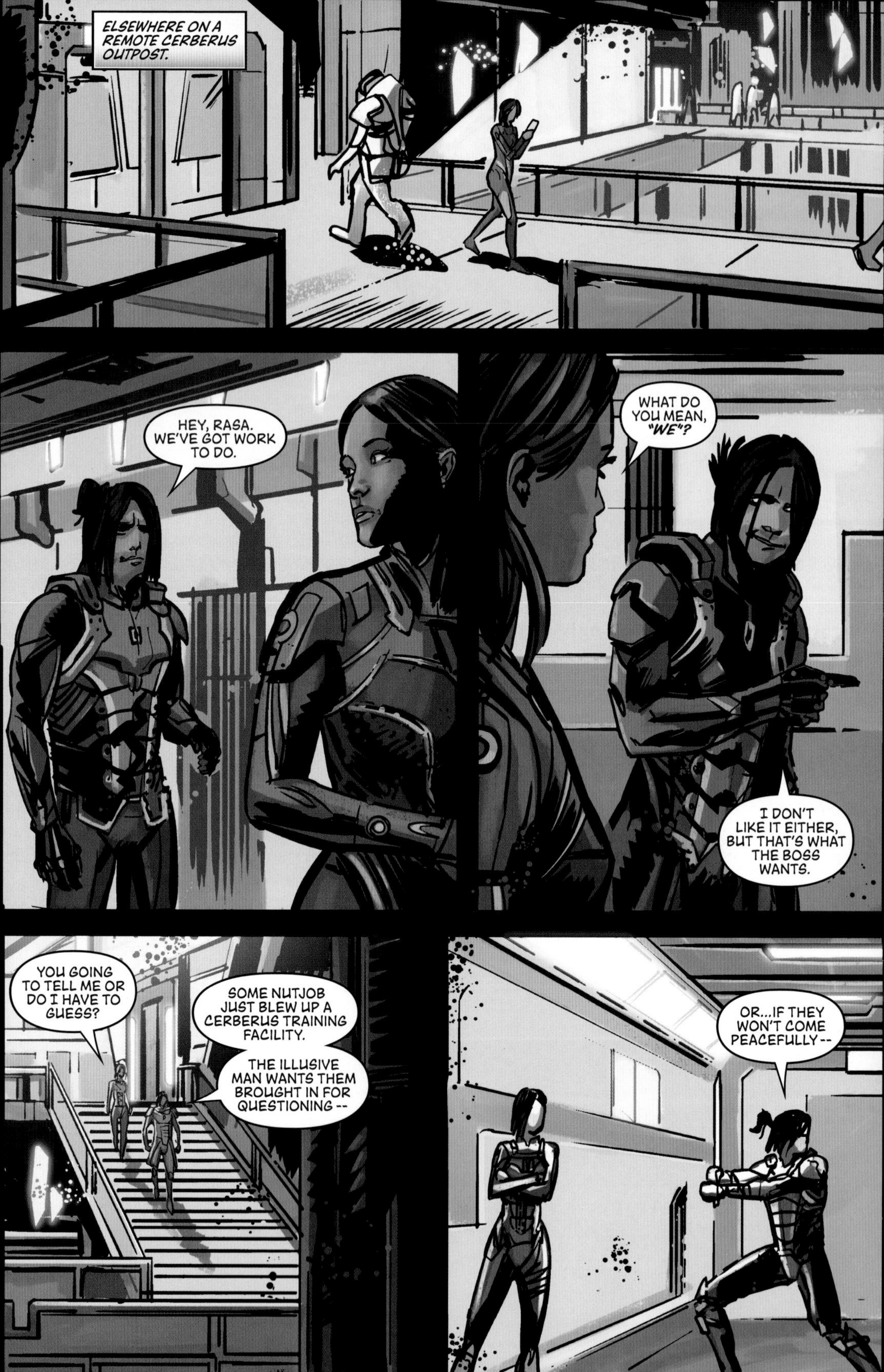
ELSEWHERE ON A REMOTE CERBERUS OUTPOST.
HEY, RASA. WE'VE GOT WORK TO DO.
WHAT DO YOU MEAN, "WE"?
I DON'T LIKE IT EITHER, BUT THAT'S WHAT THE BOSS WANTS.
YOU GOING TO TELL ME OR DO I HAVE TO GUESS?
SOME NUTJOB JUST BLEW UP A CERBERUS TRAINING FACILITY.
THE ILLUSIVE MAN WANTS THEM BROUGHT IN FOR QUESTIONING --
OR...IF THEY WON'T COME PEACEFULLY --

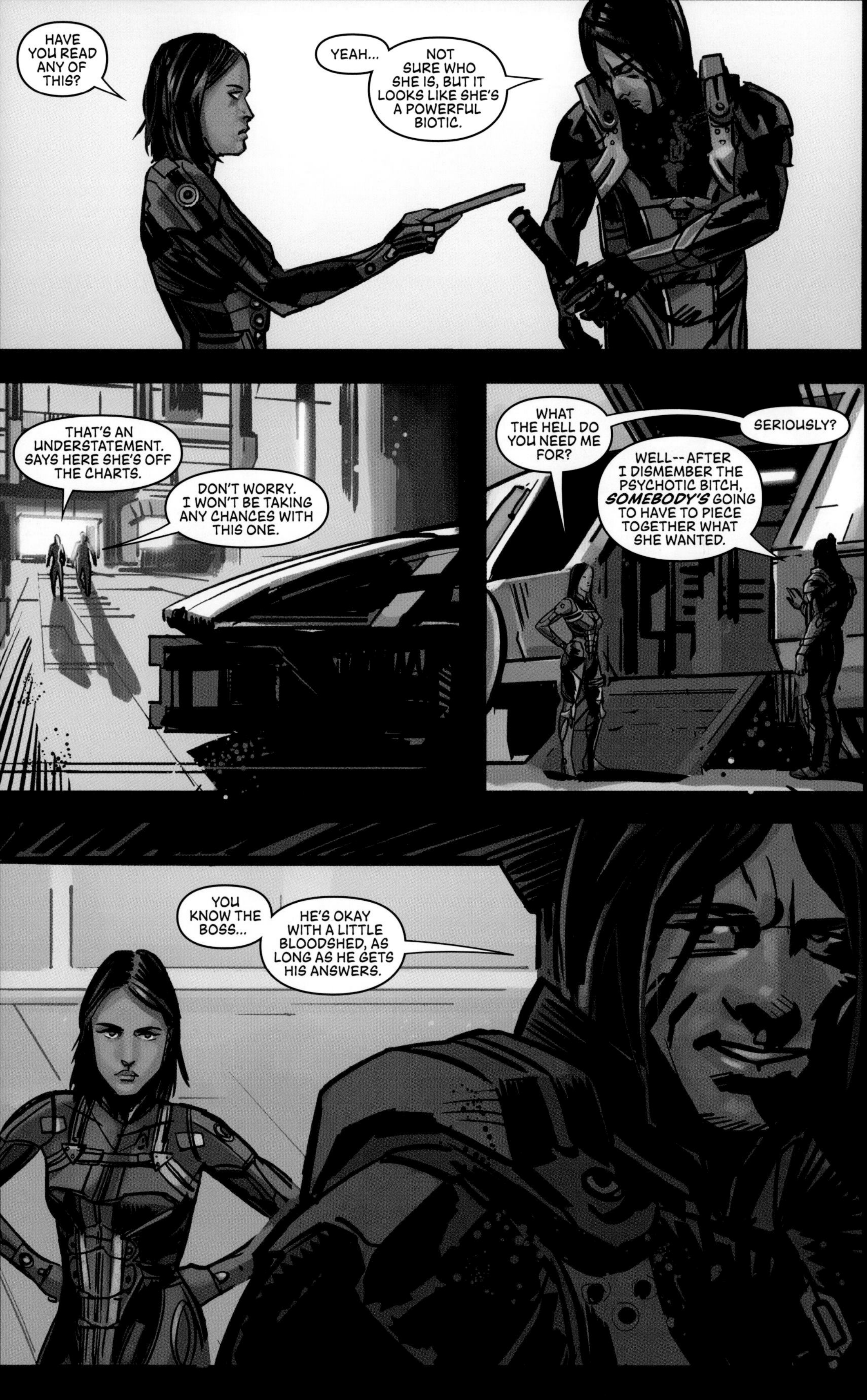
HAVE YOU READ ANY OF THIS?
YEAH...
NOT SURE WHO SHE IS, BUT IT LOOKS LIKE SHE'S A POWERFUL BIOTIC.
THAT'S AN UNDERSTATEMENT. SAYS HERE SHE'S OFF THE CHARTS.
DON'T WORRY. I WON'T BE TAKING ANY CHANCES WITH THIS ONE.
WHAT THE HELL DO YOU NEED ME FOR?
SERIOUSLY?
WELL-- AFTER I DISMEMBER THE PSYCHOTIC BITCH, *SOMEBODY'S* GOING TO HAVE TO PIECE TOGETHER WHAT SHE WANTED.
YOU KNOW THE BOSS...
HE'S OKAY WITH A LITTLE BLOODSHED, AS LONG AS HE GETS HIS ANSWERS.

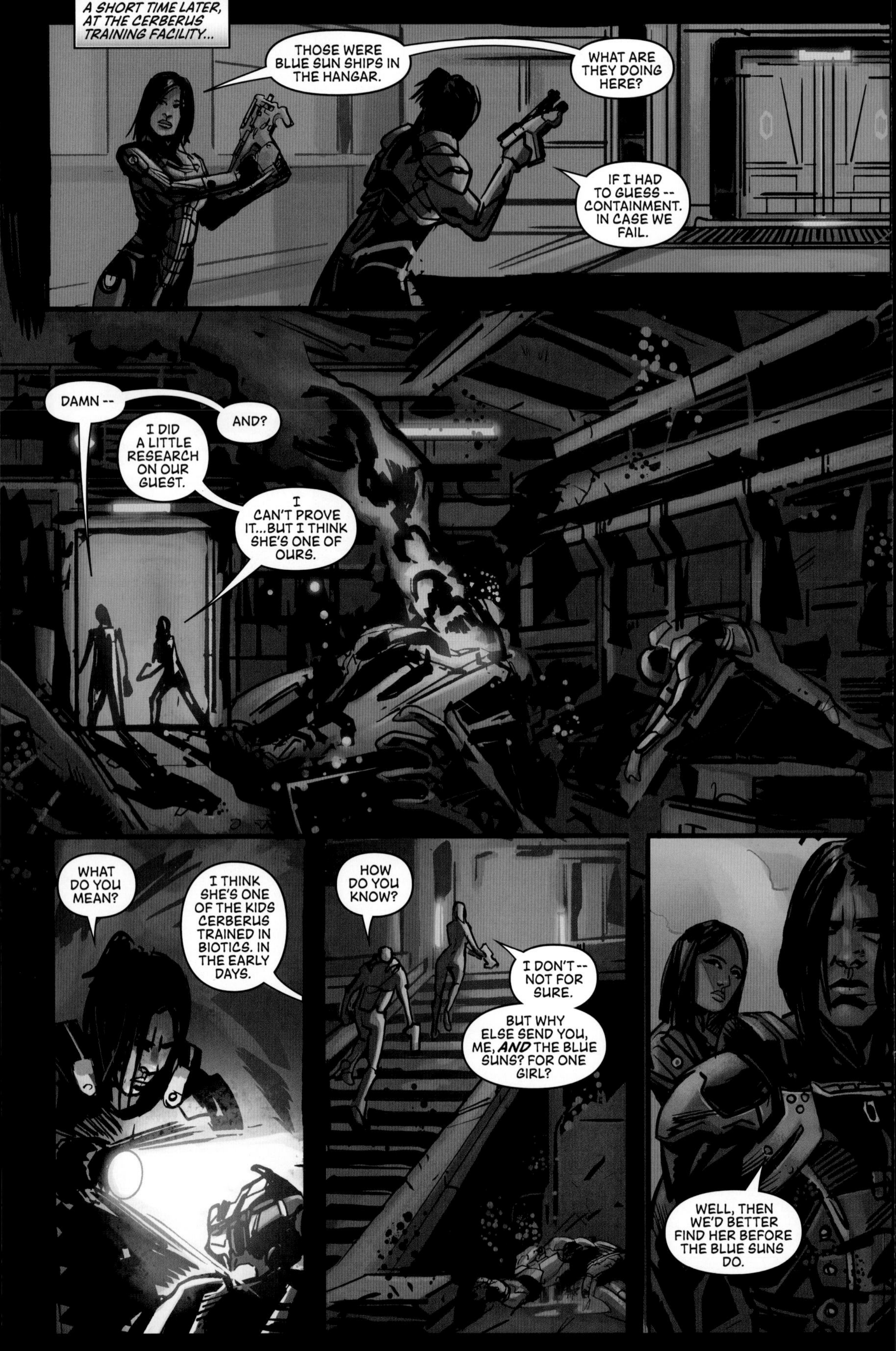
A SHORT TIME LATER, AT THE CERBERUS TRAINING FACILITY...
THOSE WERE BLUE SUN SHIPS IN THE HANGAR.
WHAT ARE THEY DOING HERE?
IF I HAD TO GUESS -- CONTAINMENT. IN CASE WE FAIL.
DAMN --
AND?
I DID A LITTLE RESEARCH ON OUR GUEST.
I CAN'T PROVE IT...BUT I THINK SHE'S ONE OF OURS.
WHAT DO YOU MEAN?
I THINK SHE'S ONE OF THE KIDS CERBERUS TRAINED IN BIOTICS. IN THE EARLY DAYS.
HOW DO YOU KNOW?
I DON'T -- NOT FOR SURE.
BUT WHY ELSE SEND YOU, ME, ***AND*** THE BLUE SUNS? FOR ONE GIRL?
WELL, THEN WE'D BETTER FIND HER BEFORE THE BLUE SUNS DO.

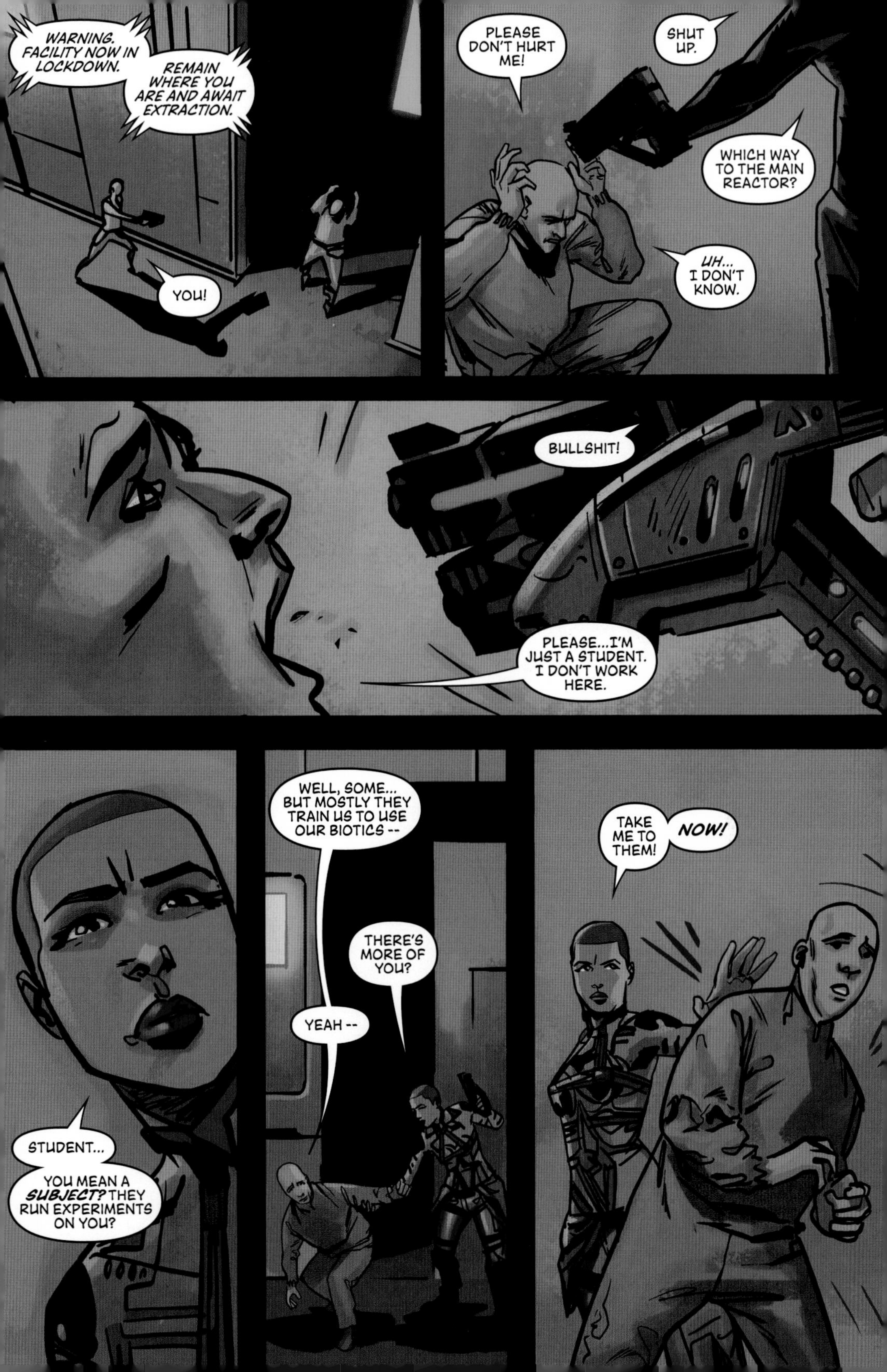
WARNING. FACILITY NOW IN LOCKDOWN.
REMAIN WHERE YOU ARE AND AWAIT EXTRACTION.
YOU!
PLEASE DON'T HURT ME!
SHUT UP.
WHICH WAY TO THE MAIN REACTOR?
UH... I DON'T KNOW.
BULLSHIT!
PLEASE...I'M JUST A STUDENT. I DON'T WORK HERE.
STUDENT...
YOU MEAN A SUBJECT? THEY RUN EXPERIMENTS ON YOU?
WELL, SOME... BUT MOSTLY THEY TRAIN US TO USE OUR BIOTICS --
THERE'S MORE OF YOU?
YEAH --
TAKE ME TO THEM!
NOW!

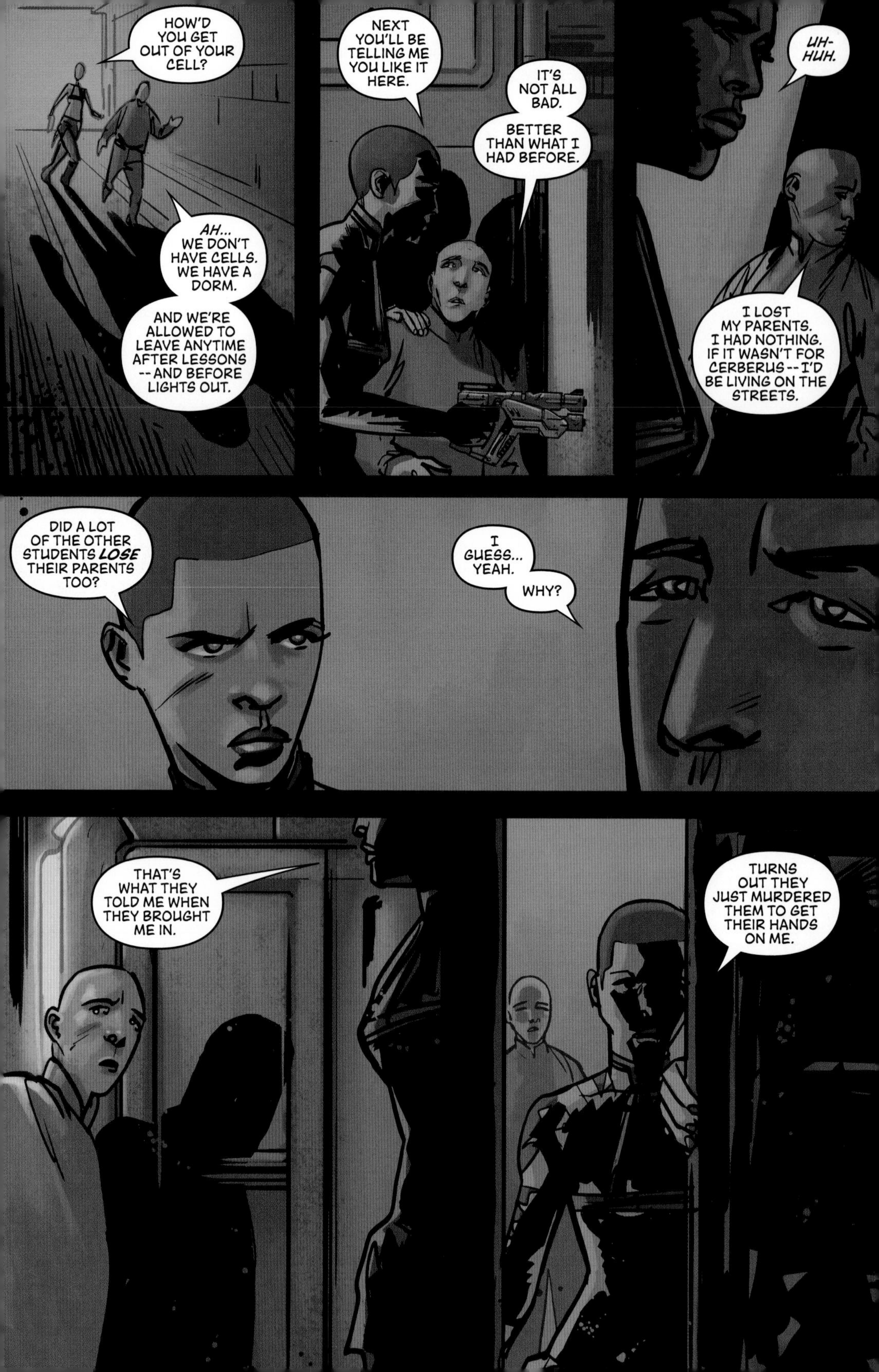
HOW'D YOU GET OUT OF YOUR CELL?
AH... WE DON'T HAVE CELLS. WE HAVE A DORM.
AND WE'RE ALLOWED TO LEAVE ANYTIME AFTER LESSONS -- AND BEFORE LIGHTS OUT.
NEXT YOU'LL BE TELLING ME YOU LIKE IT HERE.
IT'S NOT ALL BAD.
BETTER THAN WHAT I HAD BEFORE.
UH-HUH.
I LOST MY PARENTS. I HAD NOTHING. IF IT WASN'T FOR CERBERUS -- I'D BE LIVING ON THE STREETS.
DID A LOT OF THE OTHER STUDENTS LOSE THEIR PARENTS TOO?
I GUESS... YEAH.
WHY?
THAT'S WHAT THEY TOLD ME WHEN THEY BROUGHT ME IN.
TURNS OUT THEY JUST MURDERED THEM TO GET THEIR HANDS ON ME.

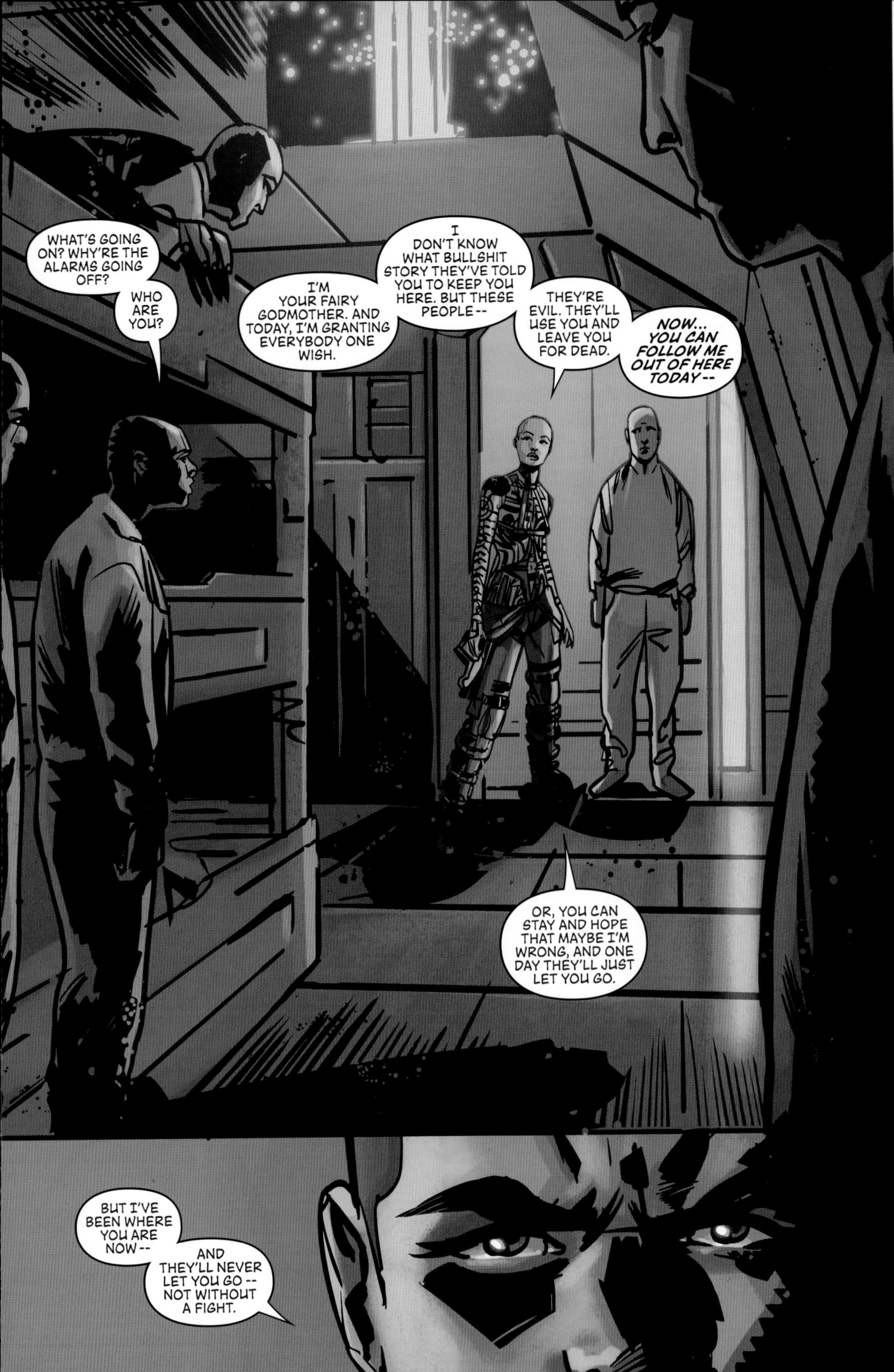
WHAT'S GOING ON? WHY'RE THE ALARMS GOING OFF?
WHO ARE YOU?
I'M YOUR FAIRY GODMOTHER. AND TODAY, I'M GRANTING EVERYBODY ONE WISH.
I DON'T KNOW WHAT BULLSHIT STORY THEY'VE TOLD YOU TO KEEP YOU HERE. BUT THESE PEOPLE --
THEY'RE EVIL. THEY'LL USE YOU AND LEAVE YOU FOR DEAD.
NOW... YOU CAN FOLLOW ME OUT OF HERE TODAY --
OR, YOU CAN STAY AND HOPE THAT MAYBE I'M WRONG, AND ONE DAY THEY'LL JUST LET YOU GO.
BUT I'VE BEEN WHERE YOU ARE NOW --
AND THEY'LL NEVER LET YOU GO -- NOT WITHOUT A FIGHT.

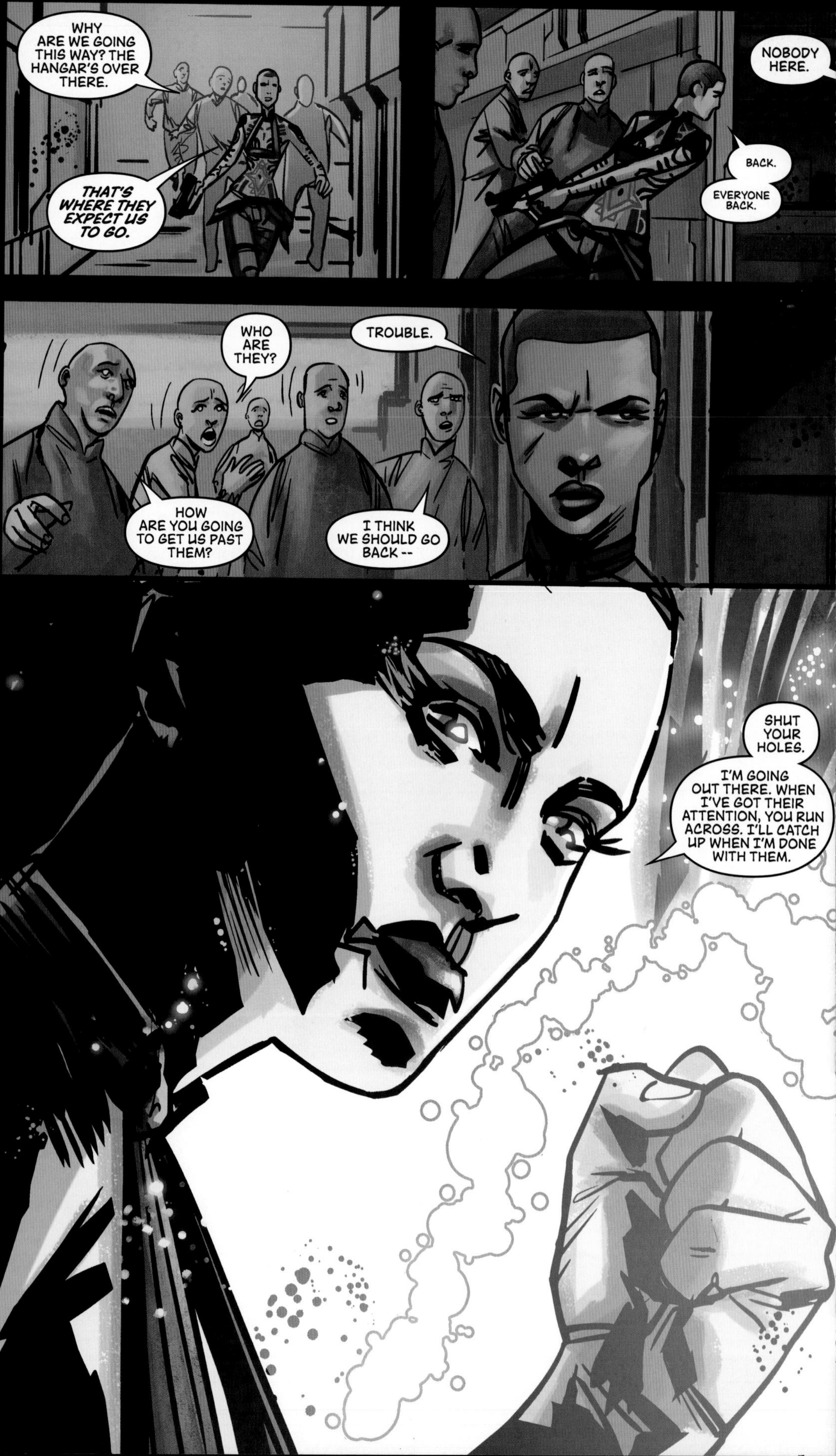
WHY ARE WE GOING THIS WAY? THE HANGAR'S OVER THERE.
THAT'S WHERE THEY EXPECT US TO GO.
NOBODY HERE.
BACK.
EVERYONE BACK.
WHO ARE THEY?
TROUBLE.
HOW ARE YOU GOING TO GET US PAST THEM?
I THINK WE SHOULD GO BACK --
SHUT YOUR HOLES.
I'M GOING OUT THERE. WHEN I'VE GOT THEIR ATTENTION, YOU RUN ACROSS. I'LL CATCH UP WHEN I'M DONE WITH THEM.

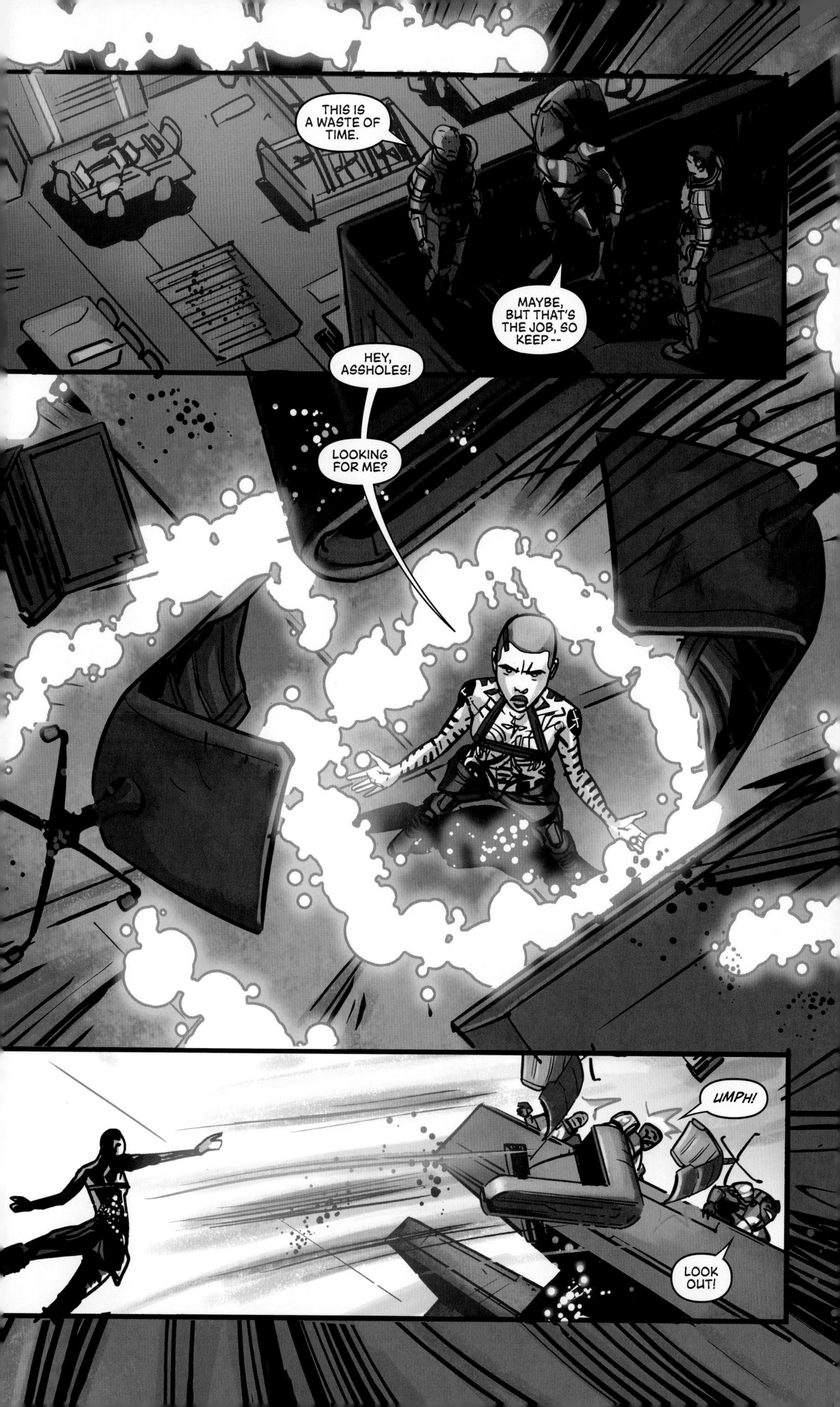
THIS IS A WASTE OF TIME.
MAYBE, BUT THAT'S THE JOB, SO KEEP --
HEY, ASSHOLES!
LOOKING FOR ME?
UMPH!
LOOK OUT!

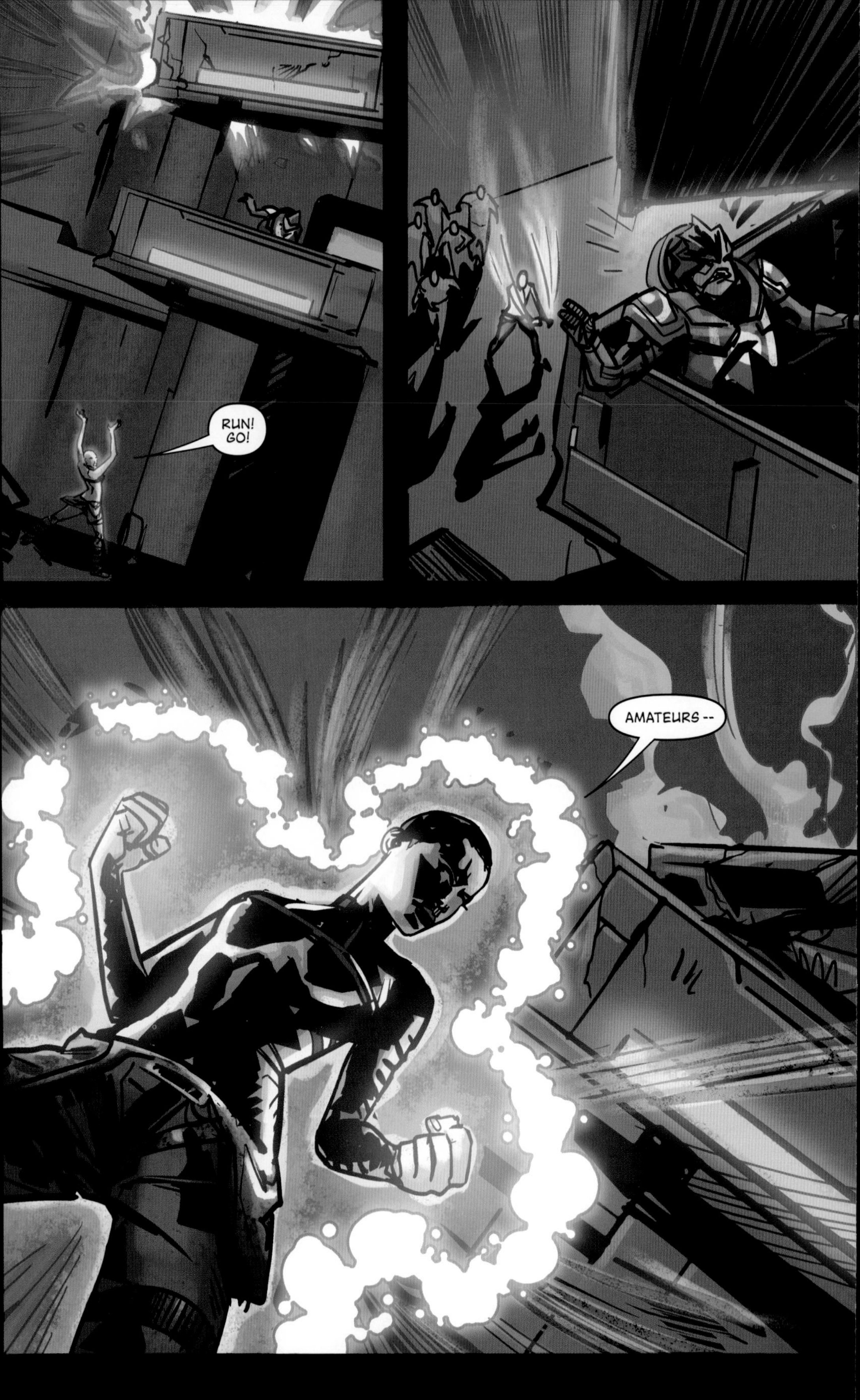
RUN! GO!
AMATEURS --

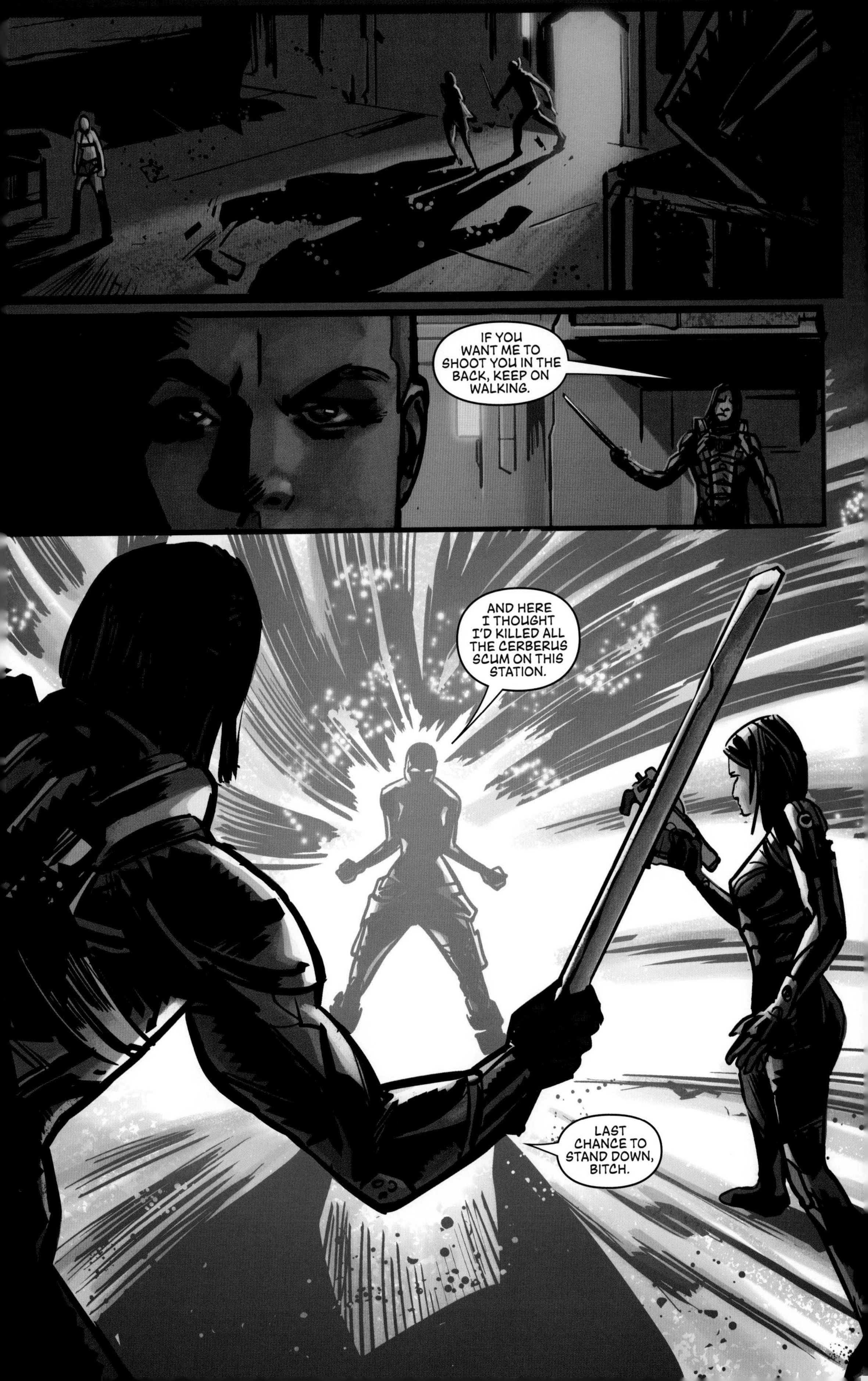
IF YOU WANT ME TO SHOOT YOU IN THE BACK, KEEP ON WALKING.
AND HERE I THOUGHT I'D KILLED ALL THE CERBERUS SCUM ON THIS STATION.
LAST CHANCE TO STAND DOWN, BITCH.

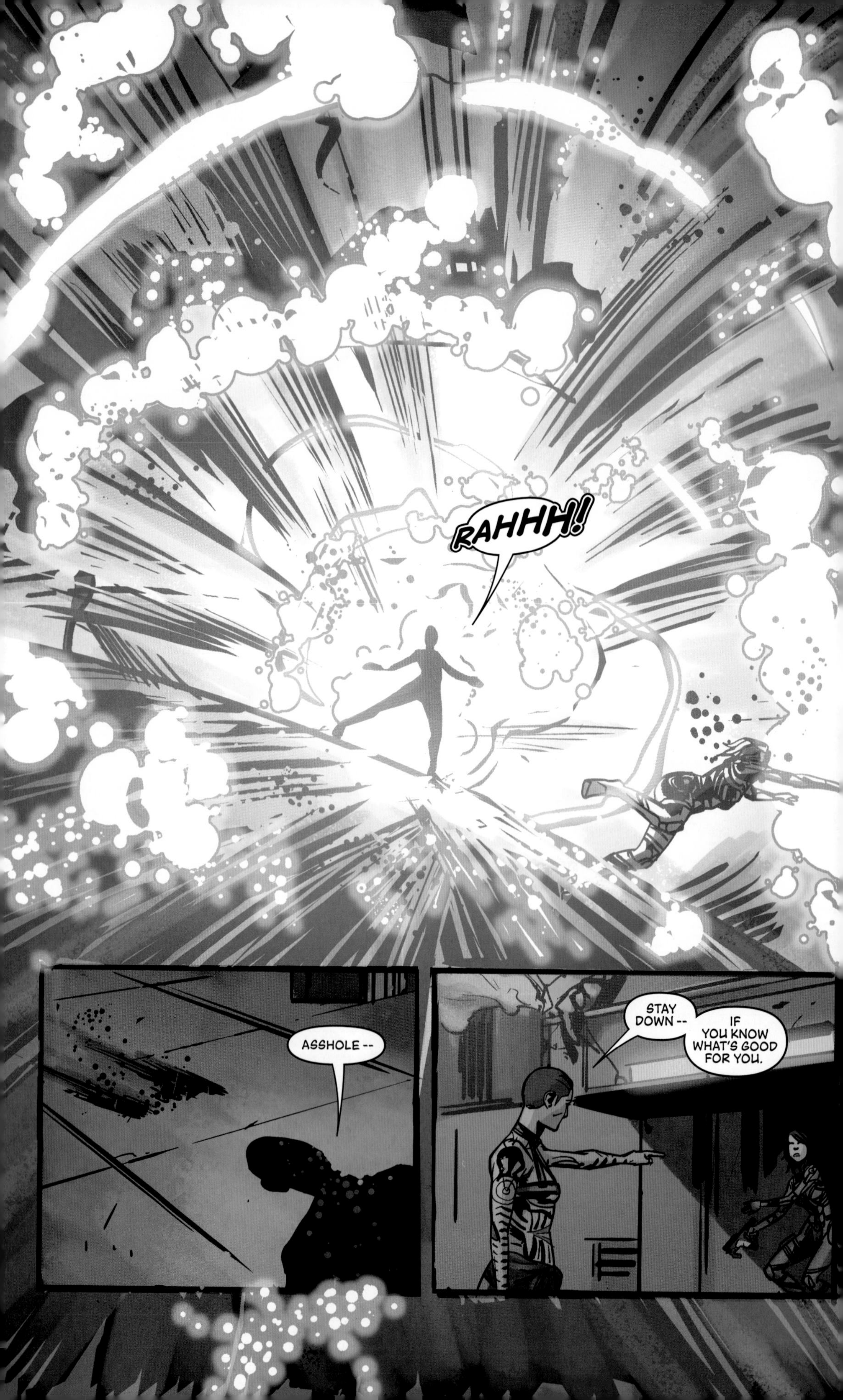
RAHHH!
ASSHOLE --
STAY DOWN --
IF YOU KNOW WHAT'S GOOD FOR YOU.

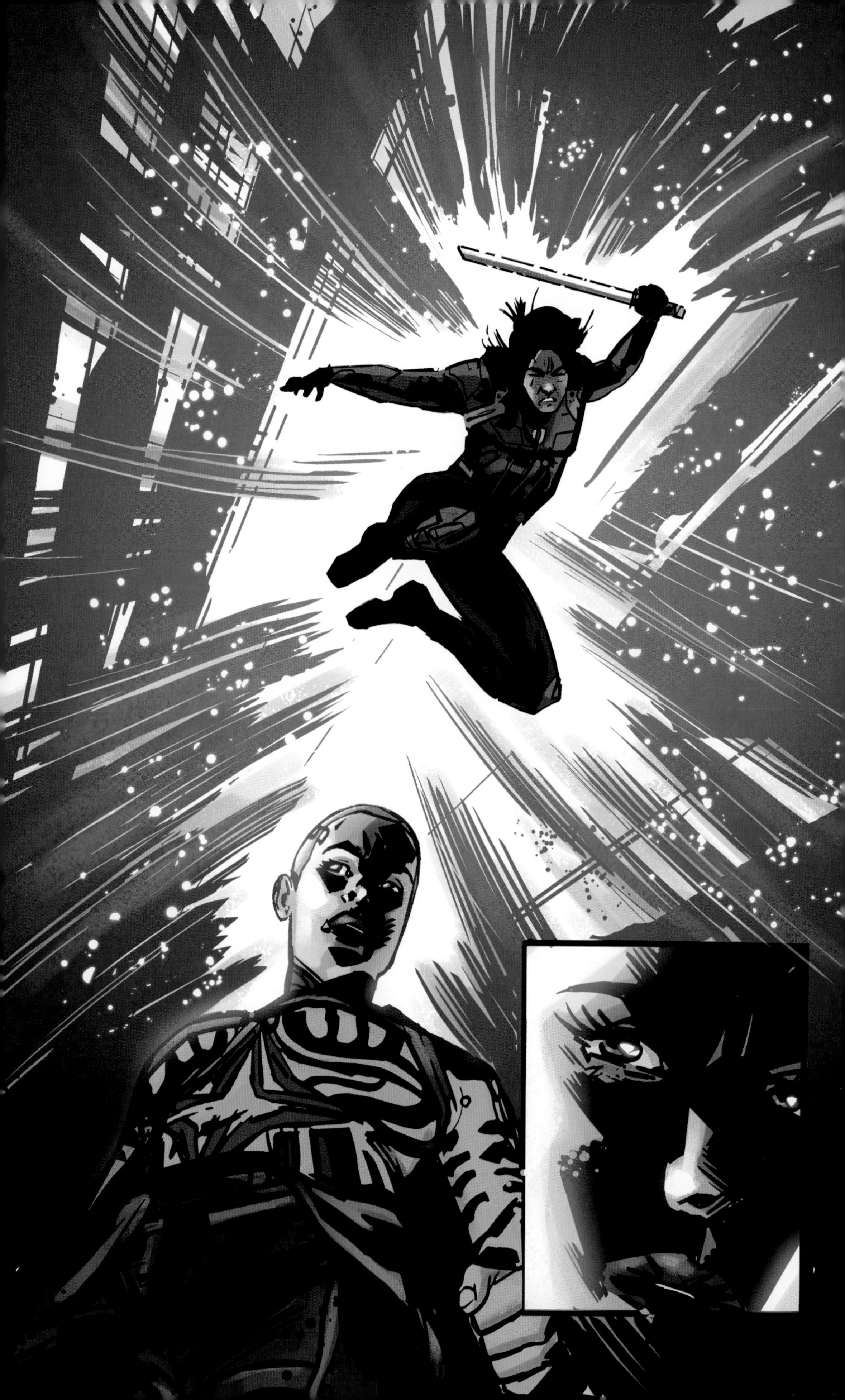

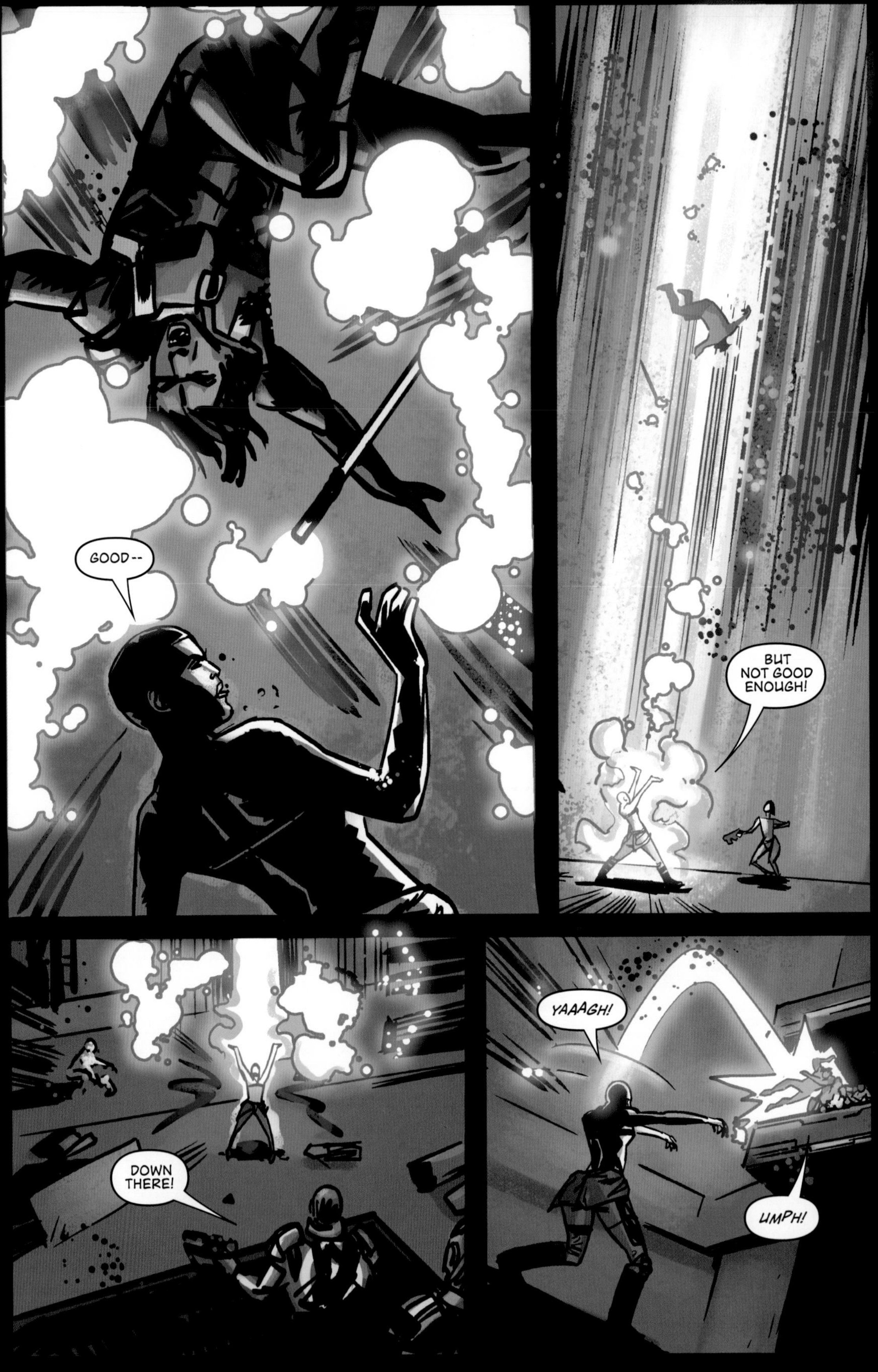
GOOD--
BUT NOT GOOD ENOUGH!
DOWN THERE!
YAAAGH!
UMPH!

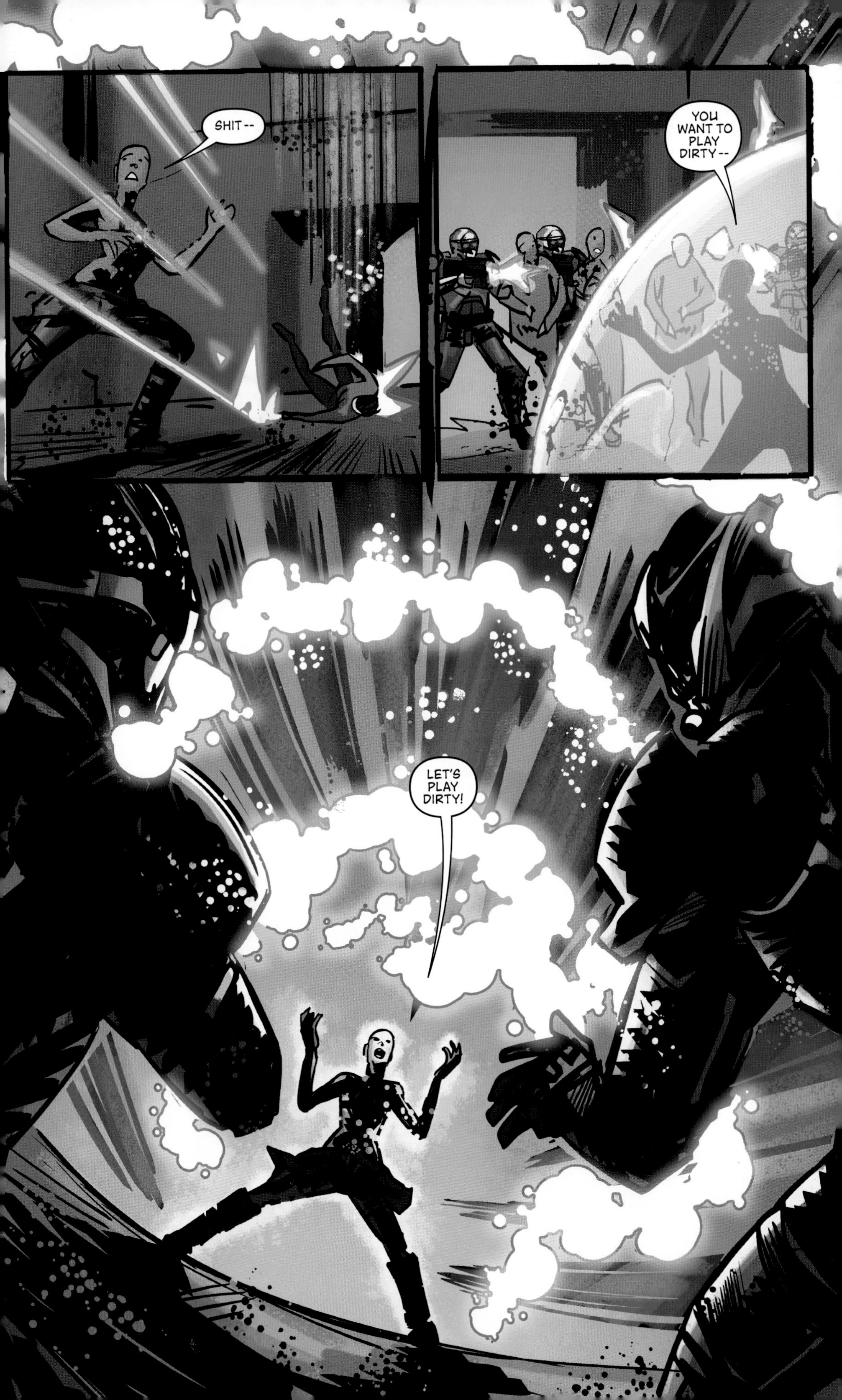
SHIT--
YOU WANT TO PLAY DIRTY--
LET'S PLAY DIRTY!

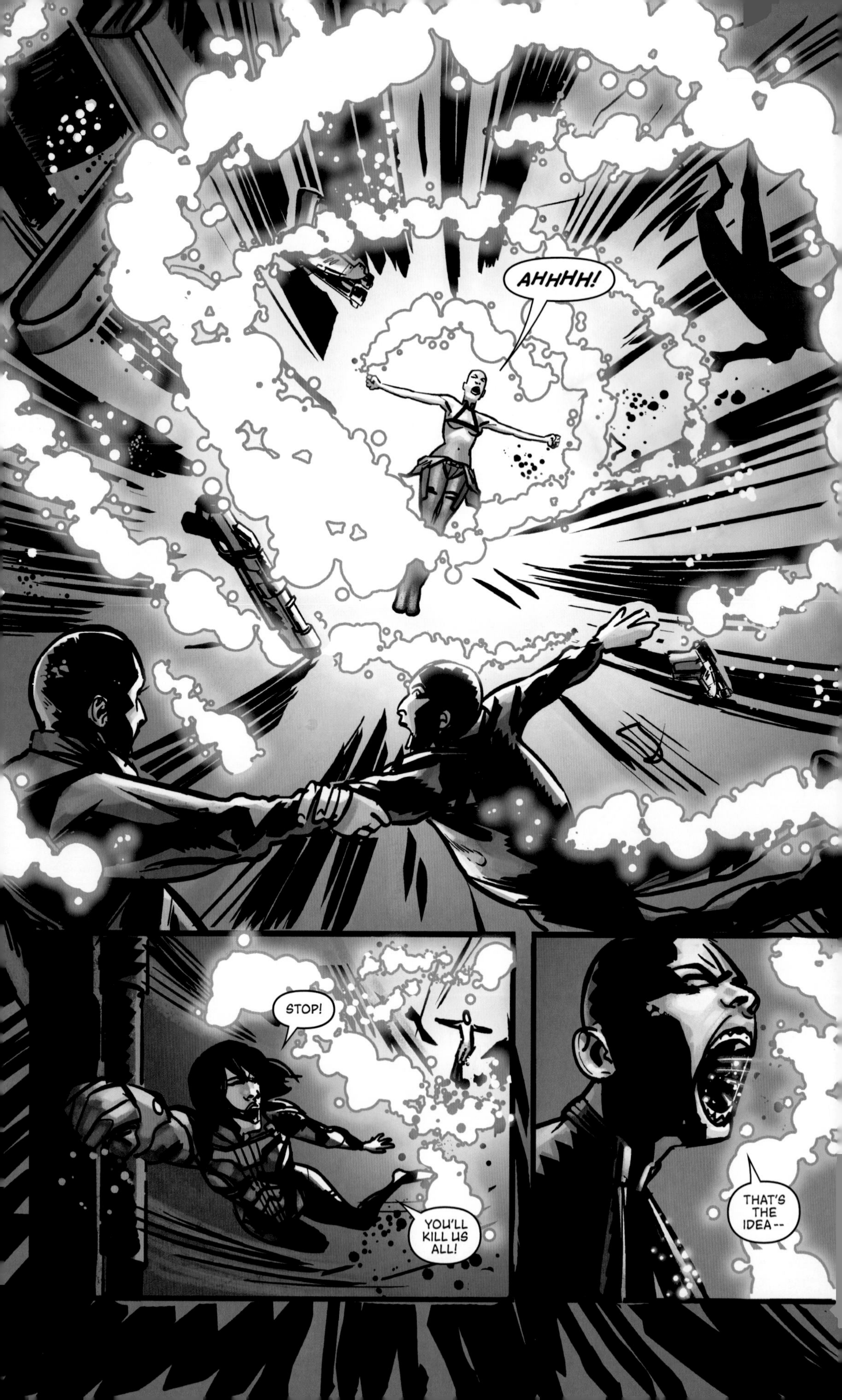
AHHHH!
STOP!
YOU'LL KILL US ALL!
THAT'S THE IDEA--

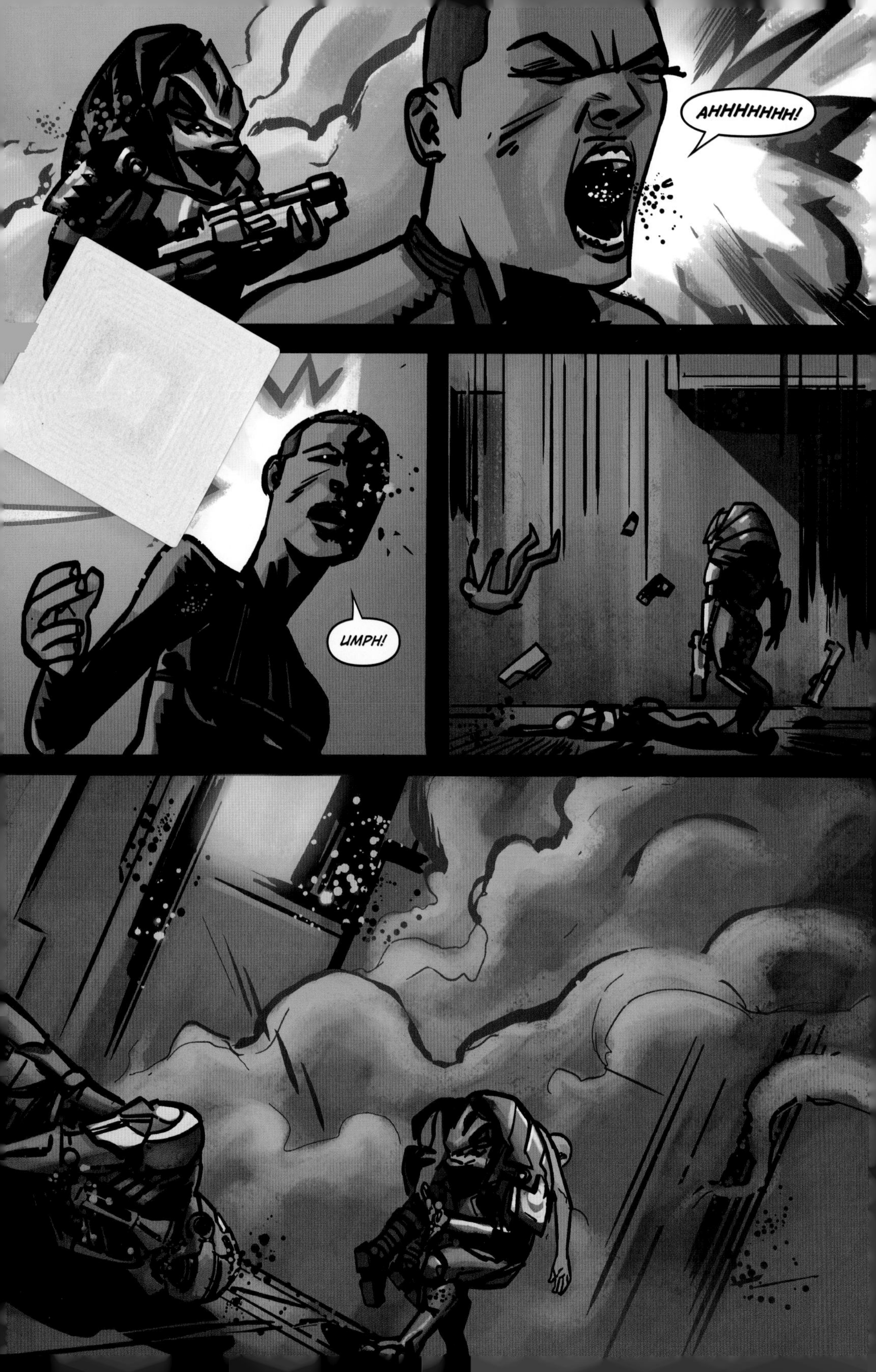
AHHHHHHH!
UMPH!

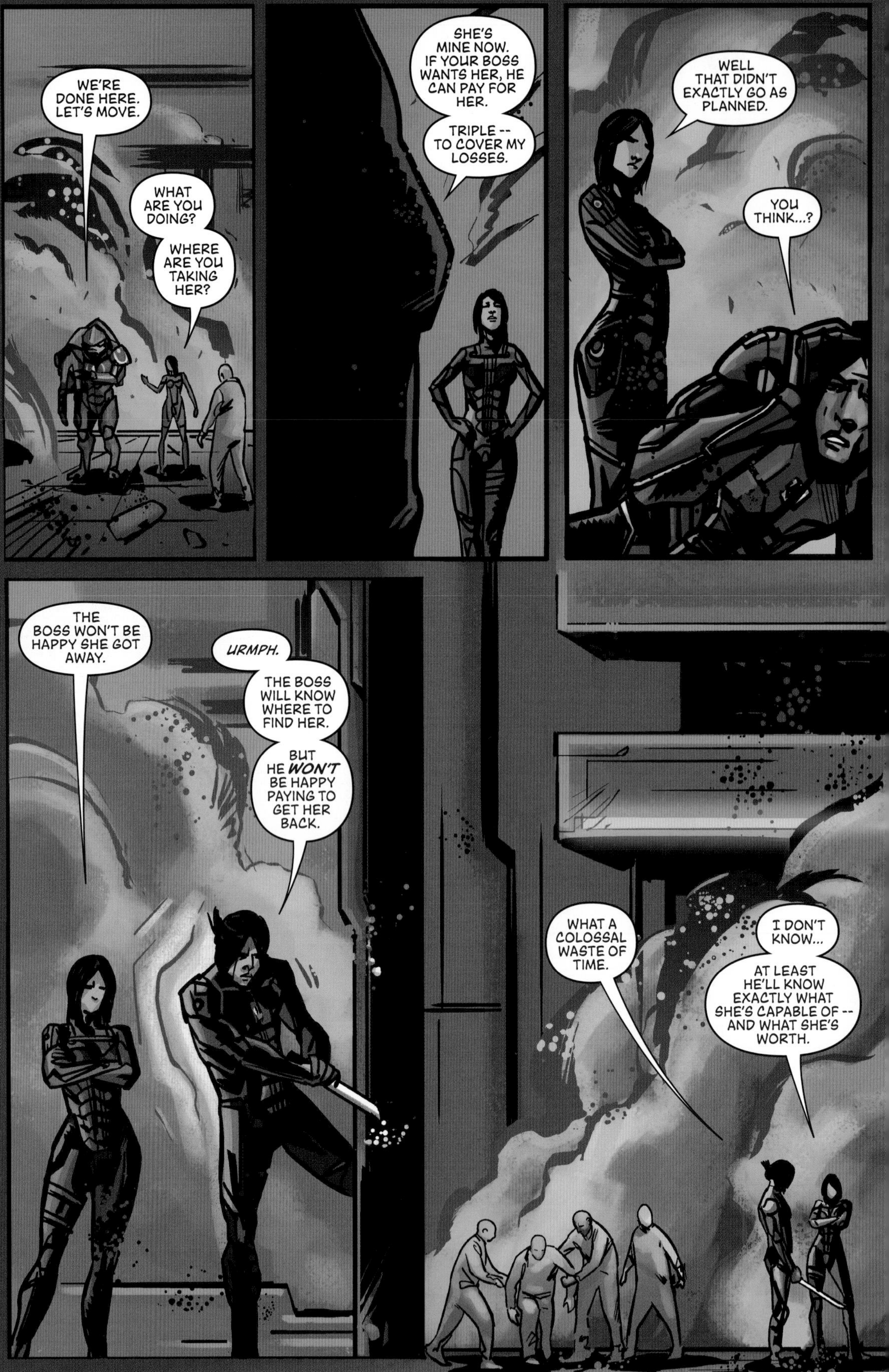
WE'RE DONE HERE. LET'S MOVE.
WHAT ARE YOU DOING?
WHERE ARE YOU TAKING HER?
SHE'S MINE NOW. IF YOUR BOSS WANTS HER, HE CAN PAY FOR HER.
TRIPLE -- TO COVER MY LOSSES.
WELL THAT DIDN'T EXACTLY GO AS PLANNED.
YOU THINK...?
THE BOSS WON'T BE HAPPY SHE GOT AWAY.
URMPH.
THE BOSS WILL KNOW WHERE TO FIND HER.
BUT HE WON'T BE HAPPY PAYING TO GET HER BACK.
WHAT A COLOSSAL WASTE OF TIME.
I DON'T KNOW...
AT LEAST HE'LL KNOW EXACTLY WHAT SHE'S CAPABLE OF -- AND WHAT SHE'S WORTH.

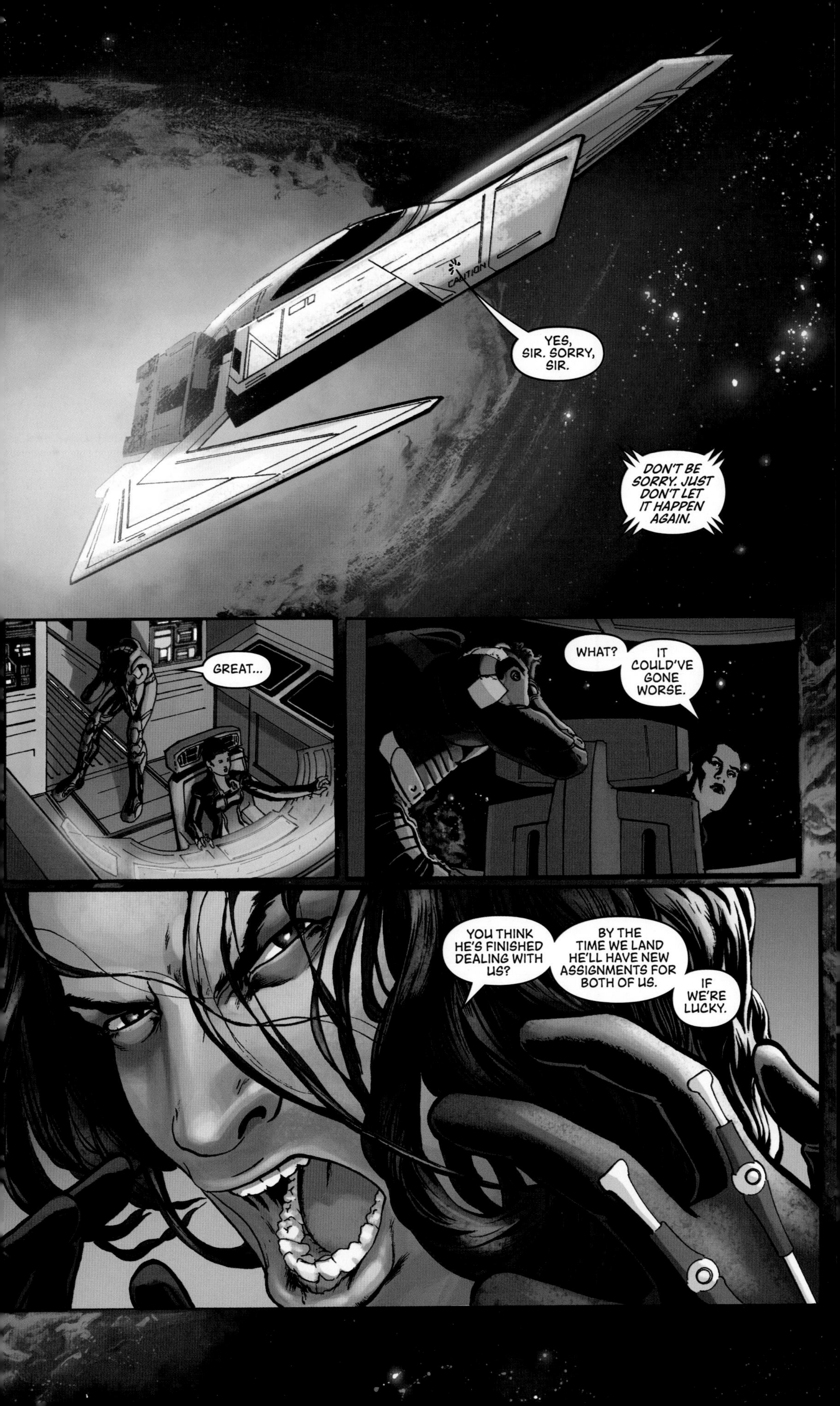
CAUTION
YES, SIR. SORRY, SIR.
DON'T BE SORRY. JUST DON'T LET IT HAPPEN AGAIN.
GREAT...
WHAT?
IT COULD'VE GONE WORSE.
YOU THINK HE'S FINISHED DEALING WITH US?
BY THE TIME WE LAND HE'LL HAVE NEW ASSIGNMENTS FOR BOTH OF US.
IF WE'RE LUCKY.

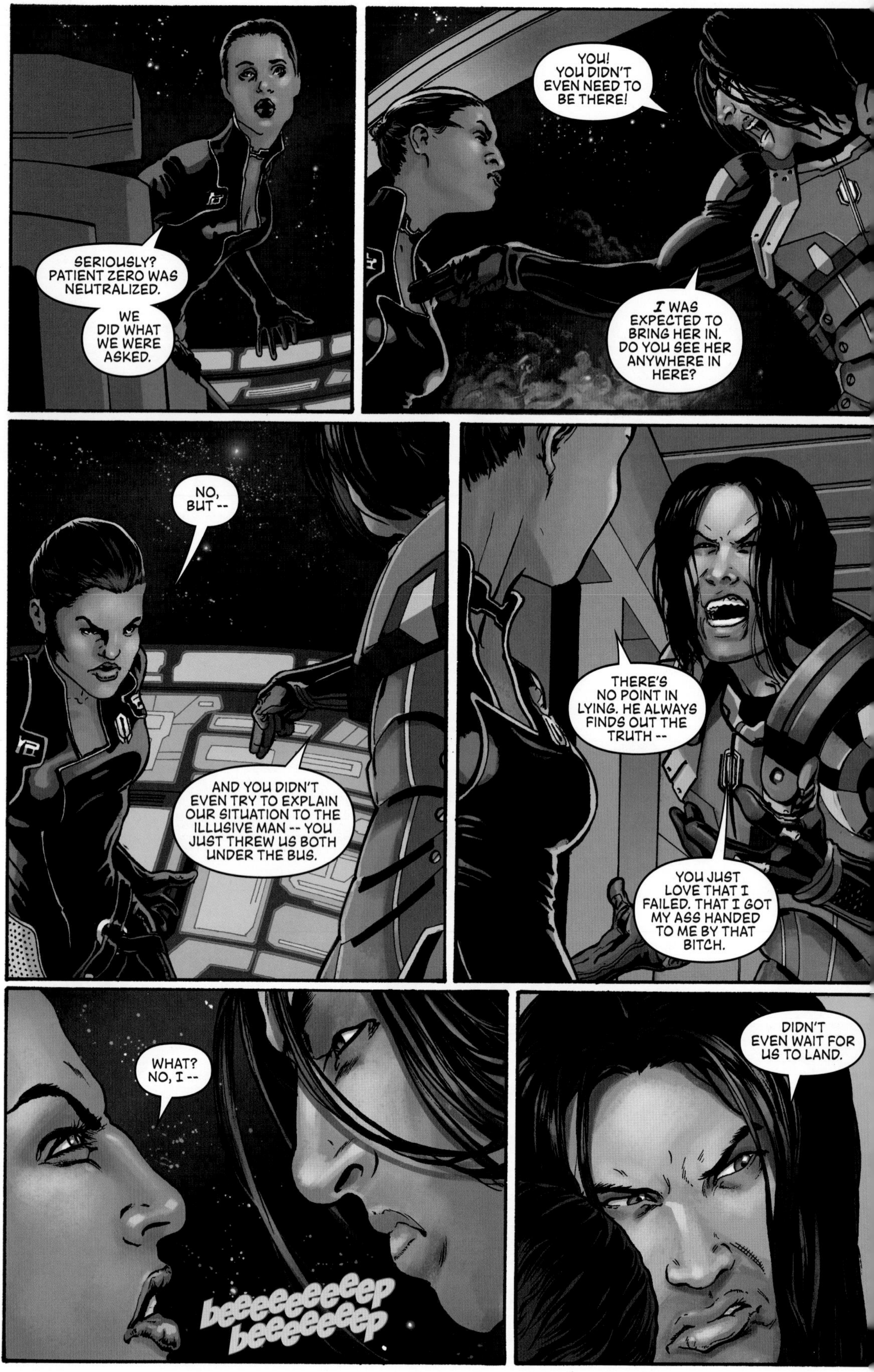

SERIOUSLY? PATIENT ZERO WAS NEUTRALIZED.
WE DID WHAT WE WERE ASKED.
YOU! YOU DIDN'T EVEN NEED TO BE THERE!
I WAS EXPECTED TO BRING HER IN. DO YOU SEE HER ANYWHERE IN HERE?
NO, BUT --
AND YOU DIDN'T EVEN TRY TO EXPLAIN OUR SITUATION TO THE ILLUSIVE MAN -- YOU JUST THREW US BOTH UNDER THE BUS.
THERE'S NO POINT IN LYING. HE ALWAYS FINDS OUT THE TRUTH --
YOU JUST LOVE THAT I FAILED. THAT I GOT MY ASS HANDED TO ME BY THAT BITCH.
WHAT? NO, I --
beeeeeeeeep
beeeeeeeep
DIDN'T EVEN WAIT FOR US TO LAND.

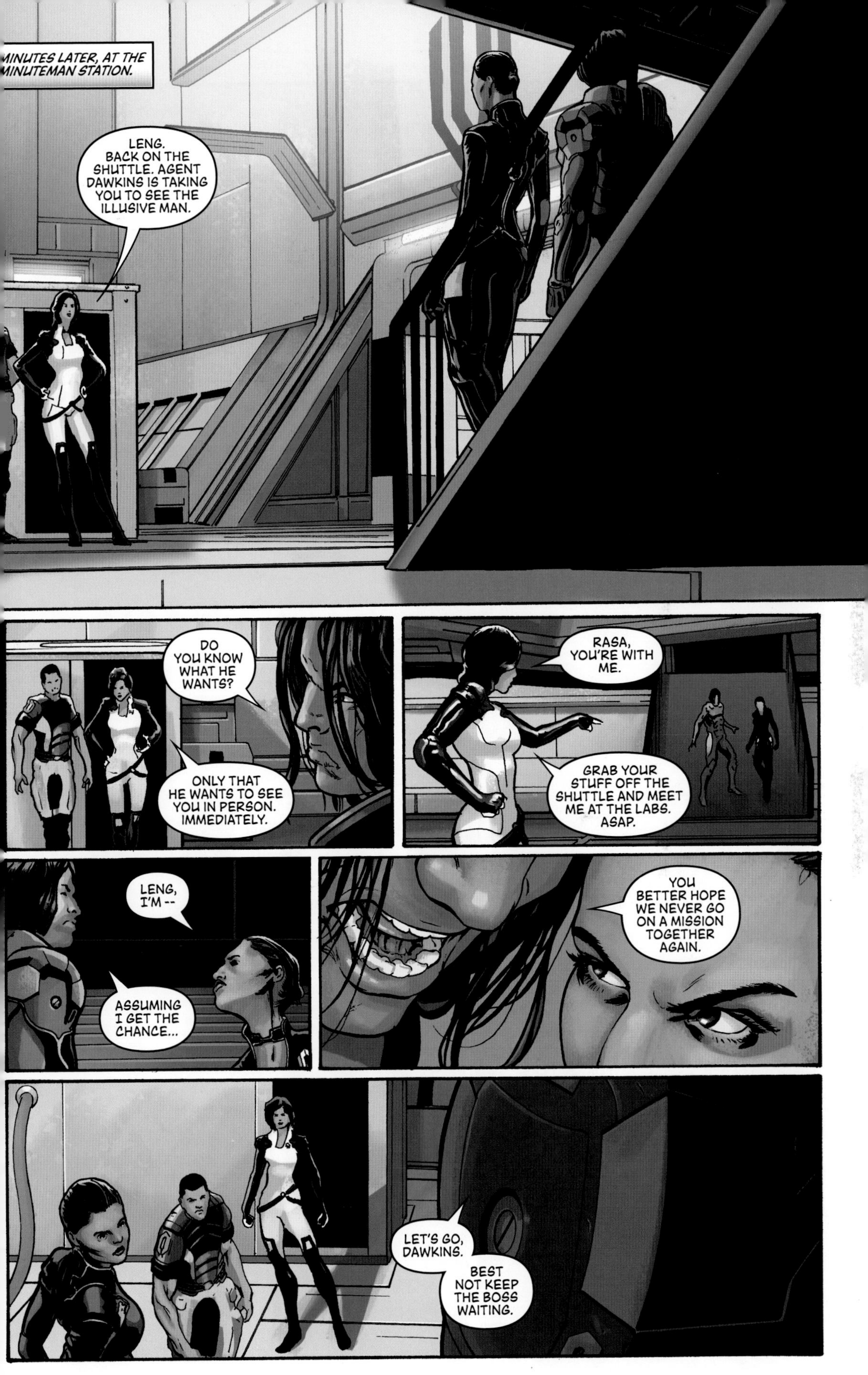
MINUTES LATER, AT THE MINUTEMAN STATION.
LENG. BACK ON THE SHUTTLE. AGENT DAWKINS IS TAKING YOU TO SEE THE ILLUSIVE MAN.
DO YOU KNOW WHAT HE WANTS?
ONLY THAT HE WANTS TO SEE YOU IN PERSON. IMMEDIATELY.
RASA, YOU'RE WITH ME.
GRAB YOUR STUFF OFF THE SHUTTLE AND MEET ME AT THE LABS. ASAP.
LENG, I'M --
ASSUMING I GET THE CHANCE...
YOU BETTER HOPE WE NEVER GO ON A MISSION TOGETHER AGAIN.
LET'S GO, DAWKINS.
BEST NOT KEEP THE BOSS WAITING.

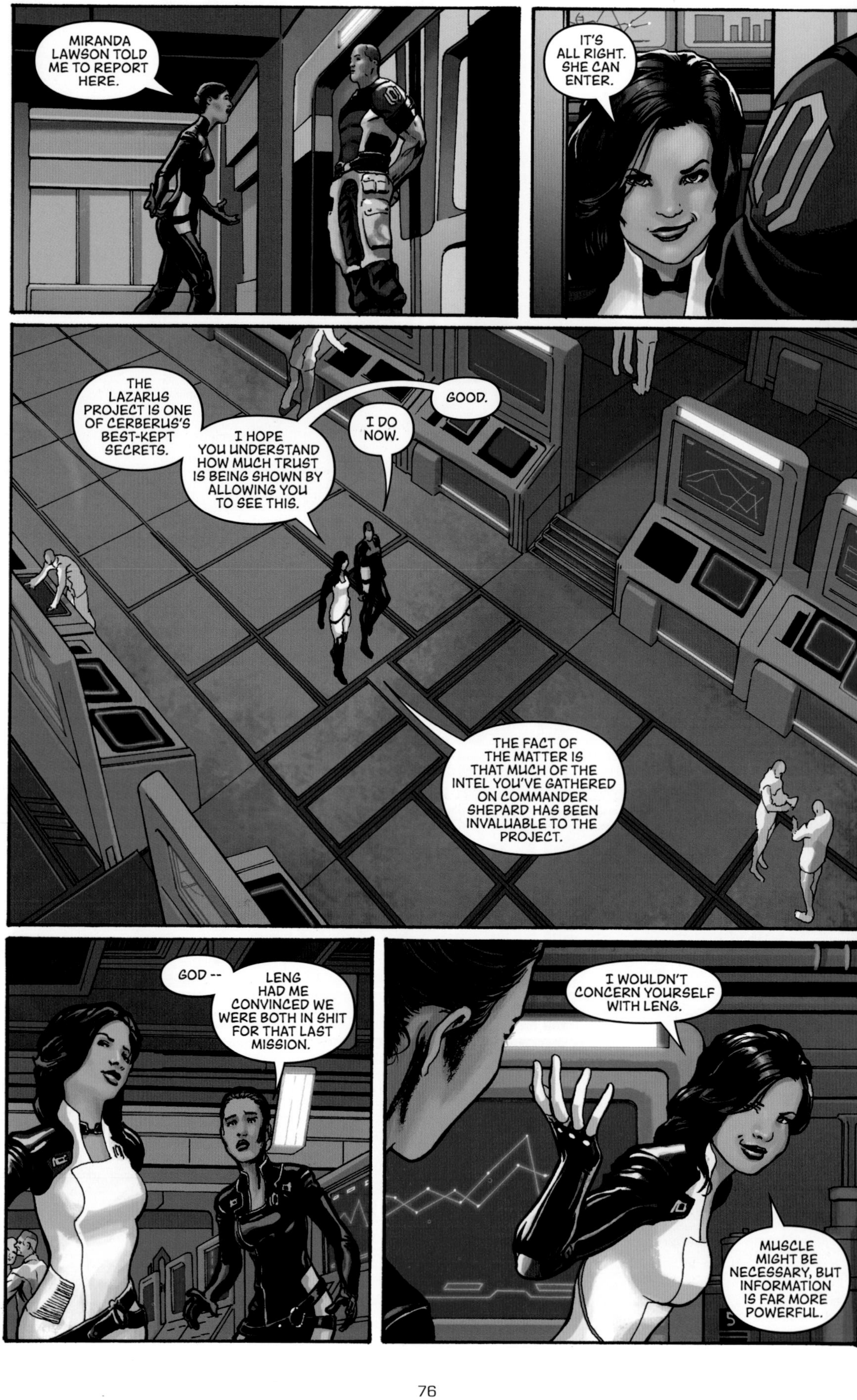
MIRANDA LAWSON TOLD ME TO REPORT HERE.
IT'S ALL RIGHT. SHE CAN ENTER.
THE LAZARUS PROJECT IS ONE OF CERBERUS'S BEST-KEPT SECRETS.
I HOPE YOU UNDERSTAND HOW MUCH TRUST IS BEING SHOWN BY ALLOWING YOU TO SEE THIS.
I DO NOW.
GOOD.
THE FACT OF THE MATTER IS THAT MUCH OF THE INTEL YOU'VE GATHERED ON COMMANDER SHEPARD HAS BEEN INVALUABLE TO THE PROJECT.
GOD --
LENG HAD ME CONVINCED WE WERE BOTH IN SHIT FOR THAT LAST MISSION.
I WOULDN'T CONCERN YOURSELF WITH LENG.
MUSCLE MIGHT BE NECESSARY, BUT INFORMATION IS FAR MORE POWERFUL.

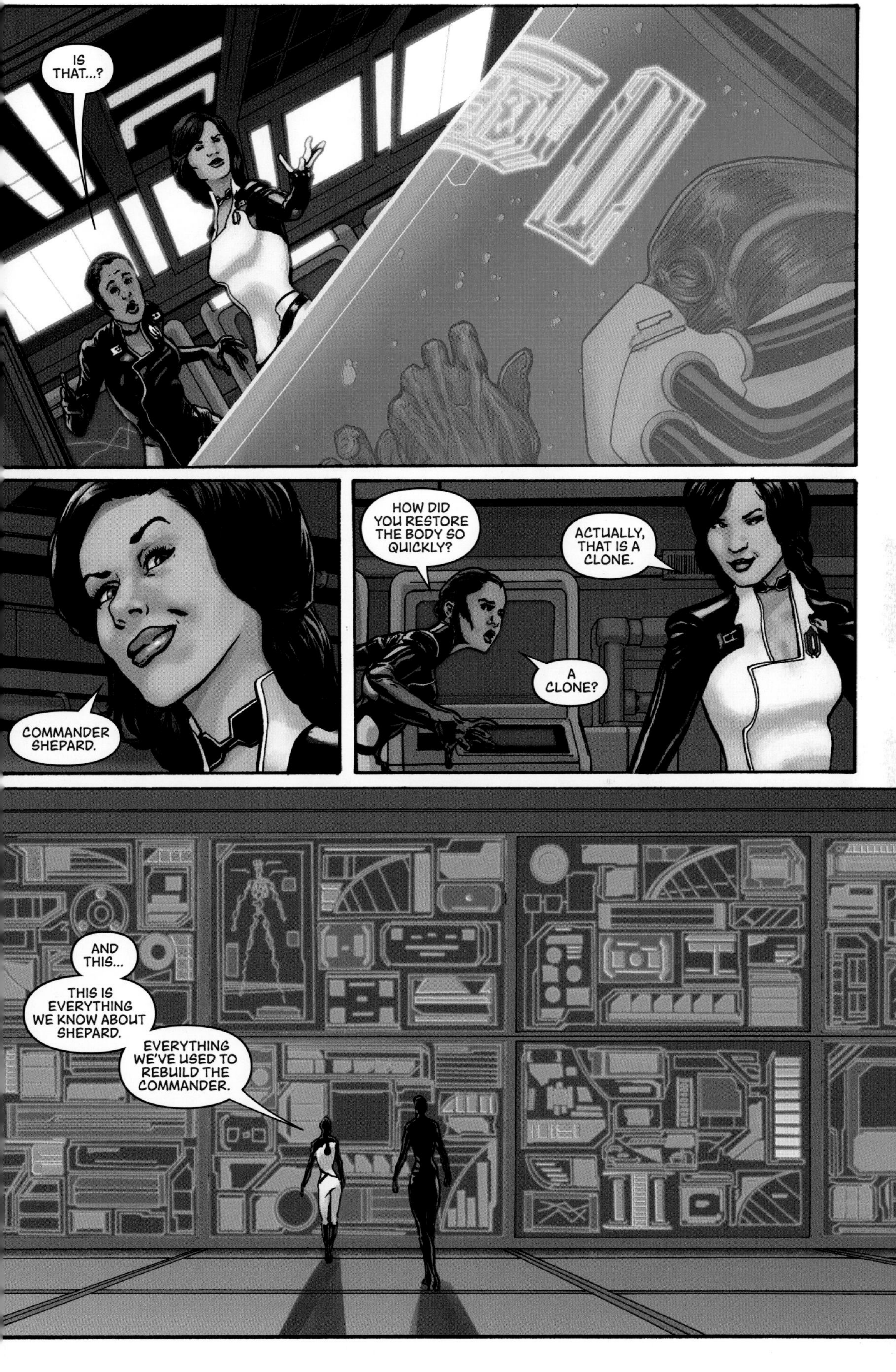
IS THAT...?
COMMANDER SHEPARD.
HOW DID YOU RESTORE THE BODY SO QUICKLY?
ACTUALLY, THAT IS A CLONE.
A CLONE?
AND THIS...
THIS IS EVERYTHING WE KNOW ABOUT SHEPARD.
EVERYTHING WE'VE USED TO REBUILD THE COMMANDER.

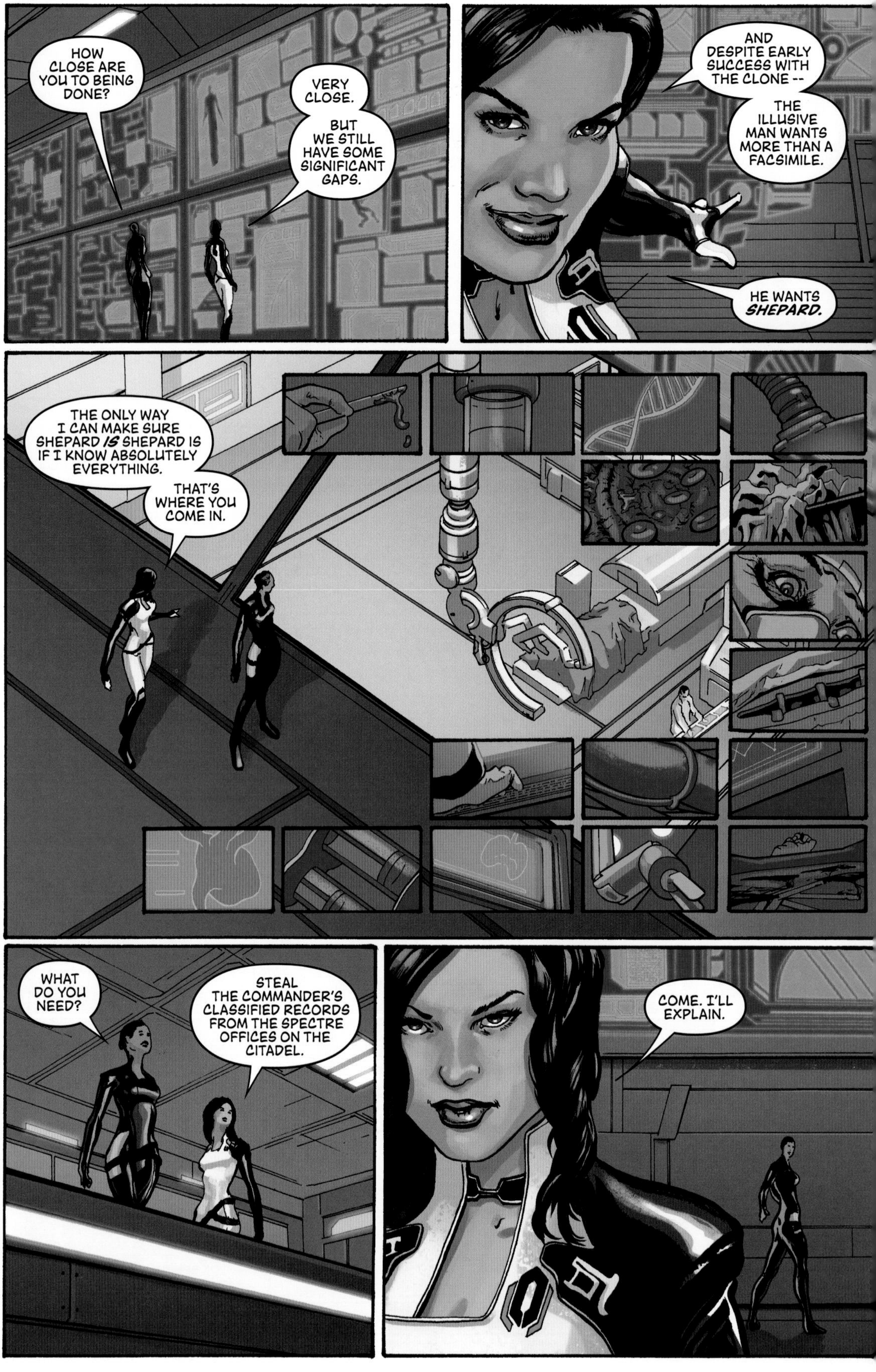
HOW CLOSE ARE YOU TO BEING DONE?
VERY CLOSE.
BUT WE STILL HAVE SOME SIGNIFICANT GAPS.
AND DESPITE EARLY SUCCESS WITH THE CLONE --
THE ILLUSIVE MAN WANTS MORE THAN A FACSIMILE.
HE WANTS *SHEPARD.*
THE ONLY WAY I CAN MAKE SURE SHEPARD *IS* SHEPARD IS IF I KNOW ABSOLUTELY EVERYTHING.
THAT'S WHERE YOU COME IN.
WHAT DO YOU NEED?
STEAL THE COMMANDER'S CLASSIFIED RECORDS FROM THE SPECTRE OFFICES ON THE CITADEL.
COME. I'LL EXPLAIN.

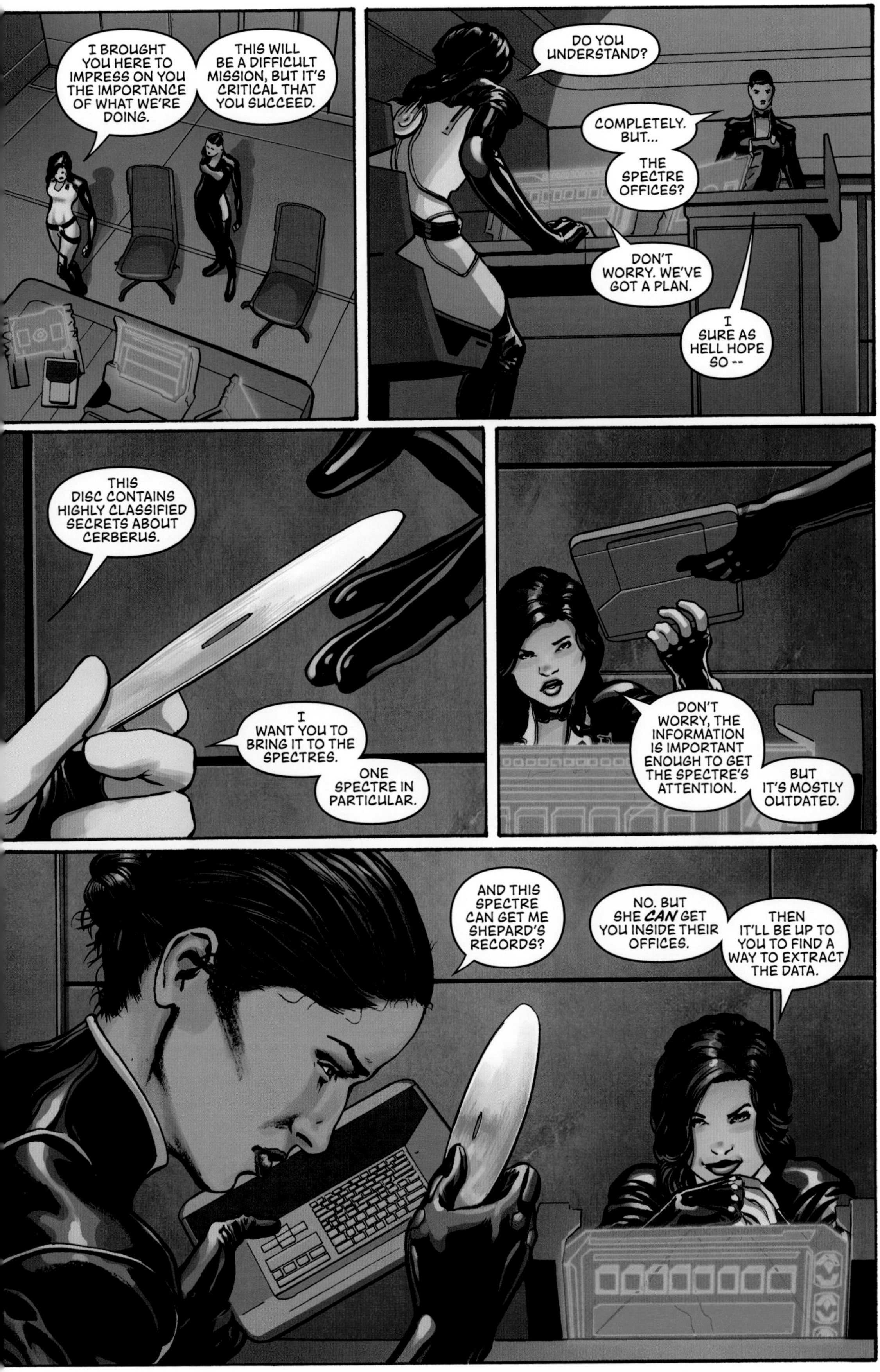
I BROUGHT YOU HERE TO IMPRESS ON YOU THE IMPORTANCE OF WHAT WE'RE DOING.
THIS WILL BE A DIFFICULT MISSION, BUT IT'S CRITICAL THAT YOU SUCCEED.
DO YOU UNDERSTAND?
COMPLETELY. BUT...
THE SPECTRE OFFICES?
DON'T WORRY. WE'VE GOT A PLAN.
I SURE AS HELL HOPE SO --
THIS DISC CONTAINS HIGHLY CLASSIFIED SECRETS ABOUT CERBERUS.
I WANT YOU TO BRING IT TO THE SPECTRES.
ONE SPECTRE IN PARTICULAR.
DON'T WORRY, THE INFORMATION IS IMPORTANT ENOUGH TO GET THE SPECTRE'S ATTENTION.
BUT IT'S MOSTLY OUTDATED.
AND THIS SPECTRE CAN GET ME SHEPARD'S RECORDS?
NO. BUT SHE *CAN* GET YOU INSIDE THEIR OFFICES.
THEN IT'LL BE UP TO YOU TO FIND A WAY TO EXTRACT THE DATA.

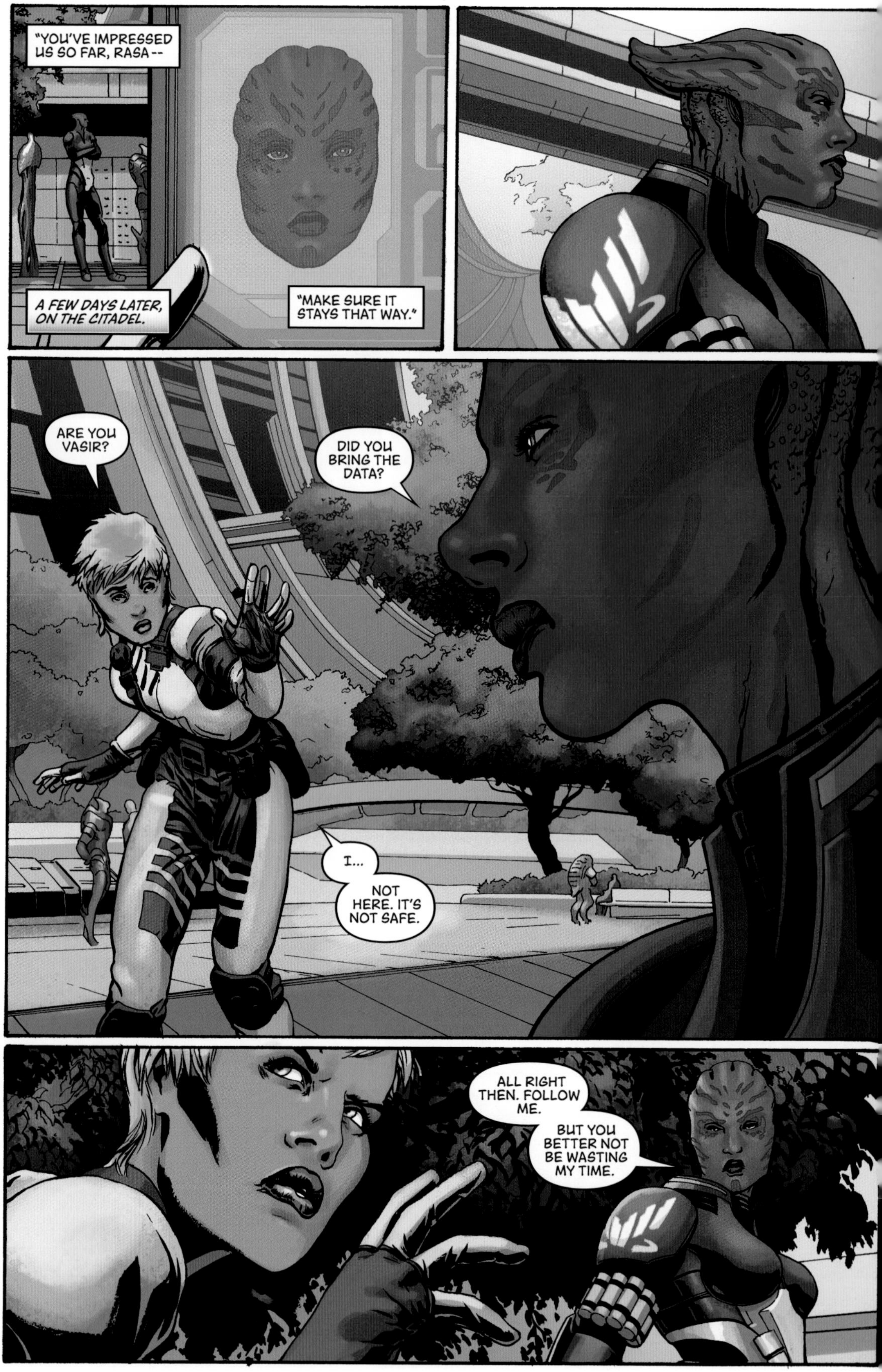
"YOU'VE IMPRESSED US SO FAR, RASA --
A FEW DAYS LATER, ON THE CITADEL.
"MAKE SURE IT STAYS THAT WAY."
ARE YOU VASIR?
DID YOU BRING THE DATA?
I...
NOT HERE. IT'S NOT SAFE.
ALL RIGHT THEN. FOLLOW ME.
BUT YOU BETTER NOT BE WASTING MY TIME.

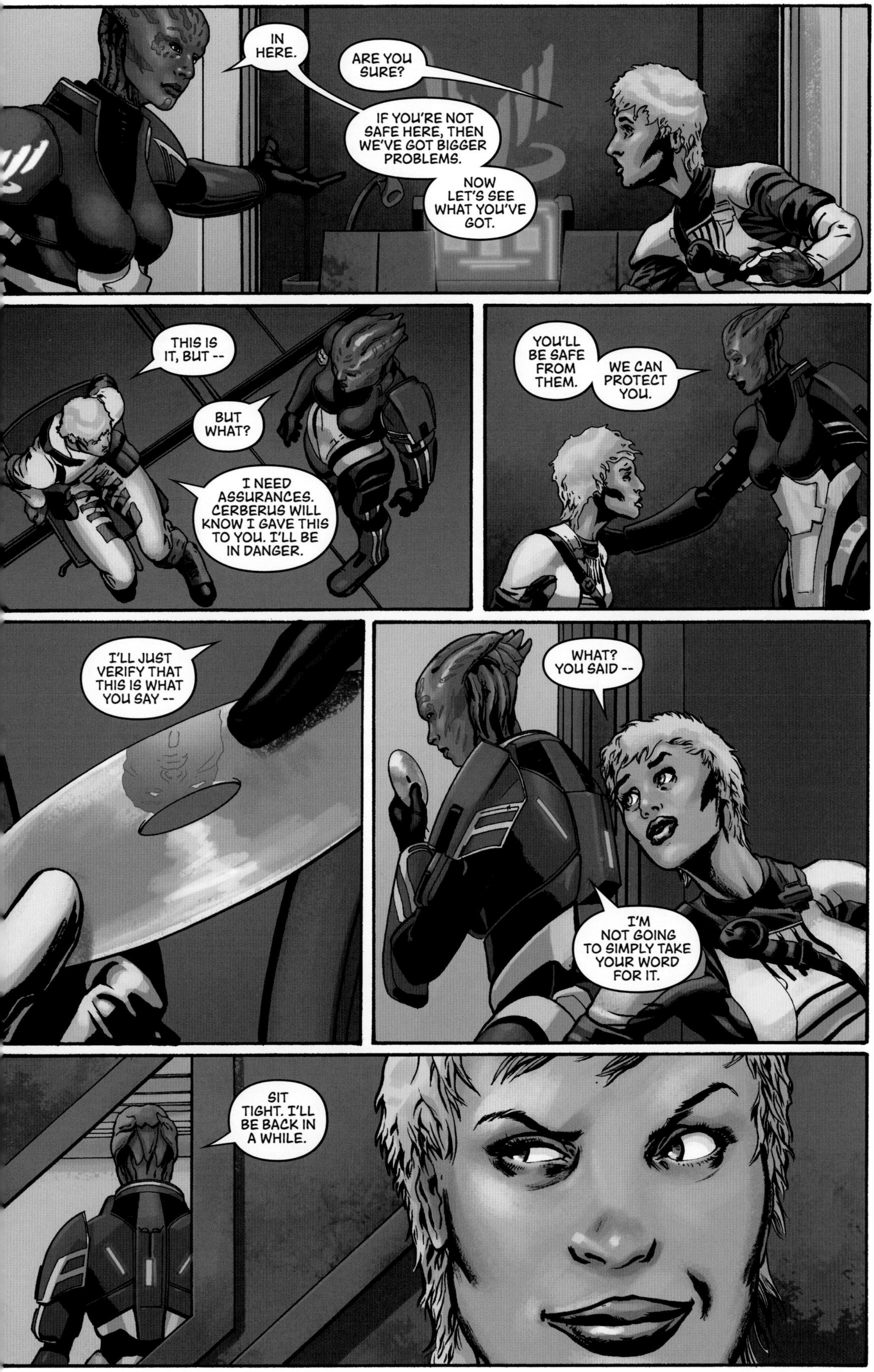
IN HERE.
ARE YOU SURE?
IF YOU'RE NOT SAFE HERE, THEN WE'VE GOT BIGGER PROBLEMS.
NOW LET'S SEE WHAT YOU'VE GOT.
THIS IS IT, BUT --
BUT WHAT?
I NEED ASSURANCES. CERBERUS WILL KNOW I GAVE THIS TO YOU. I'LL BE IN DANGER.
YOU'LL BE SAFE FROM THEM.
WE CAN PROTECT YOU.
I'LL JUST VERIFY THAT THIS IS WHAT YOU SAY --
WHAT? YOU SAID --
I'M NOT GOING TO SIMPLY TAKE YOUR WORD FOR IT.
SIT TIGHT. I'LL BE BACK IN A WHILE.

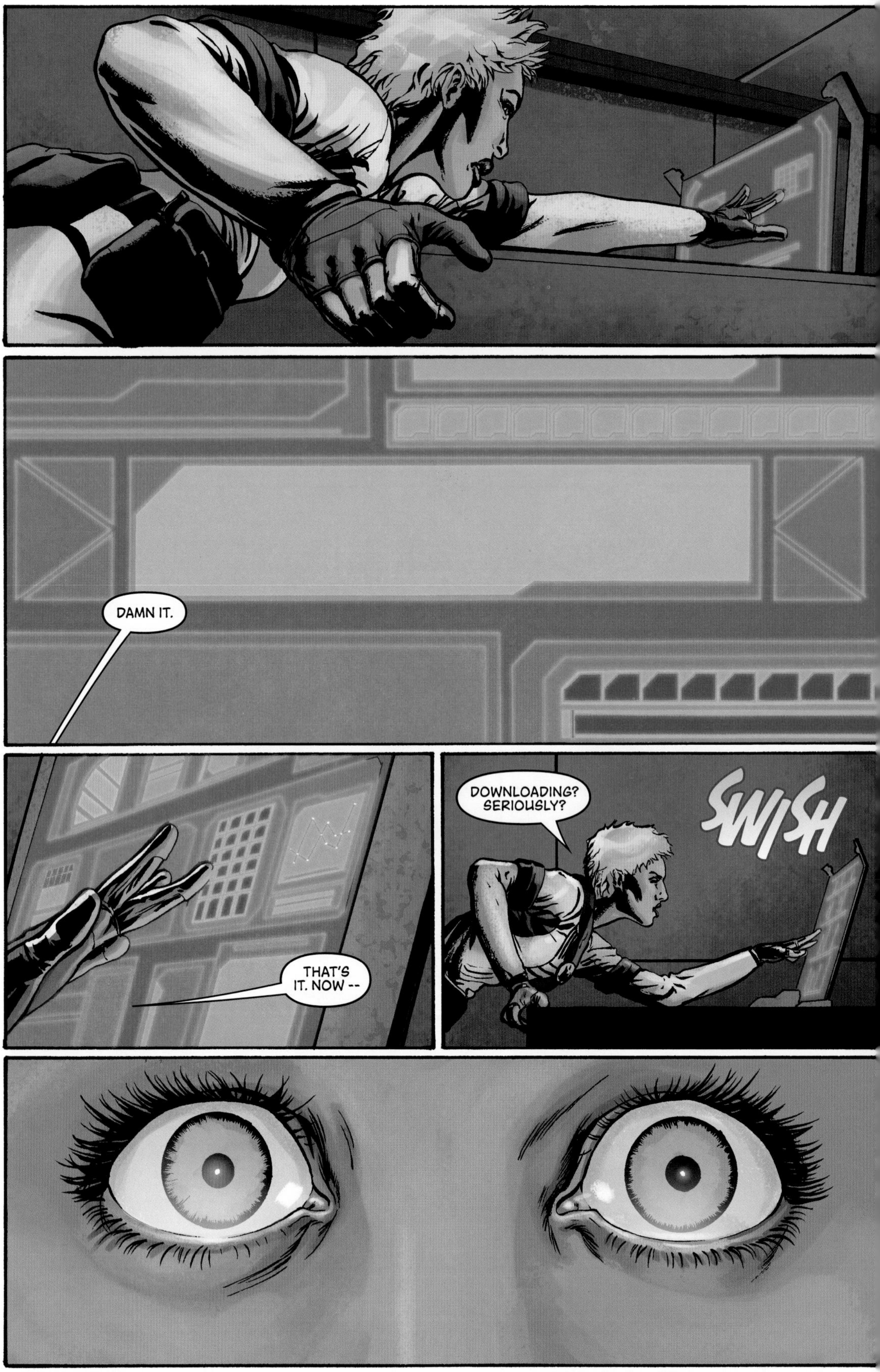
DAMN IT.
THAT'S IT. NOW --
DOWNLOADING? SERIOUSLY?
SWISH

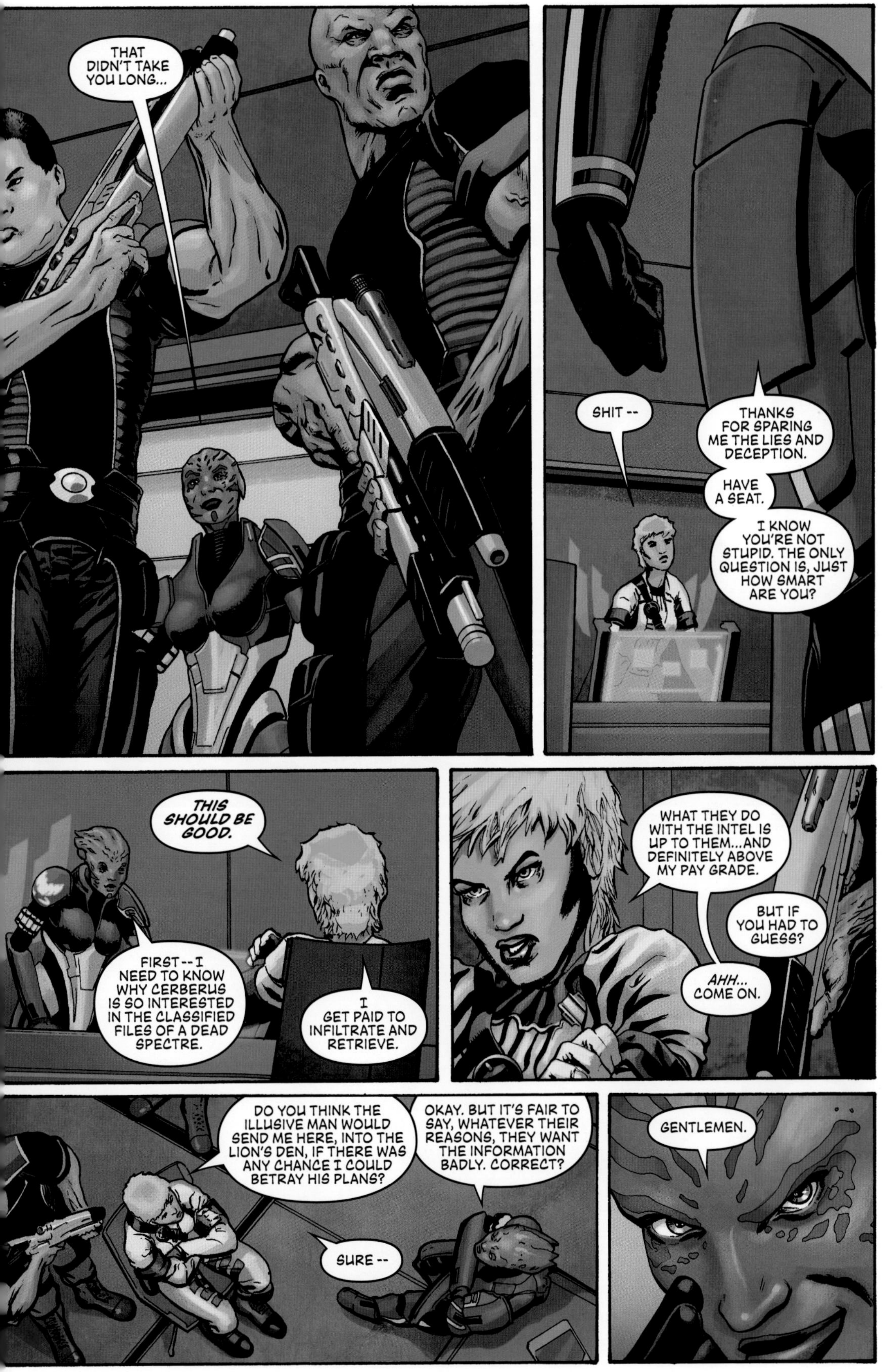
THAT DIDN'T TAKE YOU LONG...
SHIT --
THANKS FOR SPARING ME THE LIES AND DECEPTION.
HAVE A SEAT.
I KNOW YOU'RE NOT STUPID. THE ONLY QUESTION IS, JUST HOW SMART ARE YOU?
THIS SHOULD BE GOOD.
FIRST -- I NEED TO KNOW WHY CERBERUS IS SO INTERESTED IN THE CLASSIFIED FILES OF A DEAD SPECTRE.
I GET PAID TO INFILTRATE AND RETRIEVE.
WHAT THEY DO WITH THE INTEL IS UP TO THEM...AND DEFINITELY ABOVE MY PAY GRADE.
BUT IF YOU HAD TO GUESS?
AHH... COME ON.
DO YOU THINK THE ILLUSIVE MAN WOULD SEND ME HERE, INTO THE LION'S DEN, IF THERE WAS ANY CHANCE I COULD BETRAY HIS PLANS?
OKAY. BUT IT'S FAIR TO SAY, WHATEVER THEIR REASONS, THEY WANT THE INFORMATION BADLY. CORRECT?
SURE --
GENTLEMEN.

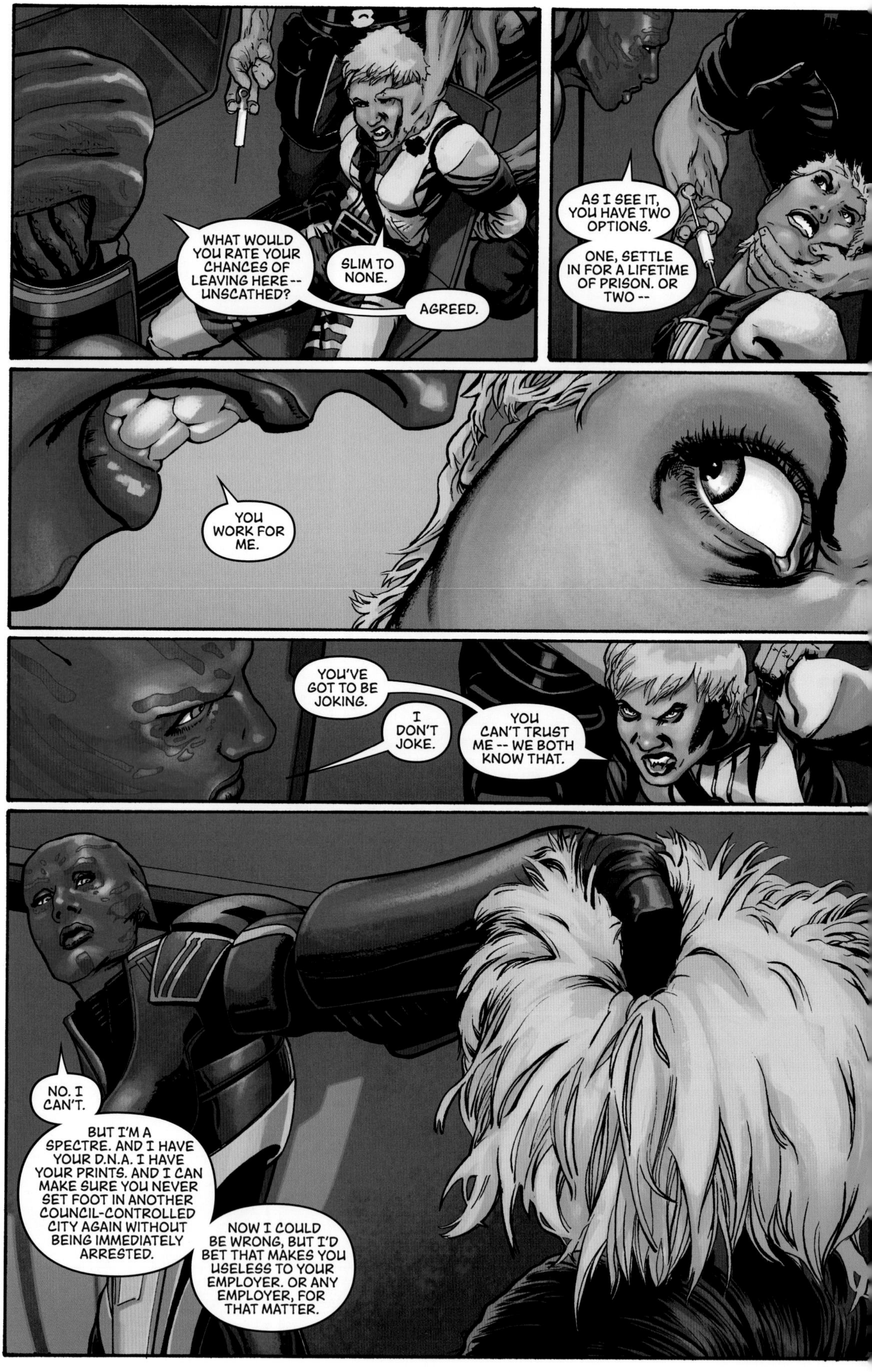
WHAT WOULD YOU RATE YOUR CHANCES OF LEAVING HERE -- UNSCATHED?
SLIM TO NONE.
AGREED.
AS I SEE IT, YOU HAVE TWO OPTIONS.
ONE, SETTLE IN FOR A LIFETIME OF PRISON. OR TWO --
YOU WORK FOR ME.
YOU'VE GOT TO BE JOKING.
I DON'T JOKE.
YOU CAN'T TRUST ME -- WE BOTH KNOW THAT.
NO. I CAN'T.
BUT I'M A SPECTRE. AND I HAVE YOUR D.N.A. I HAVE YOUR PRINTS. AND I CAN MAKE SURE YOU NEVER SET FOOT IN ANOTHER COUNCIL-CONTROLLED CITY AGAIN WITHOUT BEING IMMEDIATELY ARRESTED.
NOW I COULD BE WRONG, BUT I'D BET THAT MAKES YOU USELESS TO YOUR EMPLOYER. OR ANY EMPLOYER, FOR THAT MATTER.

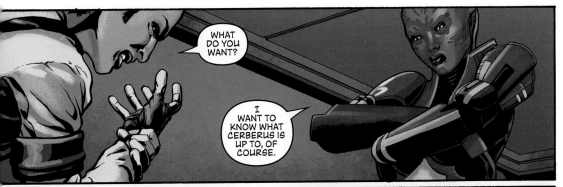

WHAT DO YOU WANT?

I WANT TO KNOW WHAT CERBERUS IS UP TO, OF COURSE.

THE ILLUSIVE MAN WOULD NEVER LET ME CLOSE ENOUGH TO GET YOU ANYTHING VALUABLE.

YOU'RE PROBABLY RIGHT. BUT HE WANTS TO KNOW ABOUT SHEPARD.

AND I CAN GIVE YOU EVERYTHING YOU NEED TO KNOW ABOUT THE DEAD SPECTRE.

HOW DOES THIS HELP YOU?

YOU'RE GOING TO TAKE THAT TO YOUR BOSS AND GIVE HIM EVERYTHING HE WANTS --

AND IN RETURN, HE'LL GIVE ME EVERYTHING I WANT.

A VIRUS?

YOU'RE CLEVER.

BUT DON'T BE TOO CLEVER.

IF THIS VIRUS DOESN'T TRIGGER, I'LL KNOW YOU WARNED THEM. AND YOU'LL BECOME A WANTED CRIMINAL THROUGHOUT THE GALAXY.

SOUNDS LIKE I DON'T HAVE MUCH CHOICE.

THERE'S ALWAYS A CHOICE.

JUST BE SURE YOU MAKE THE RIGHT ONE.

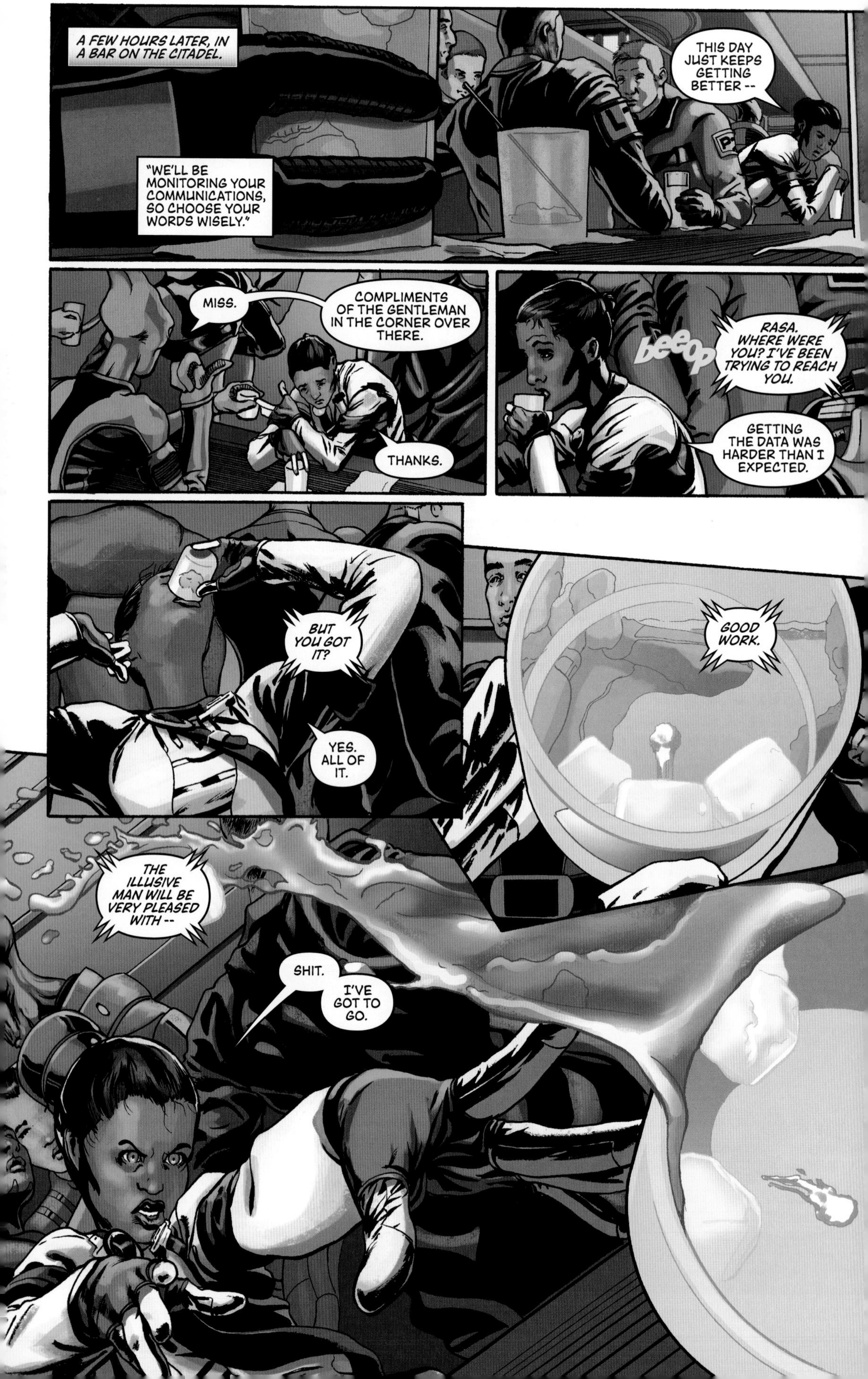
A FEW HOURS LATER, IN A BAR ON THE CITADEL.
"WE'LL BE MONITORING YOUR COMMUNICATIONS, SO CHOOSE YOUR WORDS WISELY."
THIS DAY JUST KEEPS GETTING BETTER --
MISS.
COMPLIMENTS OF THE GENTLEMAN IN THE CORNER OVER THERE.
THANKS.
beeop
RASA. WHERE WERE YOU? I'VE BEEN TRYING TO REACH YOU.
GETTING THE DATA WAS HARDER THAN I EXPECTED.
BUT YOU GOT IT?
YES. ALL OF IT.
GOOD WORK.
THE ILLUSIVE MAN WILL BE VERY PLEASED WITH --
SHIT.
I'VE GOT TO GO.

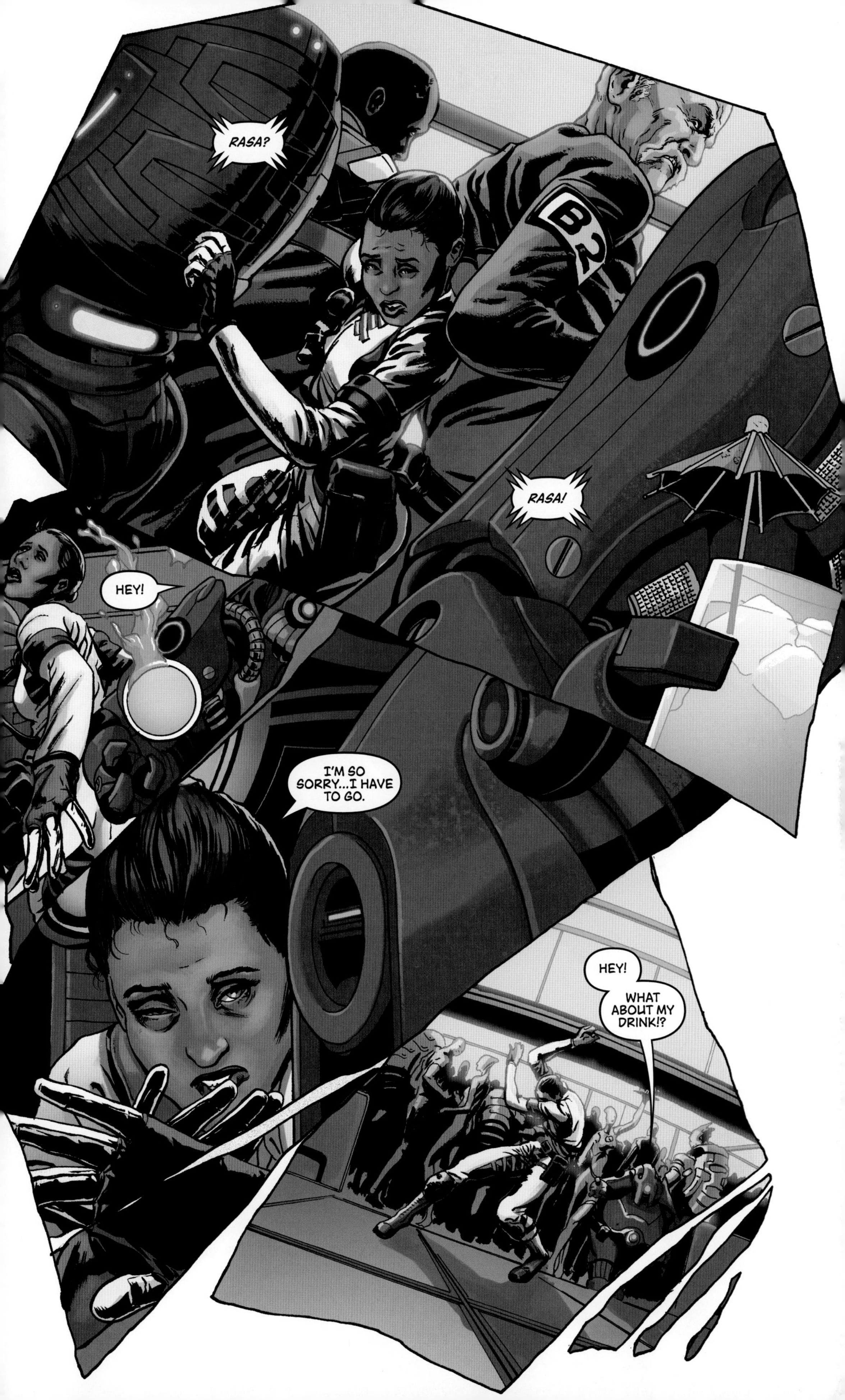
RASA?
RASA!
HEY!
I'M SO SORRY...I HAVE TO GO.
HEY!
WHAT ABOUT MY DRINK!?

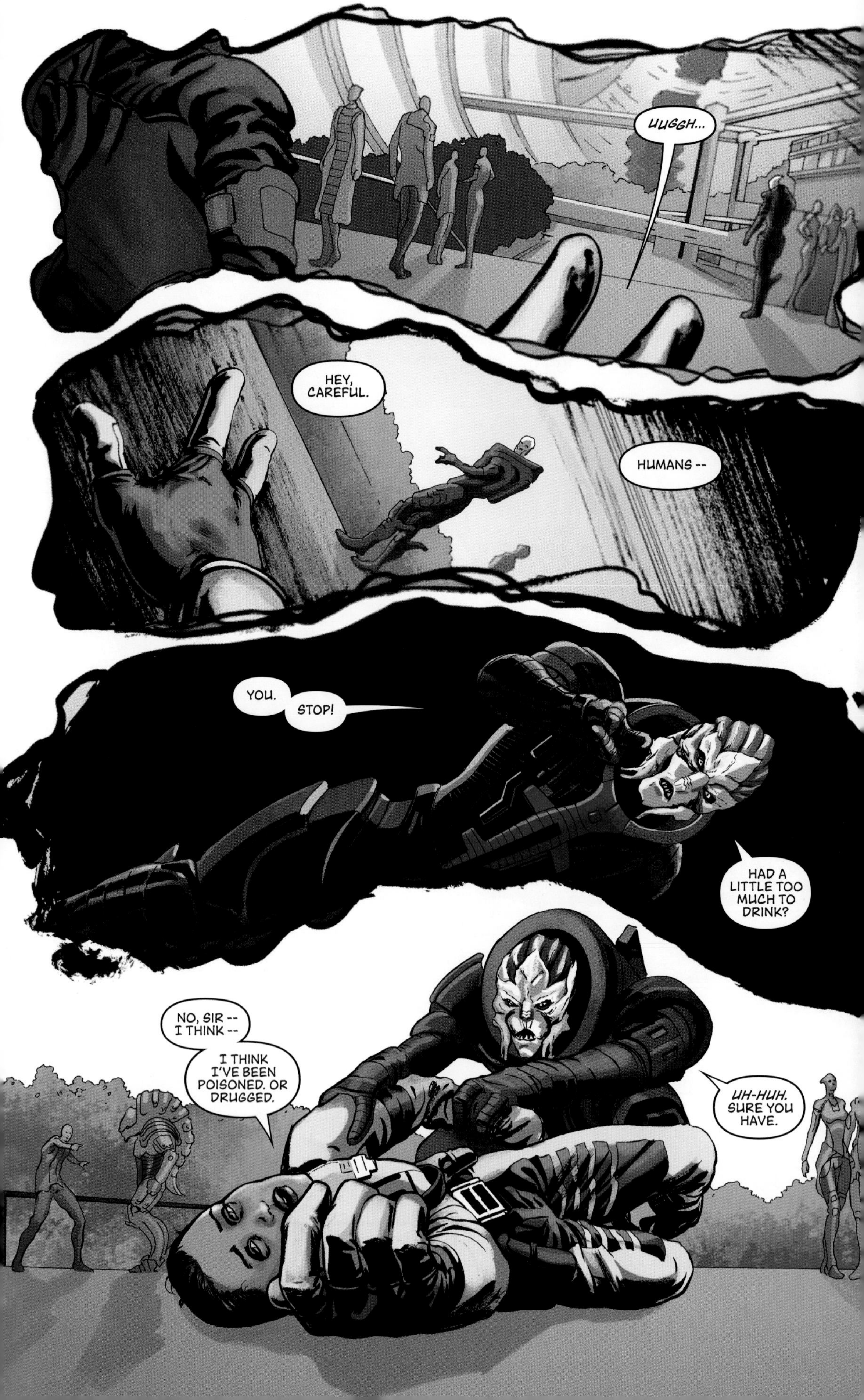
UUGGH...
HEY, CAREFUL.
HUMANS --
YOU.
STOP!
HAD A LITTLE TOO MUCH TO DRINK?
NO, SIR -- I THINK --
I THINK I'VE BEEN POISONED. OR DRUGGED.
UH-HUH. SURE YOU HAVE.

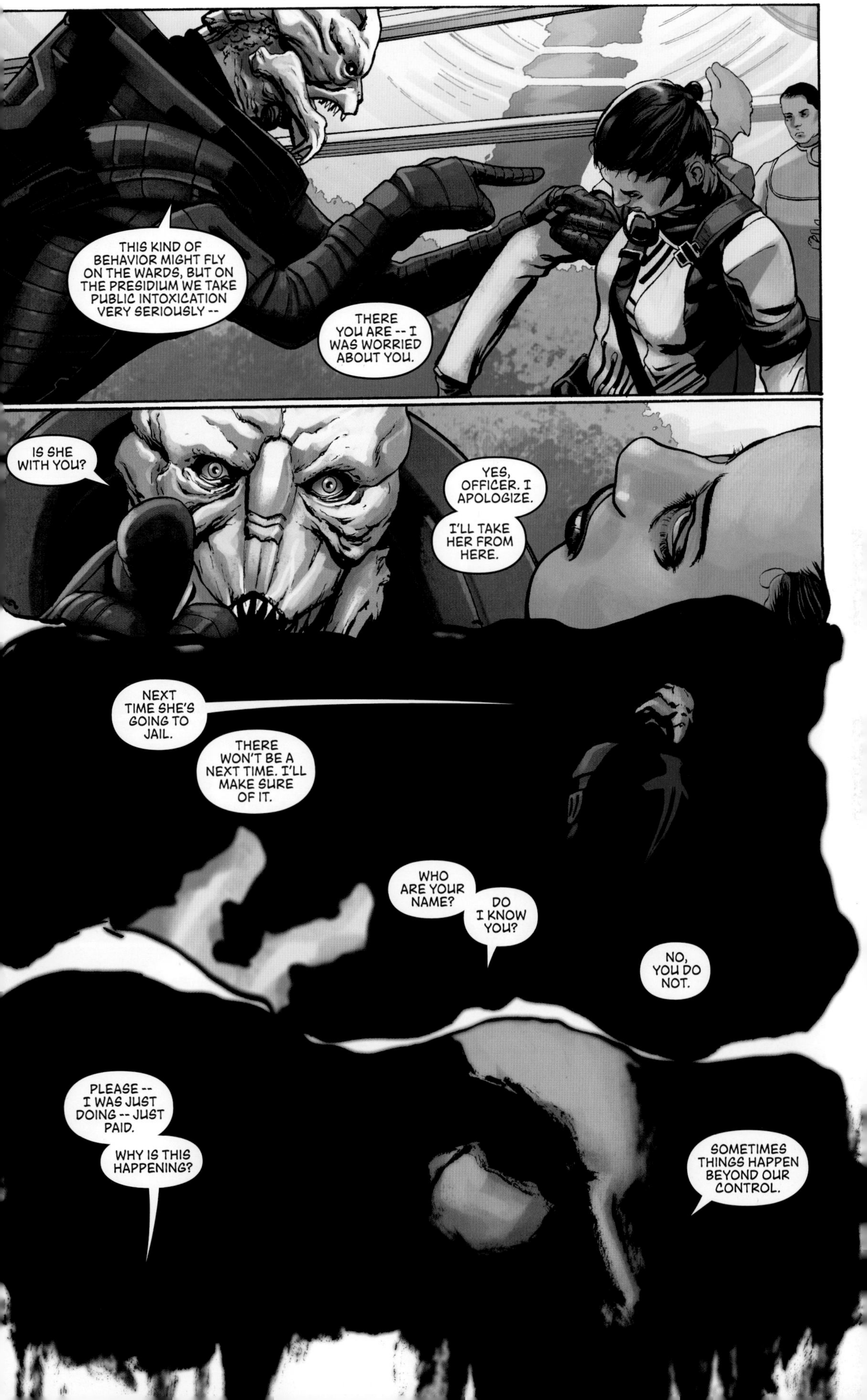
THIS KIND OF BEHAVIOR MIGHT FLY ON THE WARDS, BUT ON THE PRESIDIUM WE TAKE PUBLIC INTOXICATION VERY SERIOUSLY --
THERE YOU ARE -- I WAS WORRIED ABOUT YOU.
IS SHE WITH YOU?
YES, OFFICER. I APOLOGIZE.
I'LL TAKE HER FROM HERE.
NEXT TIME SHE'S GOING TO JAIL.
THERE WON'T BE A NEXT TIME. I'LL MAKE SURE OF IT.
WHO ARE YOUR NAME?
DO I KNOW YOU?
NO, YOU DO NOT.
PLEASE -- I WAS JUST DOING -- JUST PAID.
WHY IS THIS HAPPENING?
SOMETIMES THINGS HAPPEN BEYOND OUR CONTROL.

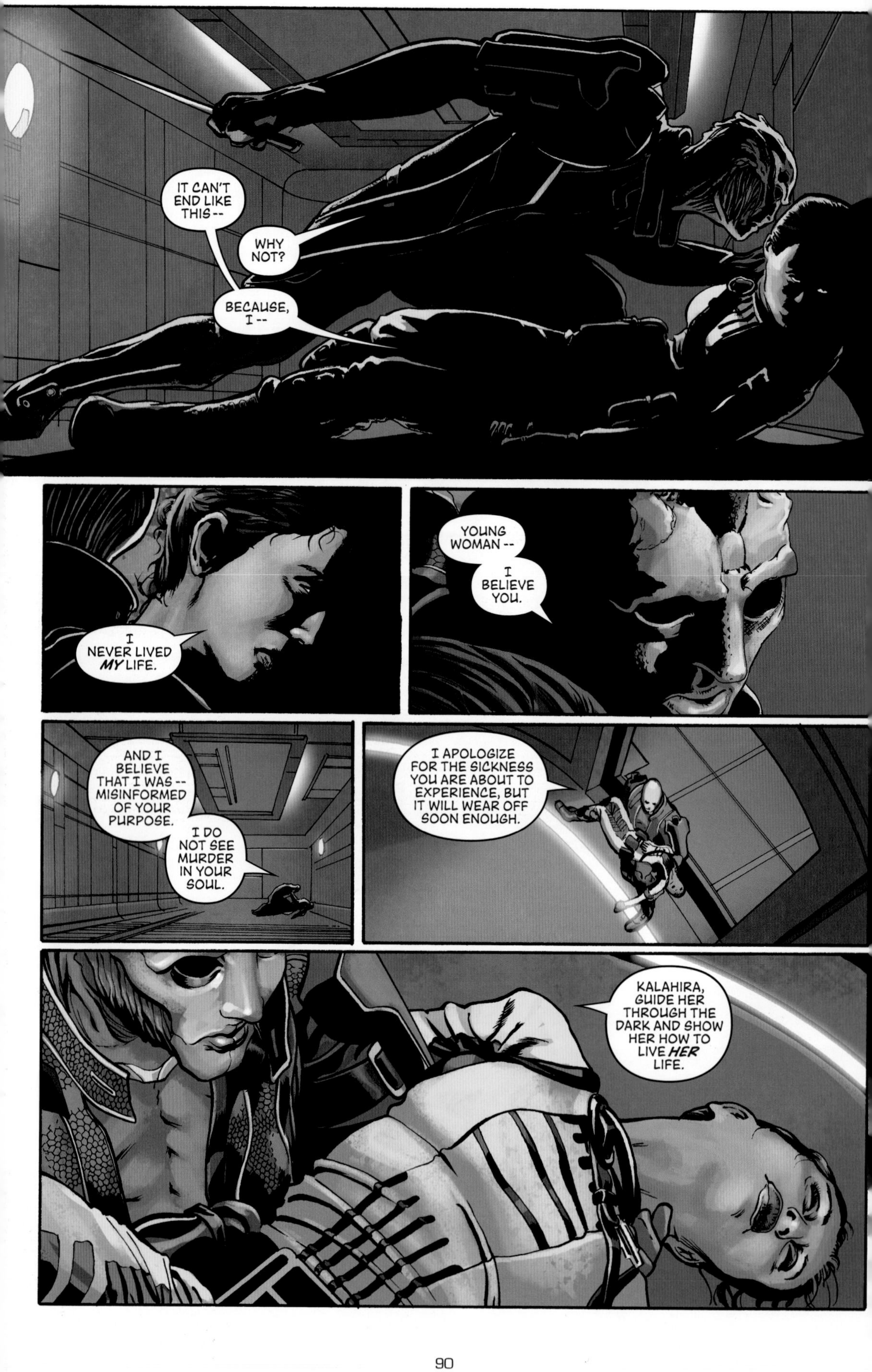
IT CAN'T END LIKE THIS--
WHY NOT?
BECAUSE, I--
I NEVER LIVED MY LIFE.
YOUNG WOMAN--
I BELIEVE YOU.
AND I BELIEVE THAT I WAS-- MISINFORMED OF YOUR PURPOSE.
I DO NOT SEE MURDER IN YOUR SOUL.
I APOLOGIZE FOR THE SICKNESS YOU ARE ABOUT TO EXPERIENCE, BUT IT WILL WEAR OFF SOON ENOUGH.
KALAHIRA, GUIDE HER THROUGH THE DARK AND SHOW HER HOW TO LIVE HER LIFE.

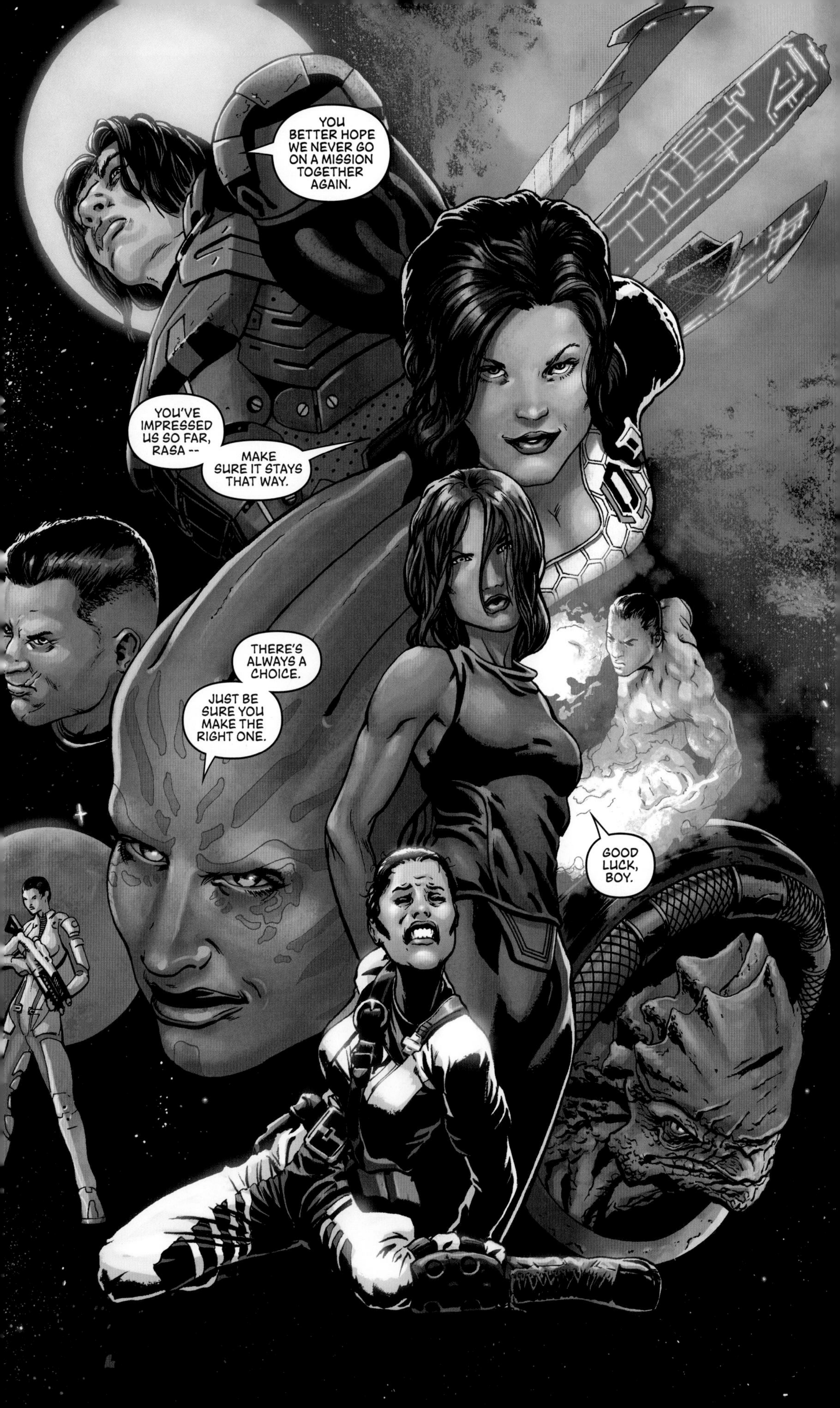

YOU BETTER HOPE WE NEVER GO ON A MISSION TOGETHER AGAIN.
YOU'VE IMPRESSED US SO FAR, RASA --
MAKE SURE IT STAYS THAT WAY.
THERE'S ALWAYS A CHOICE.
JUST BE SURE YOU MAKE THE RIGHT ONE.
GOOD LUCK, BOY.

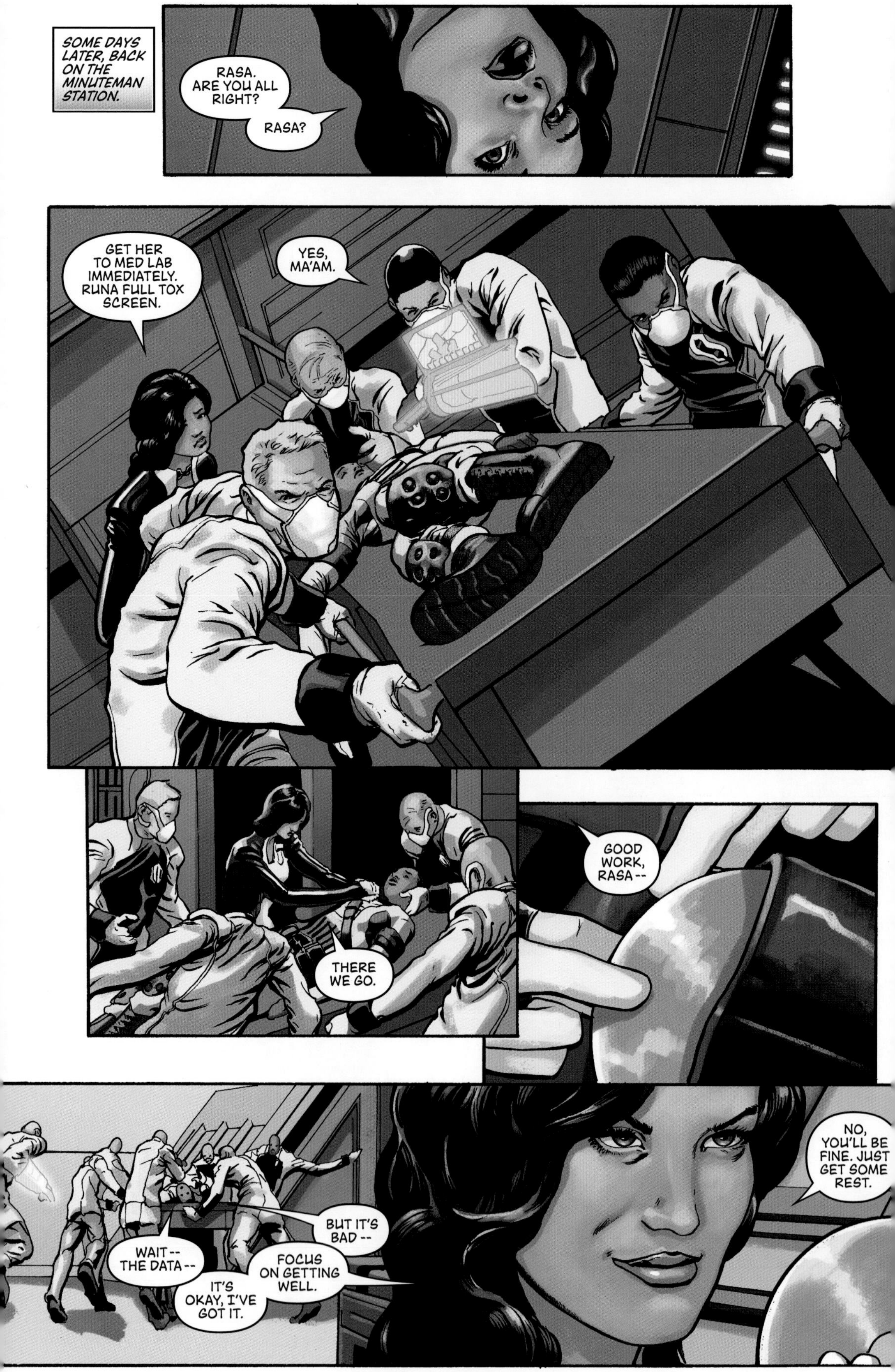
SOME DAYS LATER, BACK ON THE MINUTEMAN STATION.
RASA. ARE YOU ALL RIGHT?
RASA?
GET HER TO MED LAB IMMEDIATELY. RUN A FULL TOX SCREEN.
YES, MA'AM.
THERE WE GO.
GOOD WORK, RASA--
WAIT-- THE DATA--
BUT IT'S BAD--
IT'S OKAY, I'VE GOT IT.
FOCUS ON GETTING WELL.
NO, YOU'LL BE FINE. JUST GET SOME REST.

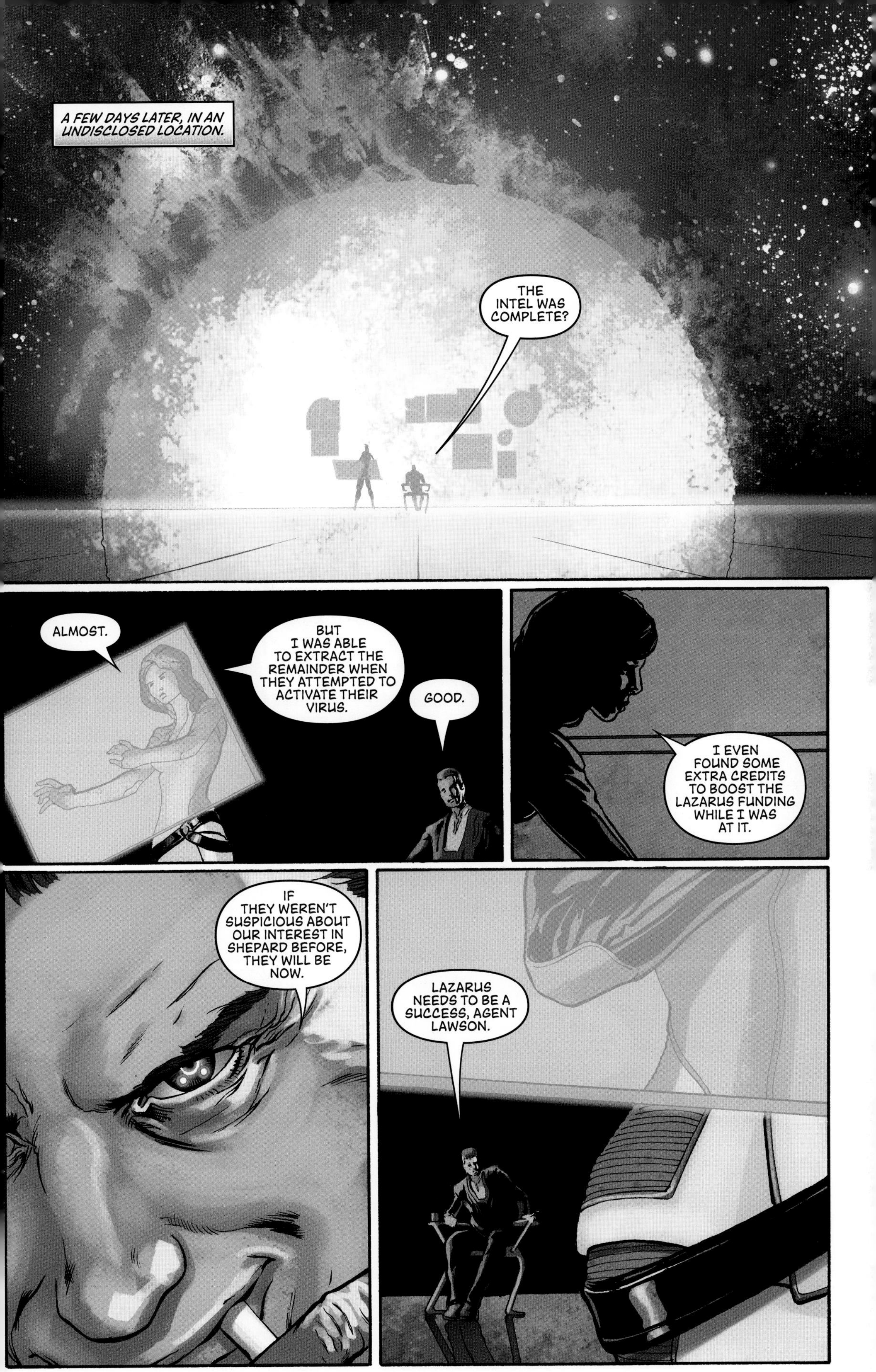
A FEW DAYS LATER, IN AN UNDISCLOSED LOCATION.
THE INTEL WAS COMPLETE?
ALMOST.
BUT I WAS ABLE TO EXTRACT THE REMAINDER WHEN THEY ATTEMPTED TO ACTIVATE THEIR VIRUS.
GOOD.
I EVEN FOUND SOME EXTRA CREDITS TO BOOST THE LAZARUS FUNDING WHILE I WAS AT IT.
IF THEY WEREN'T SUSPICIOUS ABOUT OUR INTEREST IN SHEPARD BEFORE, THEY WILL BE NOW.
LAZARUS NEEDS TO BE A SUCCESS, AGENT LAWSON.

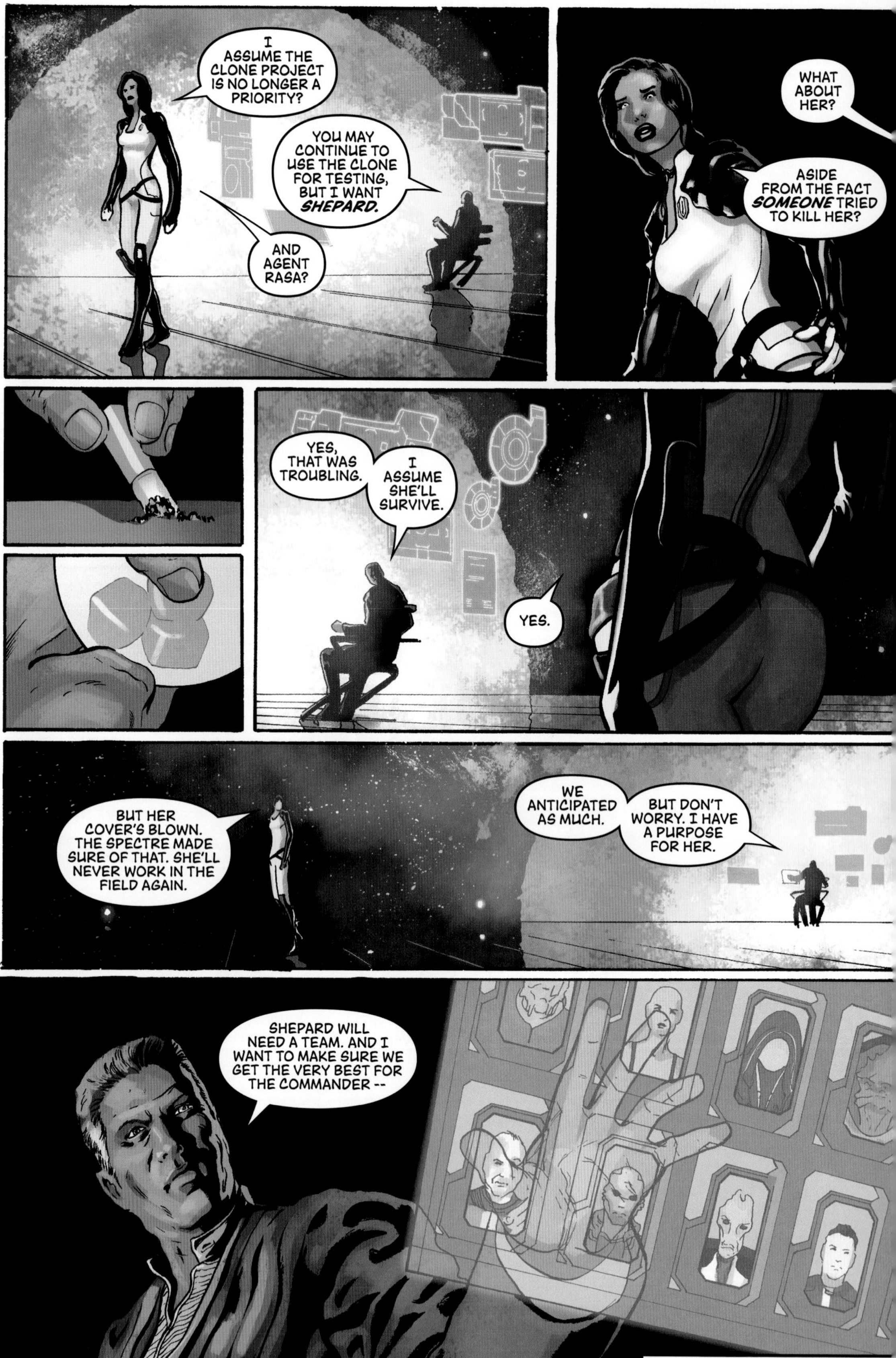

I ASSUME THE CLONE PROJECT IS NO LONGER A PRIORITY?
YOU MAY CONTINUE TO USE THE CLONE FOR TESTING, BUT I WANT *SHEPARD.*
AND AGENT RASA?
WHAT ABOUT HER?
ASIDE FROM THE FACT *SOMEONE* TRIED TO KILL HER?
YES, THAT WAS TROUBLING.
I ASSUME SHE'LL SURVIVE.
YES.
BUT HER COVER'S BLOWN. THE SPECTRE MADE SURE OF THAT. SHE'LL NEVER WORK IN THE FIELD AGAIN.
WE ANTICIPATED AS MUCH.
BUT DON'T WORRY. I HAVE A PURPOSE FOR HER.
SHEPARD WILL NEED A TEAM. AND I WANT TO MAKE SURE WE GET THE VERY BEST FOR THE COMMANDER --
TO BE CONTINUED...

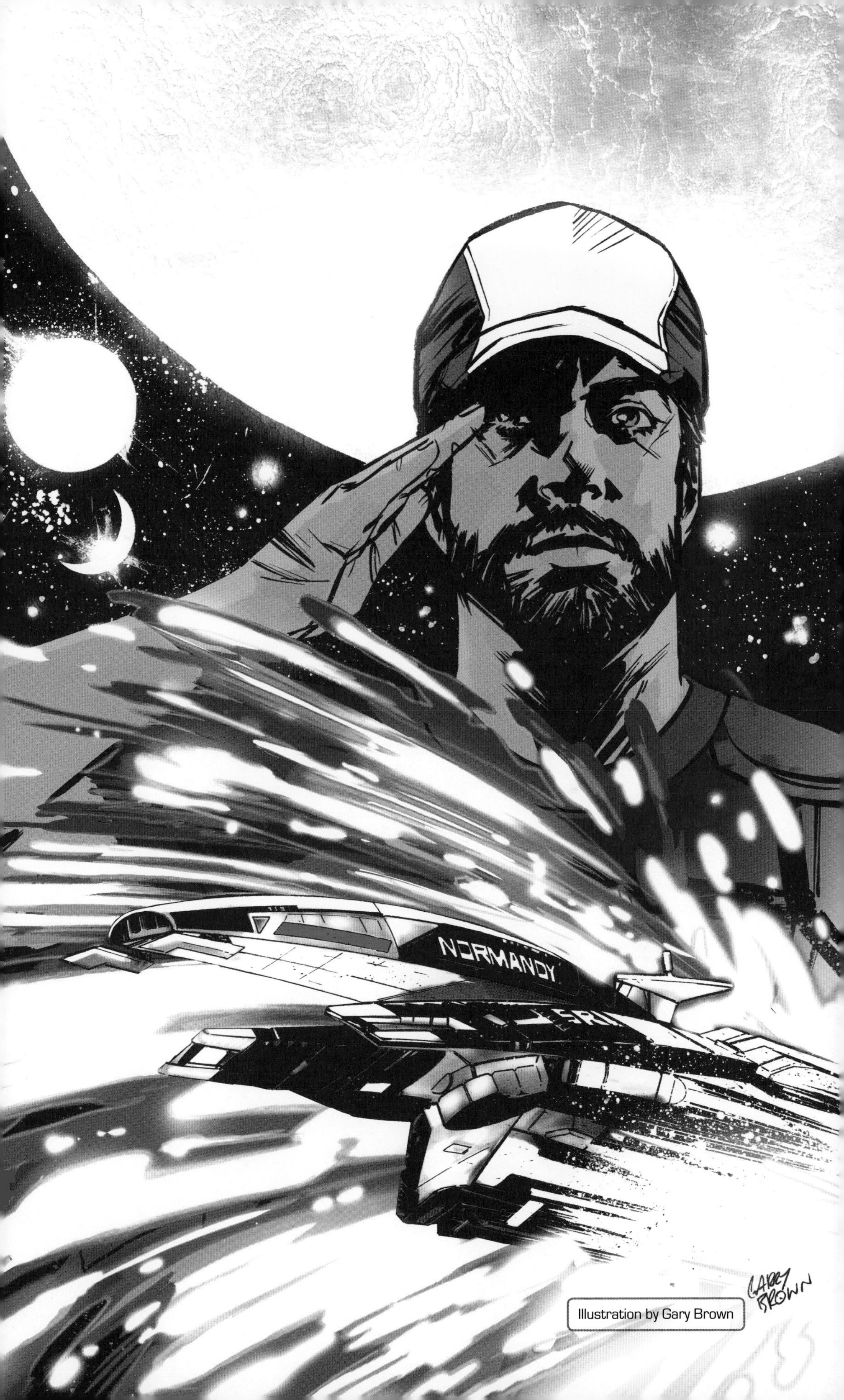
NORMANDY
GARY BROWN
Illustration by Gary Brown

HE WHO LAUGHS BEST

STORY
MAC WALTERS and JEREMY BARLOW

SCRIPT
JEREMY BARLOW

ART
GARRY BROWN

COLORS
MICHAEL ATIYEH

LETTERING
MICHAEL HEISLER

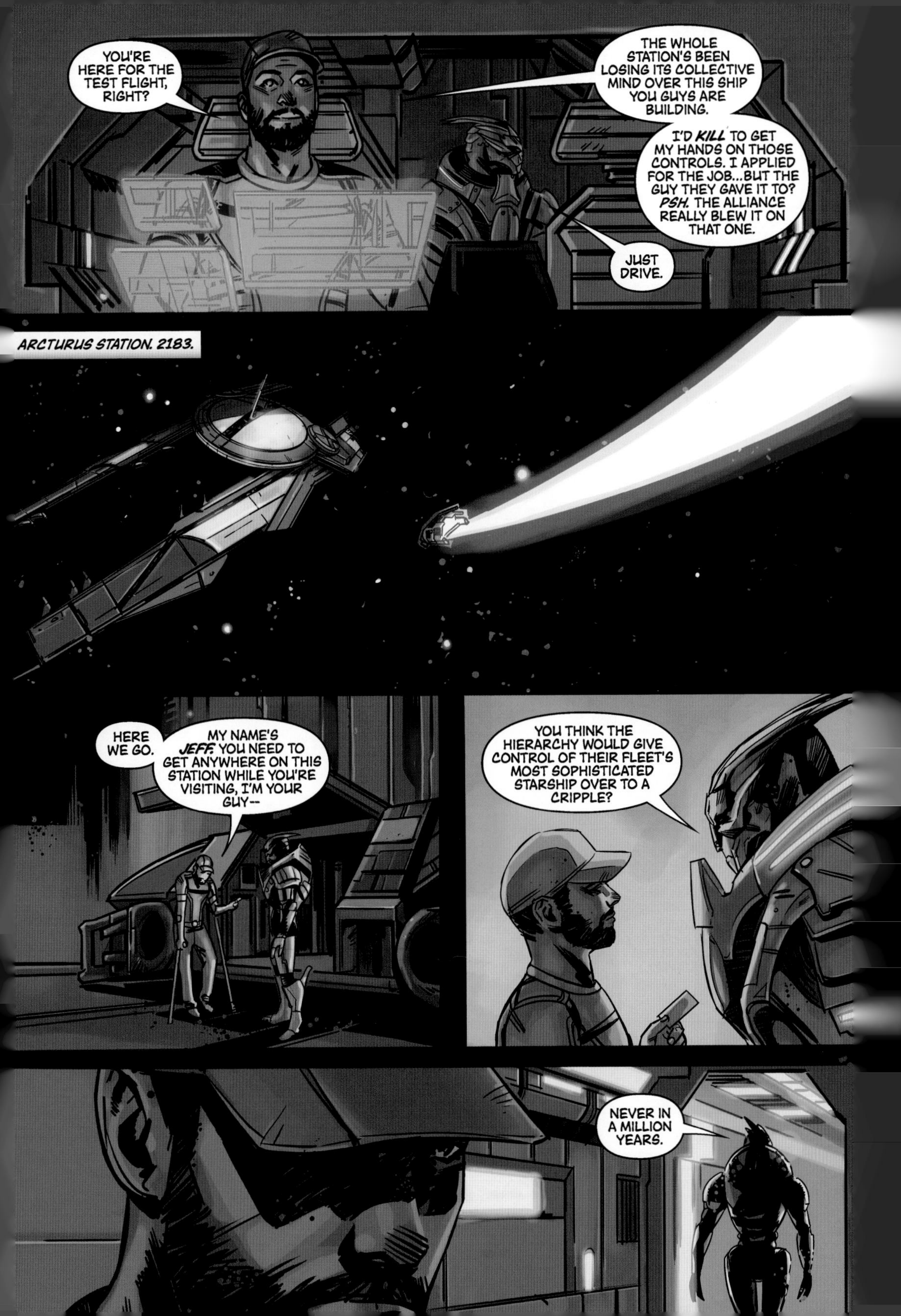
YOU'RE HERE FOR THE TEST FLIGHT, RIGHT?
THE WHOLE STATION'S BEEN LOSING ITS COLLECTIVE MIND OVER THIS SHIP YOU GUYS ARE BUILDING.
I'D KILL TO GET MY HANDS ON THOSE CONTROLS. I APPLIED FOR THE JOB...BUT THE GUY THEY GAVE IT TO? PSH. THE ALLIANCE REALLY BLEW IT ON THAT ONE.
JUST DRIVE.
ARCTURUS STATION. 2183.
HERE WE GO.
MY NAME'S JEFF. YOU NEED TO GET ANYWHERE ON THIS STATION WHILE YOU'RE VISITING, I'M YOUR GUY--
YOU THINK THE HIERARCHY WOULD GIVE CONTROL OF THEIR FLEET'S MOST SOPHISTICATED STARSHIP OVER TO A CRIPPLE?
NEVER IN A MILLION YEARS.

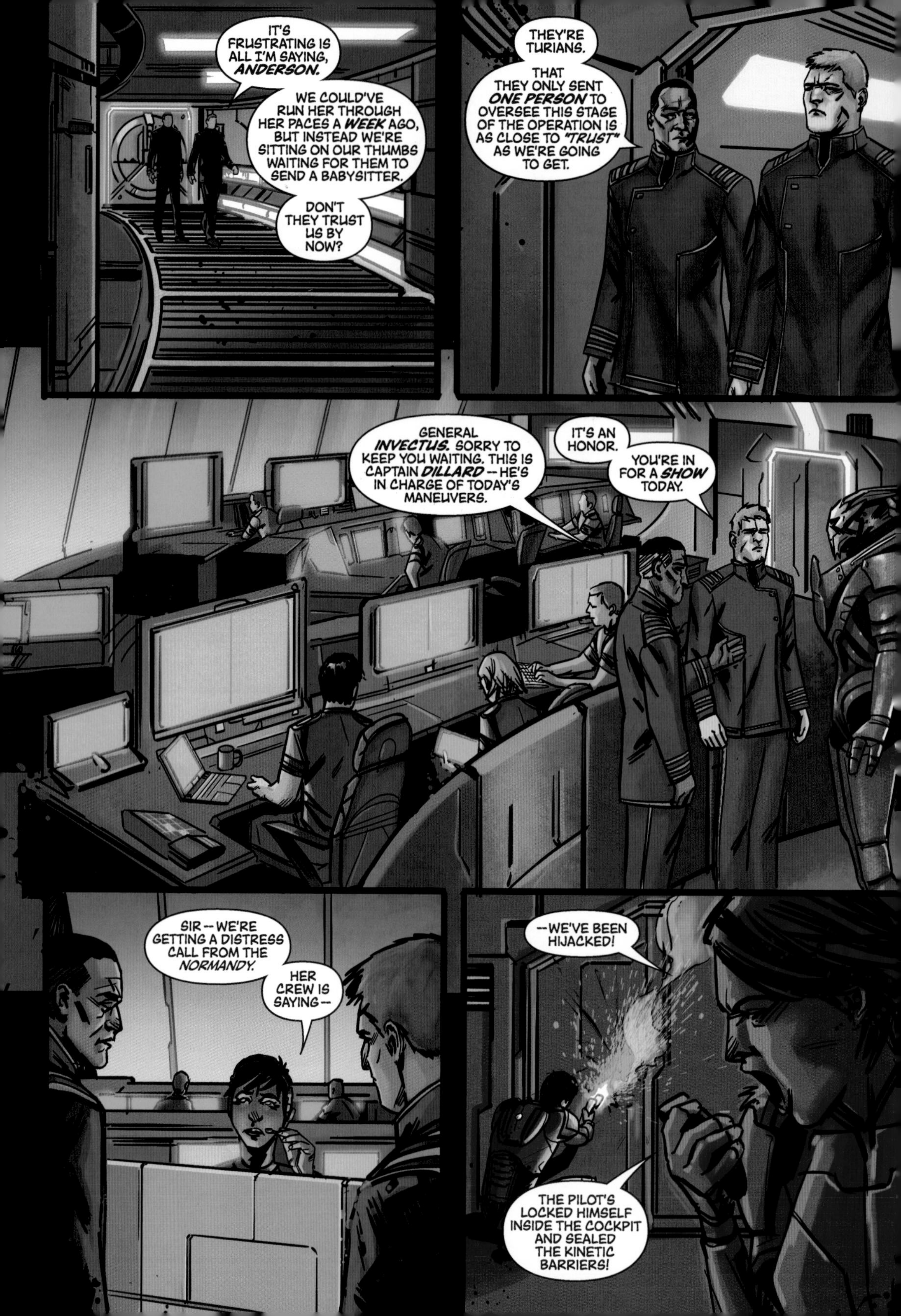

IT'S FRUSTRATING IS ALL I'M SAYING, ANDERSON.
WE COULD'VE RUN HER THROUGH HER PACES A WEEK AGO, BUT INSTEAD WE'RE SITTING ON OUR THUMBS WAITING FOR THEM TO SEND A BABYSITTER.
DON'T THEY TRUST US BY NOW?
THEY'RE TURIANS.
THAT THEY ONLY SENT ONE PERSON TO OVERSEE THIS STAGE OF THE OPERATION IS AS CLOSE TO "TRUST" AS WE'RE GOING TO GET.
GENERAL INVECTUS. SORRY TO KEEP YOU WAITING. THIS IS CAPTAIN DILLARD -- HE'S IN CHARGE OF TODAY'S MANEUVERS.
IT'S AN HONOR.
YOU'RE IN FOR A SHOW TODAY.
SIR -- WE'RE GETTING A DISTRESS CALL FROM THE NORMANDY.
HER CREW IS SAYING --
--WE'VE BEEN HIJACKED!
THE PILOT'S LOCKED HIMSELF INSIDE THE COCKPIT AND SEALED THE KINETIC BARRIERS!

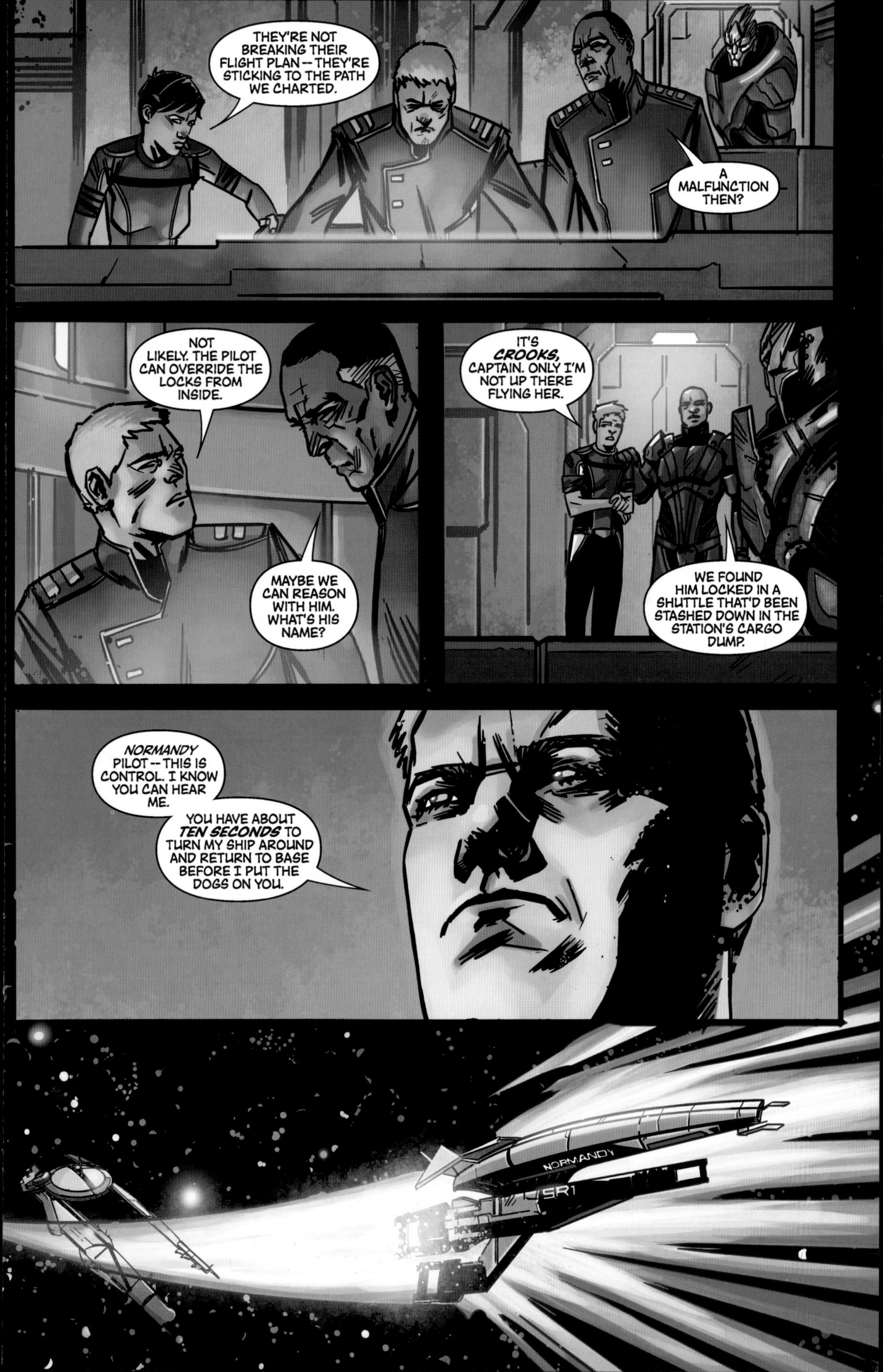
THEY'RE NOT BREAKING THEIR FLIGHT PLAN -- THEY'RE STICKING TO THE PATH WE CHARTED.
A MALFUNCTION THEN?
NOT LIKELY. THE PILOT CAN OVERRIDE THE LOCKS FROM INSIDE.
MAYBE WE CAN REASON WITH HIM. WHAT'S HIS NAME?
IT'S CROOKS, CAPTAIN. ONLY I'M NOT UP THERE FLYING HER.
WE FOUND HIM LOCKED IN A SHUTTLE THAT'D BEEN STASHED DOWN IN THE STATION'S CARGO DUMP.
NORMANDY PILOT -- THIS IS CONTROL. I KNOW YOU CAN HEAR ME.
YOU HAVE ABOUT TEN SECONDS TO TURN MY SHIP AROUND AND RETURN TO BASE BEFORE I PUT THE DOGS ON YOU.
NORMANDY
SR1

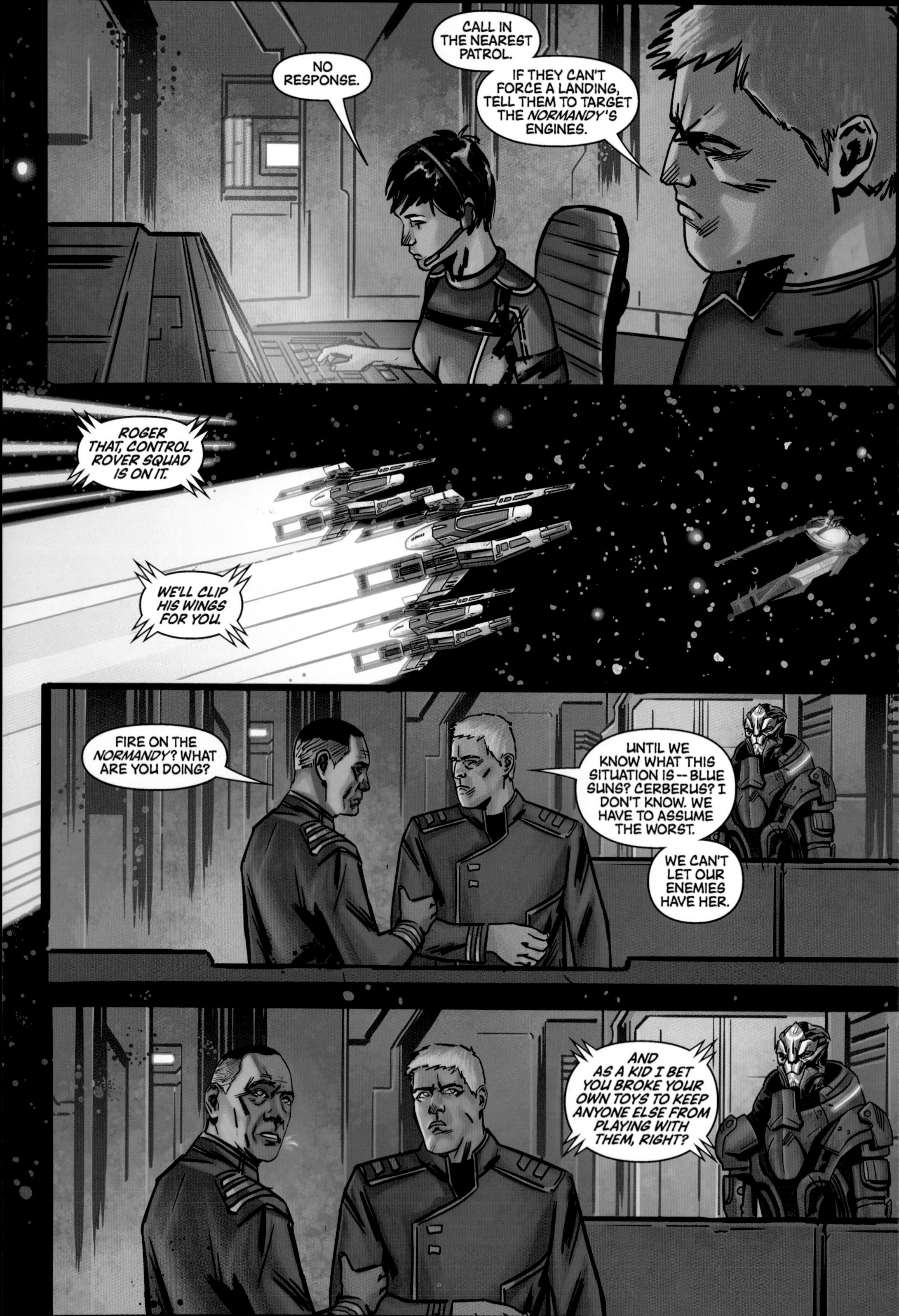
NO RESPONSE.
CALL IN THE NEAREST PATROL.
IF THEY CAN'T FORCE A LANDING, TELL THEM TO TARGET THE *NORMANDY*'S ENGINES.
ROGER THAT, CONTROL. ROVER SQUAD IS ON IT.
WE'LL CLIP HIS WINGS FOR YOU.
FIRE ON THE *NORMANDY*? WHAT ARE YOU DOING?
UNTIL WE KNOW WHAT THIS SITUATION IS -- BLUE SUNS? CERBERUS? I DON'T KNOW. WE HAVE TO ASSUME THE WORST.
WE CAN'T LET OUR ENEMIES HAVE HER.
AND AS A KID I BET YOU BROKE YOUR OWN TOYS TO KEEP ANYONE ELSE FROM PLAYING WITH THEM, RIGHT?

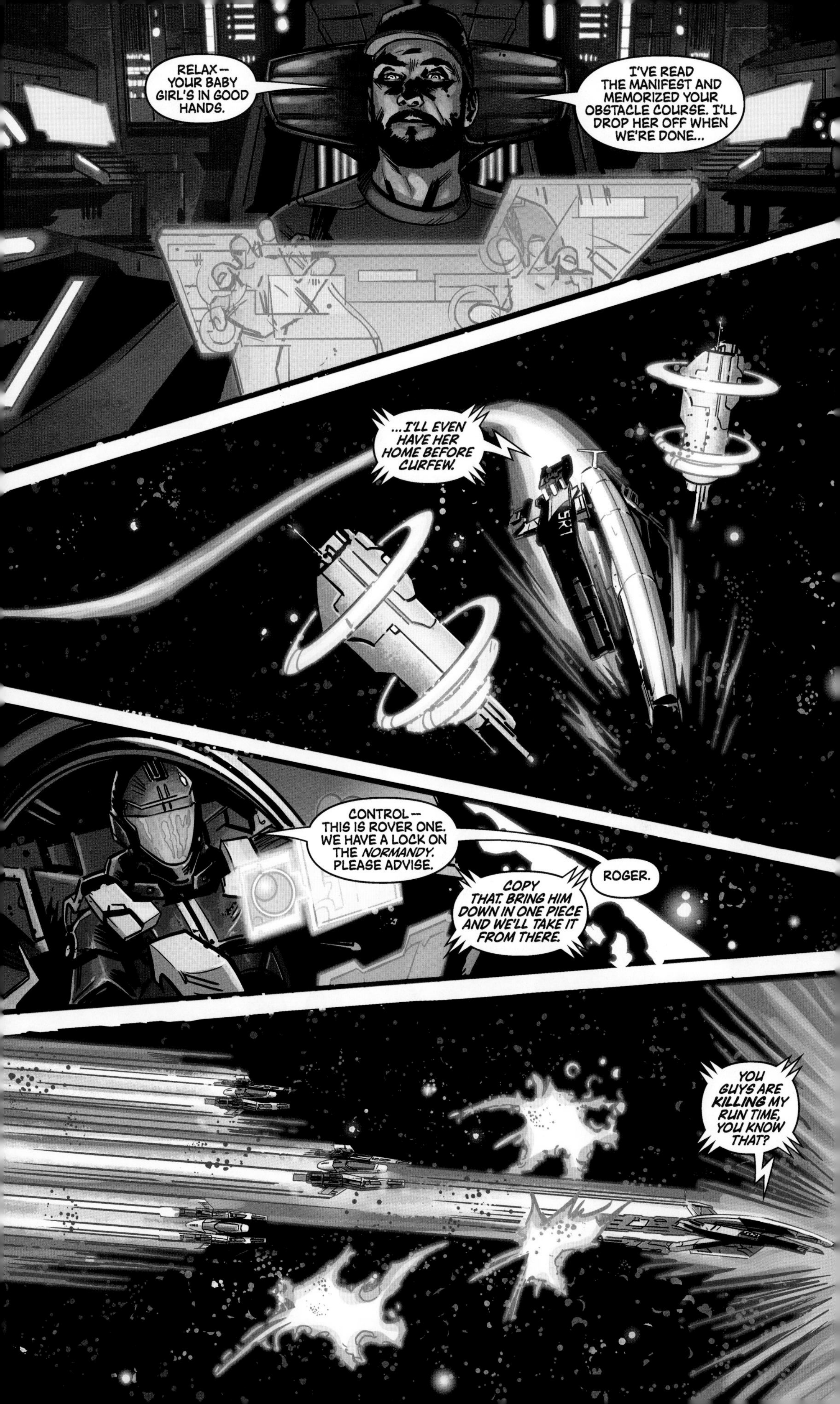
RELAX-- YOUR BABY GIRL'S IN GOOD HANDS.
I'VE READ THE MANIFEST AND MEMORIZED YOUR OBSTACLE COURSE. I'LL DROP HER OFF WHEN WE'RE DONE...
...I'LL EVEN HAVE HER HOME BEFORE CURFEW.
CONTROL-- THIS IS ROVER ONE. WE HAVE A LOCK ON THE *NORMANDY*. PLEASE ADVISE.
COPY THAT. BRING HIM DOWN IN ONE PIECE AND WE'LL TAKE IT FROM THERE.
ROGER.
YOU GUYS ARE **KILLING** MY RUN TIME, YOU KNOW THAT?

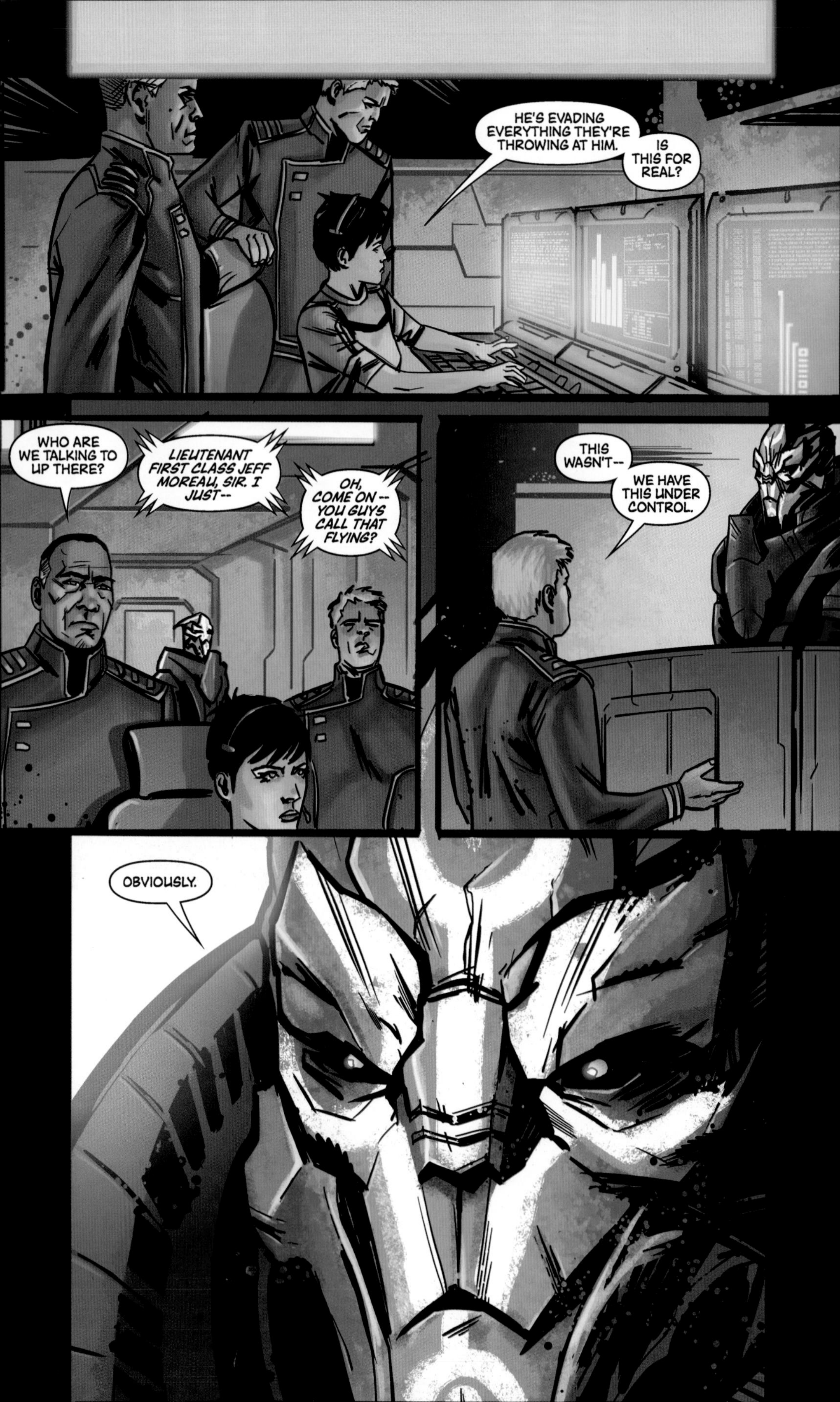
HE'S EVADING EVERYTHING THEY'RE THROWING AT HIM.
IS THIS FOR REAL?
WHO ARE WE TALKING TO UP THERE?
LIEUTENANT FIRST CLASS JEFF MOREAU, SIR. I JUST--
OH, COME ON -- YOU GUYS CALL THAT FLYING?
THIS WASN'T--
WE HAVE THIS UNDER CONTROL.
OBVIOUSLY.

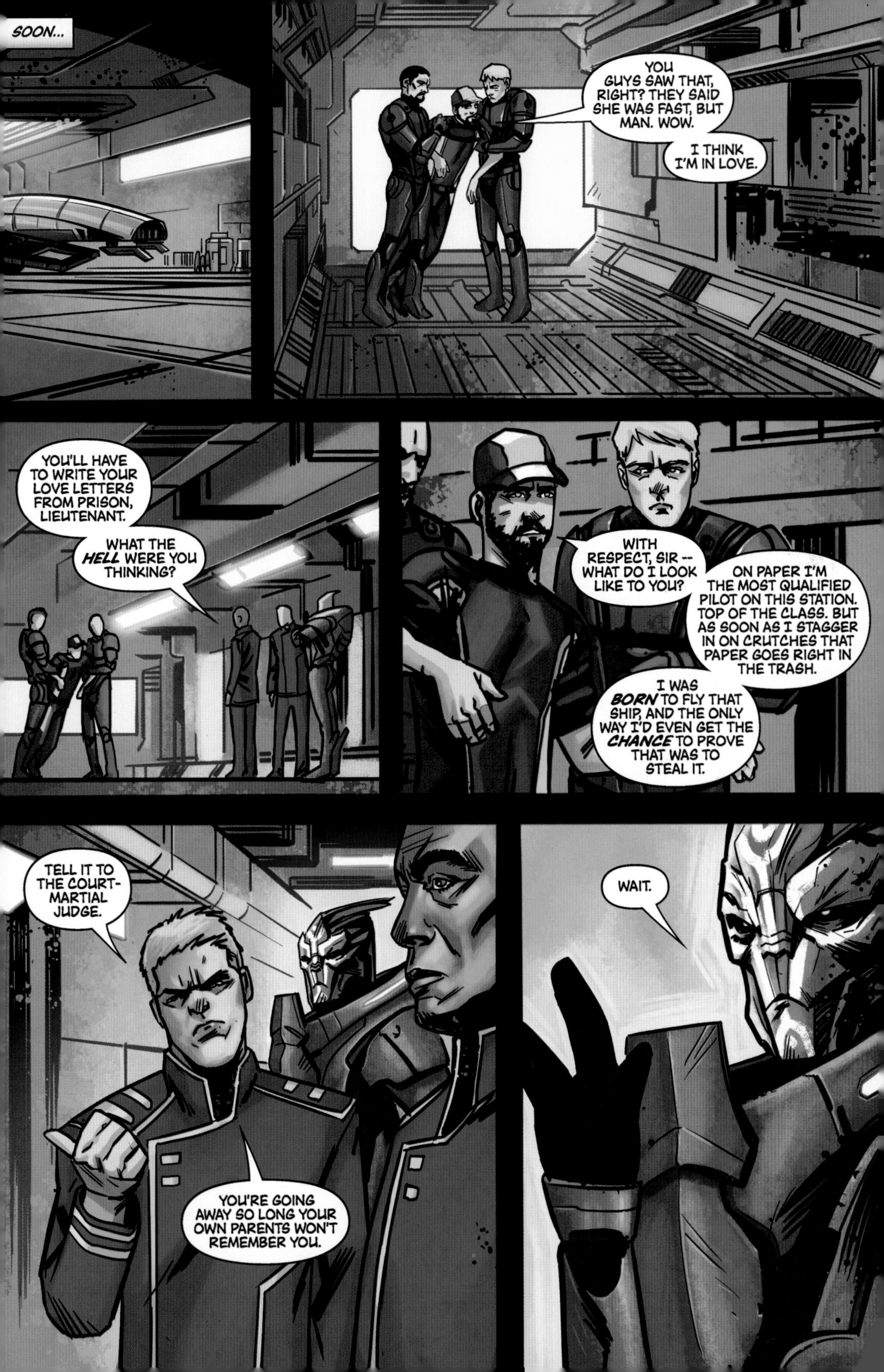
SOON...
YOU GUYS SAW THAT, RIGHT? THEY SAID SHE WAS FAST, BUT MAN. WOW.
I THINK I'M IN LOVE.
YOU'LL HAVE TO WRITE YOUR LOVE LETTERS FROM PRISON, LIEUTENANT.
WHAT THE HELL WERE YOU THINKING?
WITH RESPECT, SIR -- WHAT DO I LOOK LIKE TO YOU?
ON PAPER I'M THE MOST QUALIFIED PILOT ON THIS STATION. TOP OF THE CLASS. BUT AS SOON AS I STAGGER IN ON CRUTCHES THAT PAPER GOES RIGHT IN THE TRASH.
I WAS BORN TO FLY THAT SHIP, AND THE ONLY WAY I'D EVEN GET THE CHANCE TO PROVE THAT WAS TO STEAL IT.
TELL IT TO THE COURT-MARTIAL JUDGE.
YOU'RE GOING AWAY SO LONG YOUR OWN PARENTS WON'T REMEMBER YOU.
WAIT.

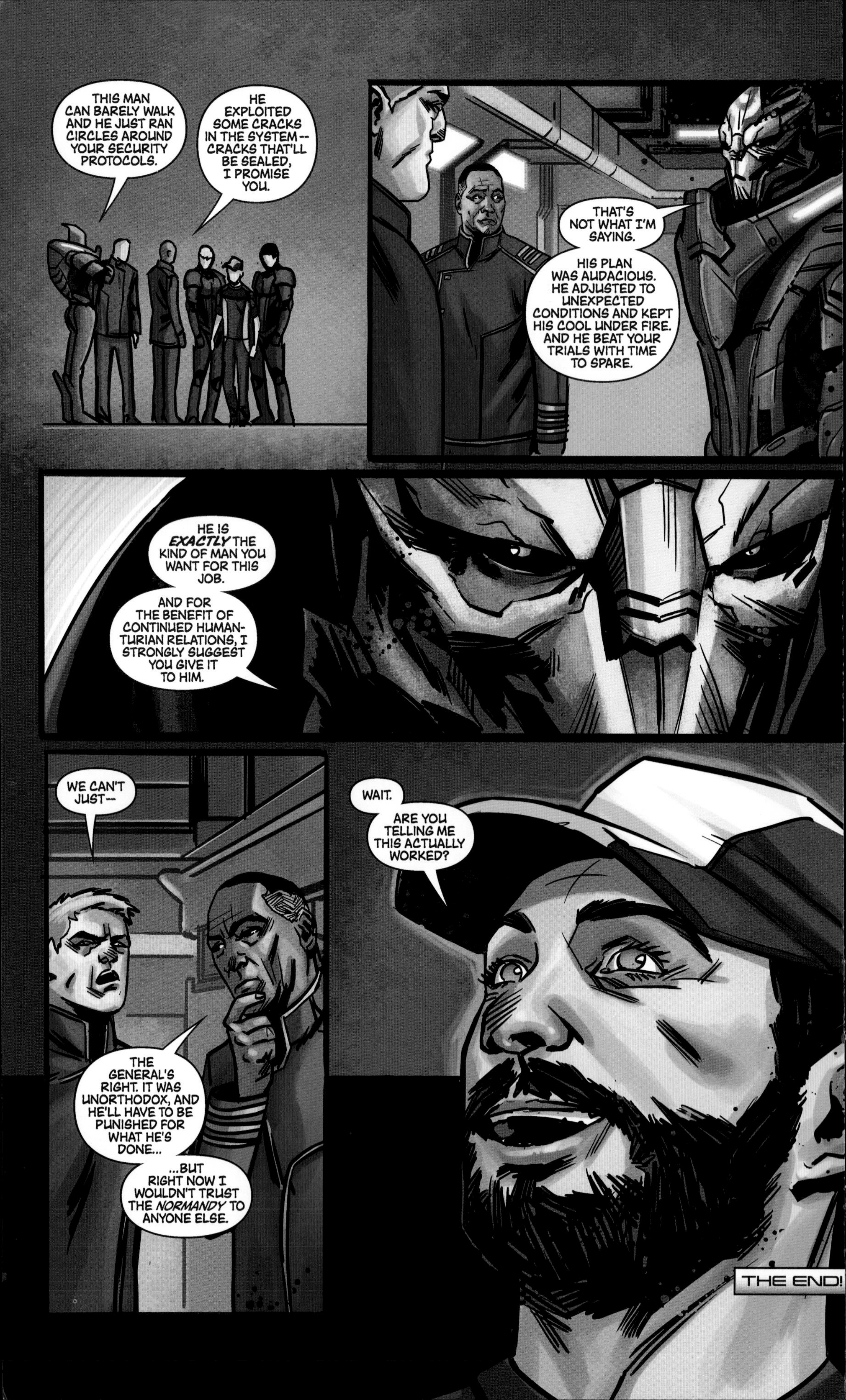
THIS MAN CAN BARELY WALK AND HE JUST RAN CIRCLES AROUND YOUR SECURITY PROTOCOLS.
HE EXPLOITED SOME CRACKS IN THE SYSTEM -- CRACKS THAT'LL BE SEALED, I PROMISE YOU.
THAT'S NOT WHAT I'M SAYING.
HIS PLAN WAS AUDACIOUS. HE ADJUSTED TO UNEXPECTED CONDITIONS AND KEPT HIS COOL UNDER FIRE. AND HE BEAT YOUR TRIALS WITH TIME TO SPARE.
HE IS *EXACTLY* THE KIND OF MAN YOU WANT FOR THIS JOB.
AND FOR THE BENEFIT OF CONTINUED HUMAN-TURIAN RELATIONS, I STRONGLY SUGGEST YOU GIVE IT TO HIM.
WE CAN'T JUST--
THE GENERAL'S RIGHT. IT WAS UNORTHODOX, AND HE'LL HAVE TO BE PUNISHED FOR WHAT HE'S DONE...
...BUT RIGHT NOW I WOULDN'T TRUST THE *NORMANDY* TO ANYONE ELSE.
WAIT.
ARE YOU TELLING ME THIS ACTUALLY WORKED?
THE END!

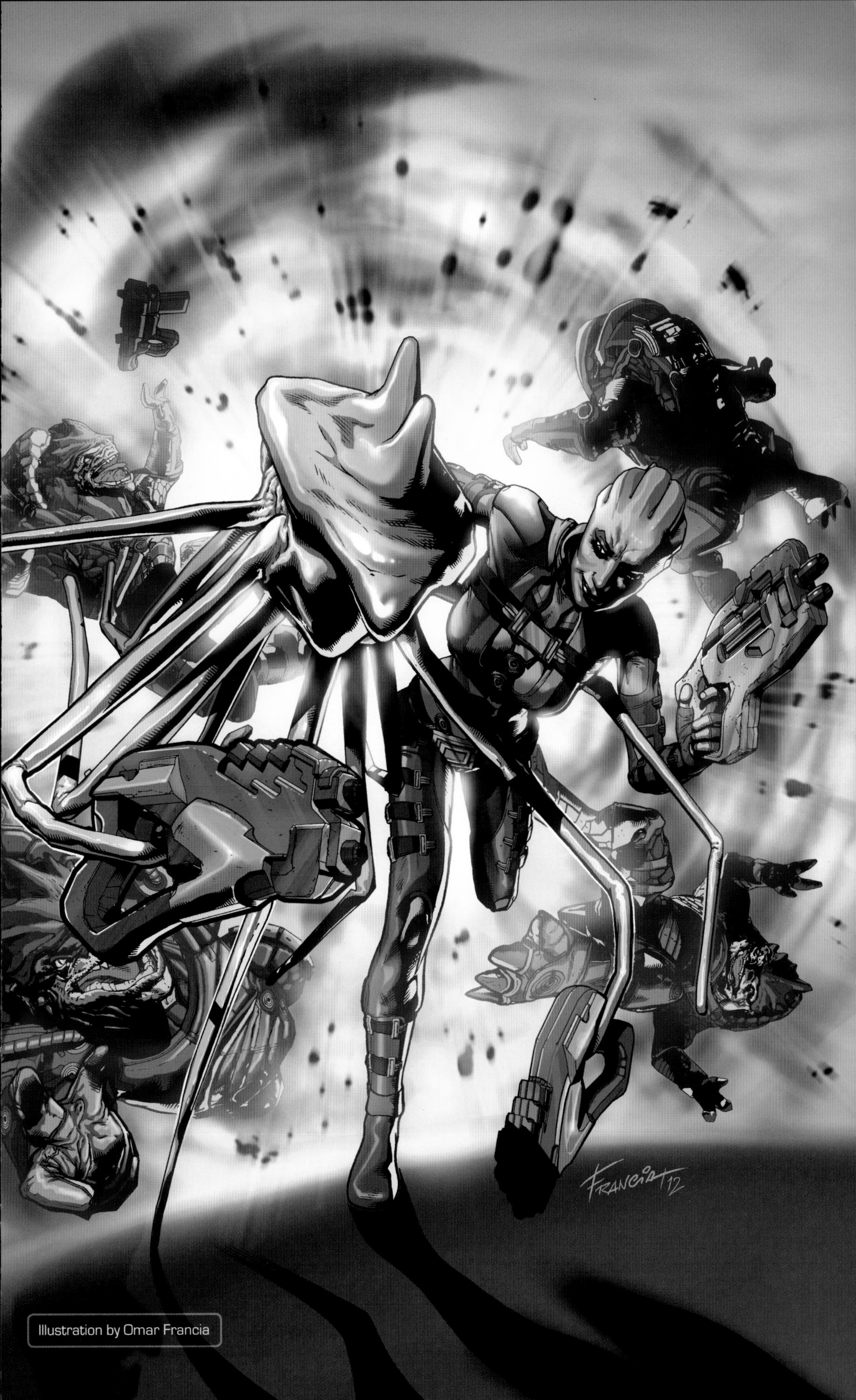
FRANCIA '12

Illustration by Omar Francia

BLASTO: ETERNITY IS FOREVER

STORY
MAC WALTERS

ART
OMAR FRANCIA

COLORS
MICHAEL ATIYEH

LETTERING
MICHAEL HEISLER

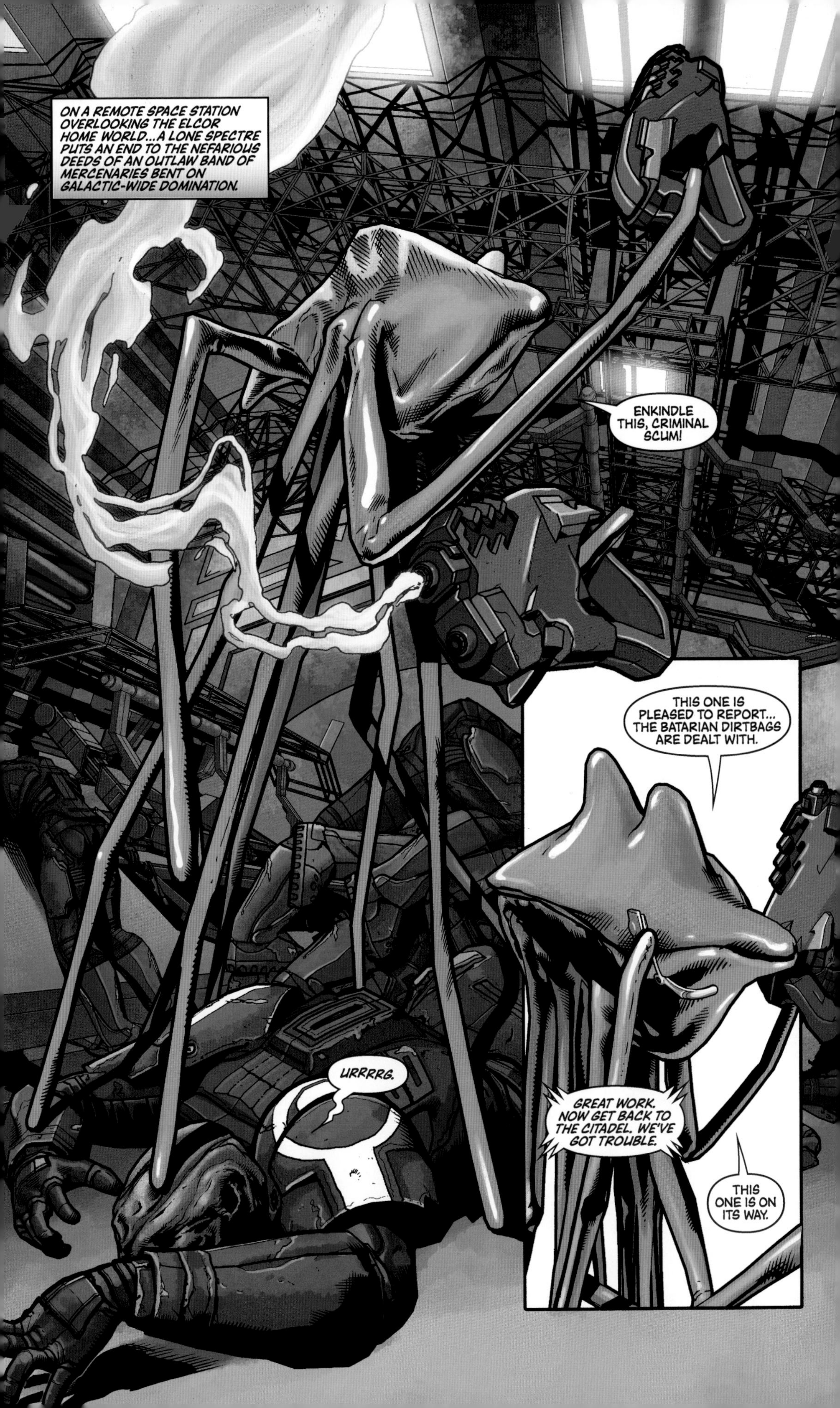
ON A REMOTE SPACE STATION OVERLOOKING THE ELCOR HOME WORLD...A LONE SPECTRE PUTS AN END TO THE NEFARIOUS DEEDS OF AN OUTLAW BAND OF MERCENARIES BENT ON GALACTIC-WIDE DOMINATION.
ENKINDLE THIS, CRIMINAL SCUM!
THIS ONE IS PLEASED TO REPORT... THE BATARIAN DIRTBAGS ARE DEALT WITH.
URRRRG.
GREAT WORK. NOW GET BACK TO THE CITADEL. WE'VE GOT TROUBLE.
THIS ONE IS ON ITS WAY.

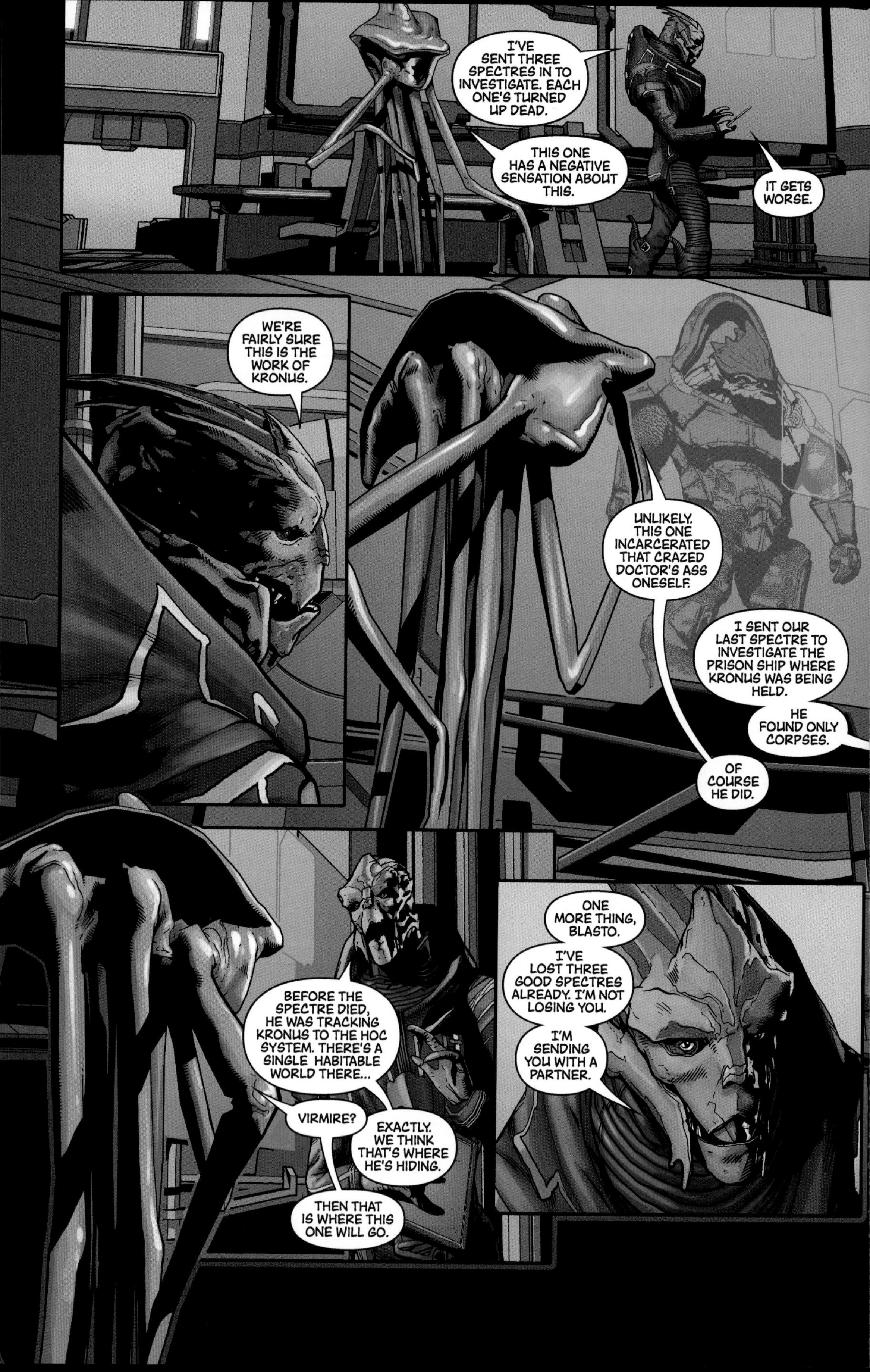
I'VE SENT THREE SPECTRES IN TO INVESTIGATE. EACH ONE'S TURNED UP DEAD.
THIS ONE HAS A NEGATIVE SENSATION ABOUT THIS.
IT GETS WORSE.
WE'RE FAIRLY SURE THIS IS THE WORK OF KRONUS.
UNLIKELY. THIS ONE INCARCERATED THAT CRAZED DOCTOR'S ASS ONESELF.
I SENT OUR LAST SPECTRE TO INVESTIGATE THE PRISON SHIP WHERE KRONUS WAS BEING HELD.
HE FOUND ONLY CORPSES.
OF COURSE HE DID.
BEFORE THE SPECTRE DIED, HE WAS TRACKING KRONUS TO THE HOC SYSTEM. THERE'S A SINGLE HABITABLE WORLD THERE...
VIRMIRE?
EXACTLY. WE THINK THAT'S WHERE HE'S HIDING.
THEN THAT IS WHERE THIS ONE WILL GO.
ONE MORE THING, BLASTO.
I'VE LOST THREE GOOD SPECTRES ALREADY. I'M NOT LOSING YOU.
I'M SENDING YOU WITH A PARTNER.

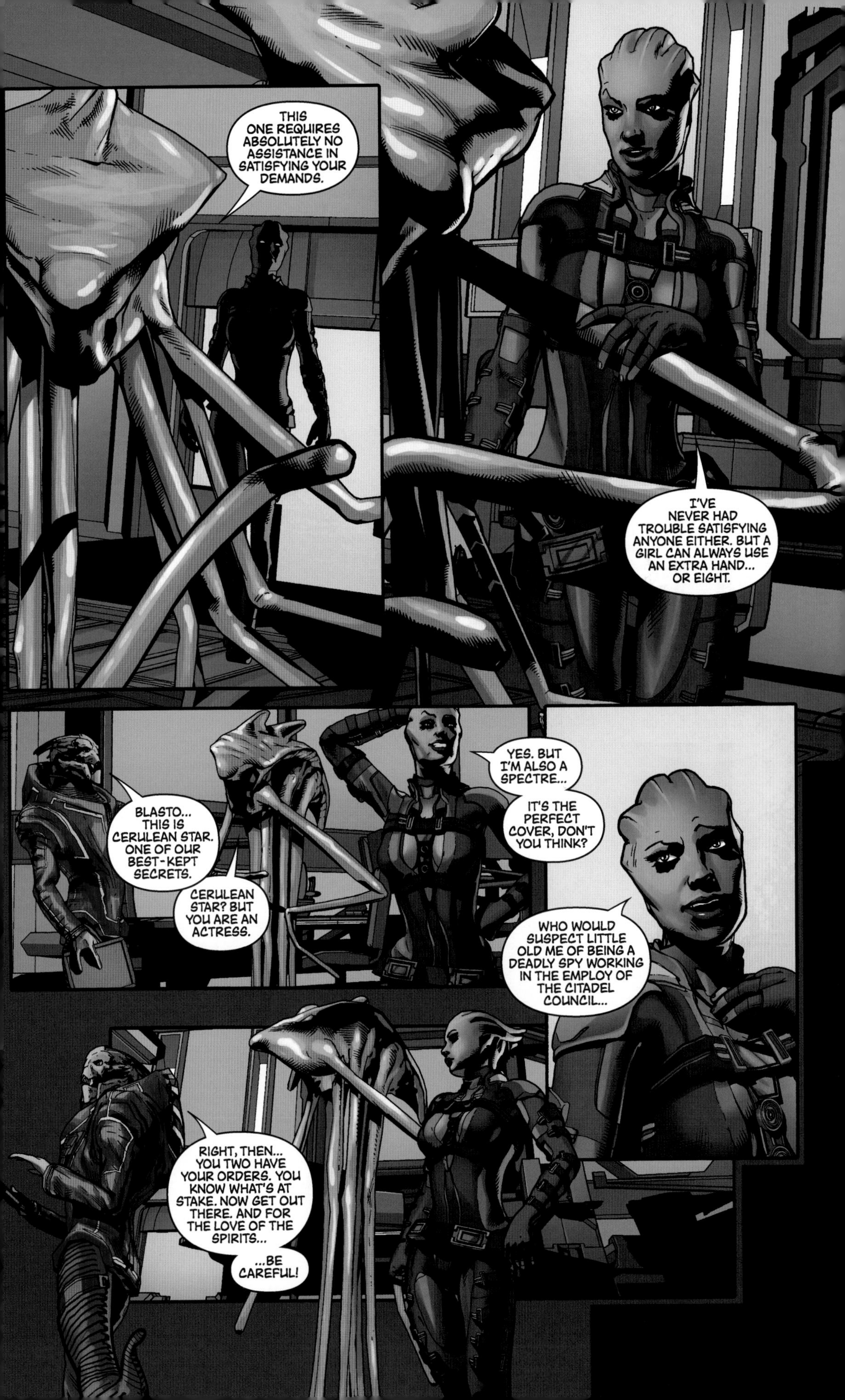
THIS ONE REQUIRES ABSOLUTELY NO ASSISTANCE IN SATISFYING YOUR DEMANDS.
I'VE NEVER HAD TROUBLE SATISFYING ANYONE EITHER. BUT A GIRL CAN ALWAYS USE AN EXTRA HAND... OR EIGHT.
BLASTO... THIS IS CERULEAN STAR. ONE OF OUR BEST-KEPT SECRETS.
CERULEAN STAR? BUT YOU ARE AN ACTRESS.
YES. BUT I'M ALSO A SPECTRE...
IT'S THE PERFECT COVER, DON'T YOU THINK?
WHO WOULD SUSPECT LITTLE OLD ME OF BEING A DEADLY SPY WORKING IN THE EMPLOY OF THE CITADEL COUNCIL...
RIGHT, THEN... YOU TWO HAVE YOUR ORDERS. YOU KNOW WHAT'S AT STAKE. NOW GET OUT THERE. AND FOR THE LOVE OF THE SPIRITS...
...BE CAREFUL!

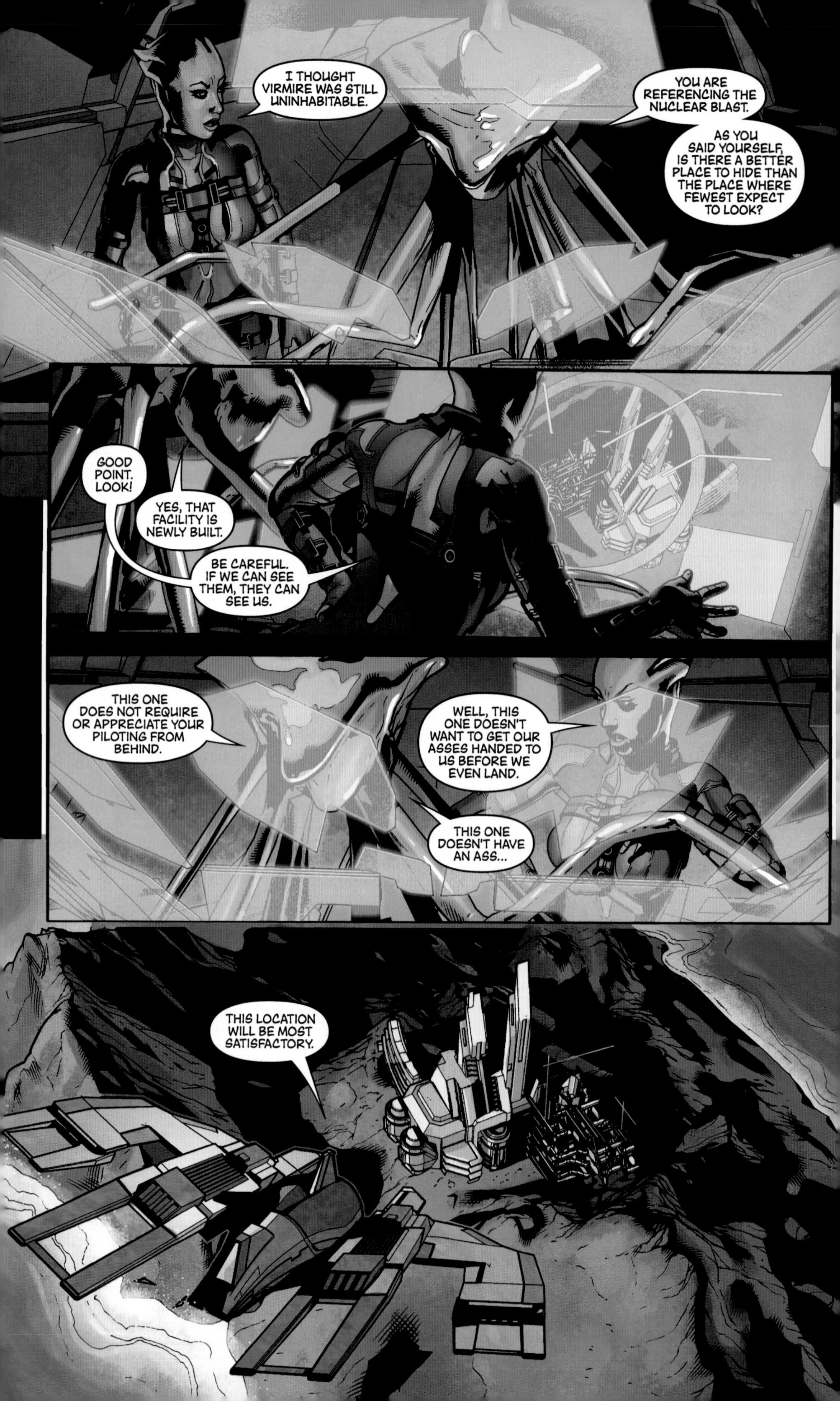
I THOUGHT VIRMIRE WAS STILL UNINHABITABLE.
YOU ARE REFERENCING THE NUCLEAR BLAST.
AS YOU SAID YOURSELF, IS THERE A BETTER PLACE TO HIDE THAN THE PLACE WHERE FEWEST EXPECT TO LOOK?
GOOD POINT. LOOK!
YES, THAT FACILITY IS NEWLY BUILT.
BE CAREFUL. IF WE CAN SEE THEM, THEY CAN SEE US.
THIS ONE DOES NOT REQUIRE OR APPRECIATE YOUR PILOTING FROM BEHIND.
WELL, THIS ONE DOESN'T WANT TO GET OUR ASSES HANDED TO US BEFORE WE EVEN LAND.
THIS ONE DOESN'T HAVE AN ASS...
THIS LOCATION WILL BE MOST SATISFACTORY.

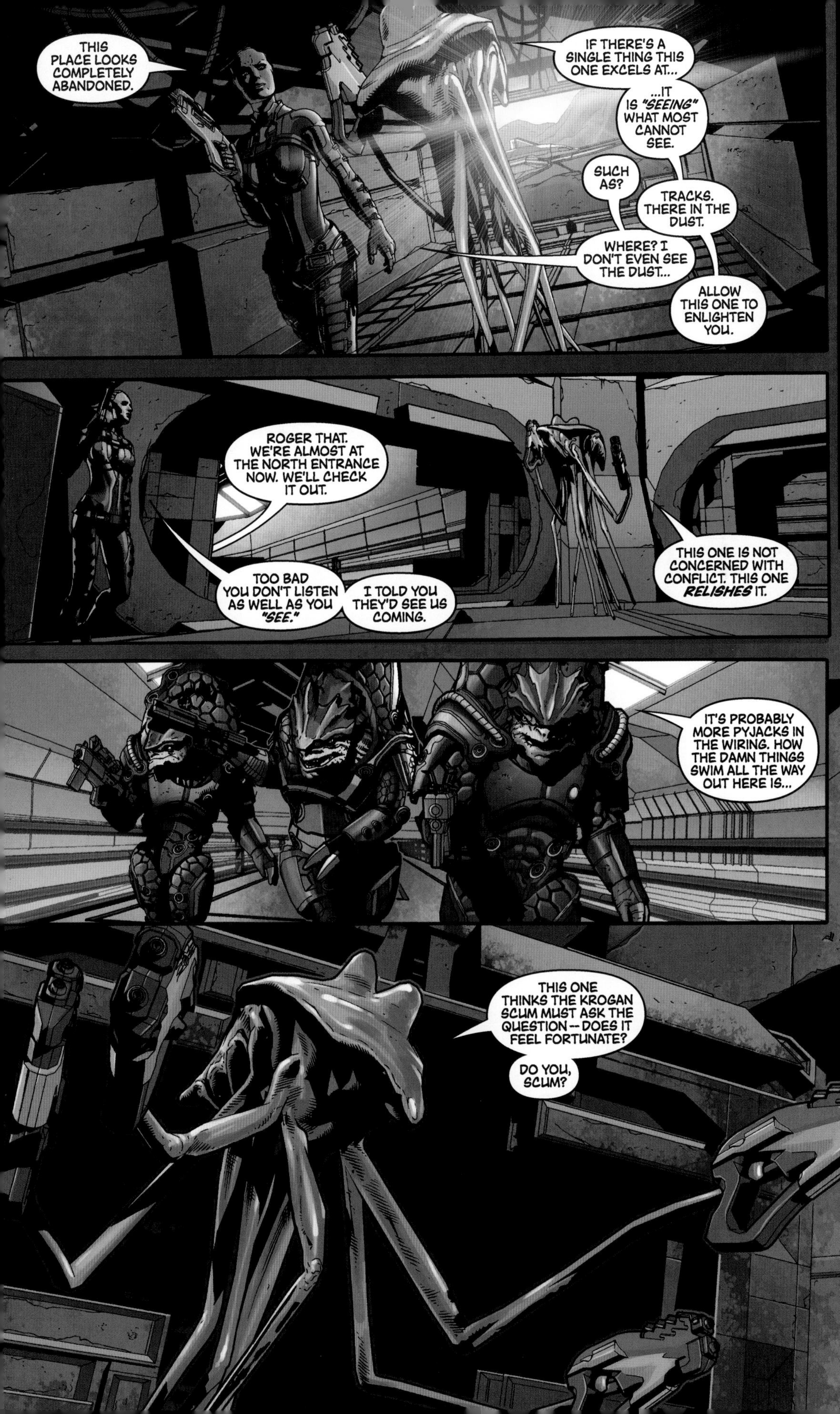
THIS PLACE LOOKS COMPLETELY ABANDONED.
IF THERE'S A SINGLE THING THIS ONE EXCELS AT...
...IT IS *"SEEING"* WHAT MOST CANNOT SEE.
SUCH AS?
TRACKS. THERE IN THE DUST.
WHERE? I DON'T EVEN SEE THE DUST...
ALLOW THIS ONE TO ENLIGHTEN YOU.
ROGER THAT. WE'RE ALMOST AT THE NORTH ENTRANCE NOW. WE'LL CHECK IT OUT.
TOO BAD YOU DON'T LISTEN AS WELL AS YOU *"SEE."*
I TOLD YOU THEY'D SEE US COMING.
THIS ONE IS NOT CONCERNED WITH CONFLICT. THIS ONE ***RELISHES*** IT.
IT'S PROBABLY MORE PYJACKS IN THE WIRING. HOW THE DAMN THINGS SWIM ALL THE WAY OUT HERE IS...
THIS ONE THINKS THE KROGAN SCUM MUST ASK THE QUESTION -- DOES IT FEEL FORTUNATE?
DO YOU, SCUM?

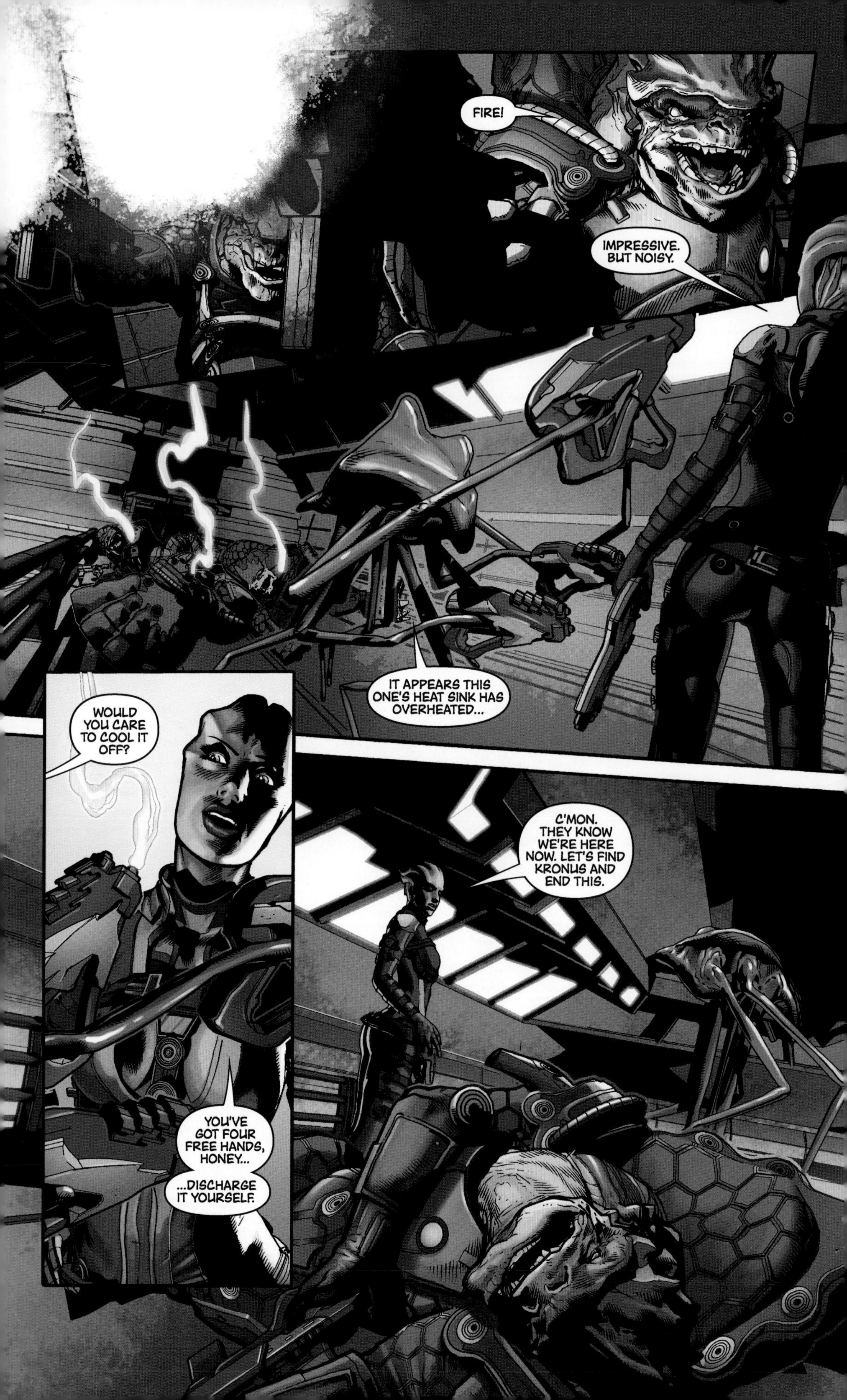
FIRE!
IMPRESSIVE. BUT NOISY.
IT APPEARS THIS ONE'S HEAT SINK HAS OVERHEATED...
WOULD YOU CARE TO COOL IT OFF?
C'MON. THEY KNOW WE'RE HERE NOW. LET'S FIND KRONUS AND END THIS.
YOU'VE GOT FOUR FREE HANDS, HONEY...
...DISCHARGE IT YOURSELF.

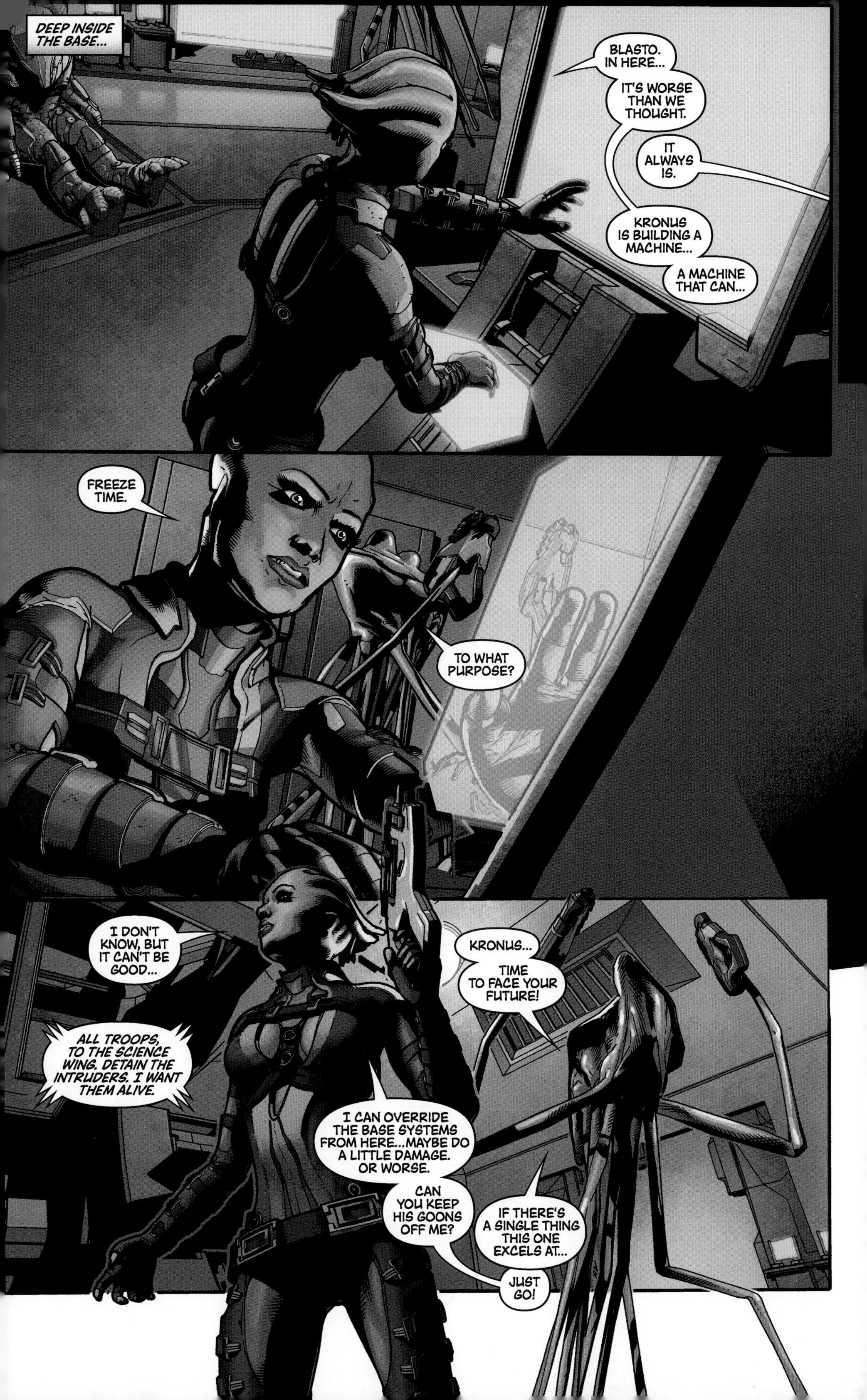
DEEP INSIDE THE BASE...
BLASTO. IN HERE...
IT'S WORSE THAN WE THOUGHT.
IT ALWAYS IS.
KRONUS IS BUILDING A MACHINE...
A MACHINE THAT CAN...
FREEZE TIME.
TO WHAT PURPOSE?
I DON'T KNOW, BUT IT CAN'T BE GOOD...
ALL TROOPS, TO THE SCIENCE WING. DETAIN THE INTRUDERS. I WANT THEM ALIVE.
KRONUS...
TIME TO FACE YOUR FUTURE!
I CAN OVERRIDE THE BASE SYSTEMS FROM HERE...MAYBE DO A LITTLE DAMAGE. OR WORSE.
CAN YOU KEEP HIS GOONS OFF ME?
IF THERE'S A SINGLE THING THIS ONE EXCELS AT...
JUST GO!

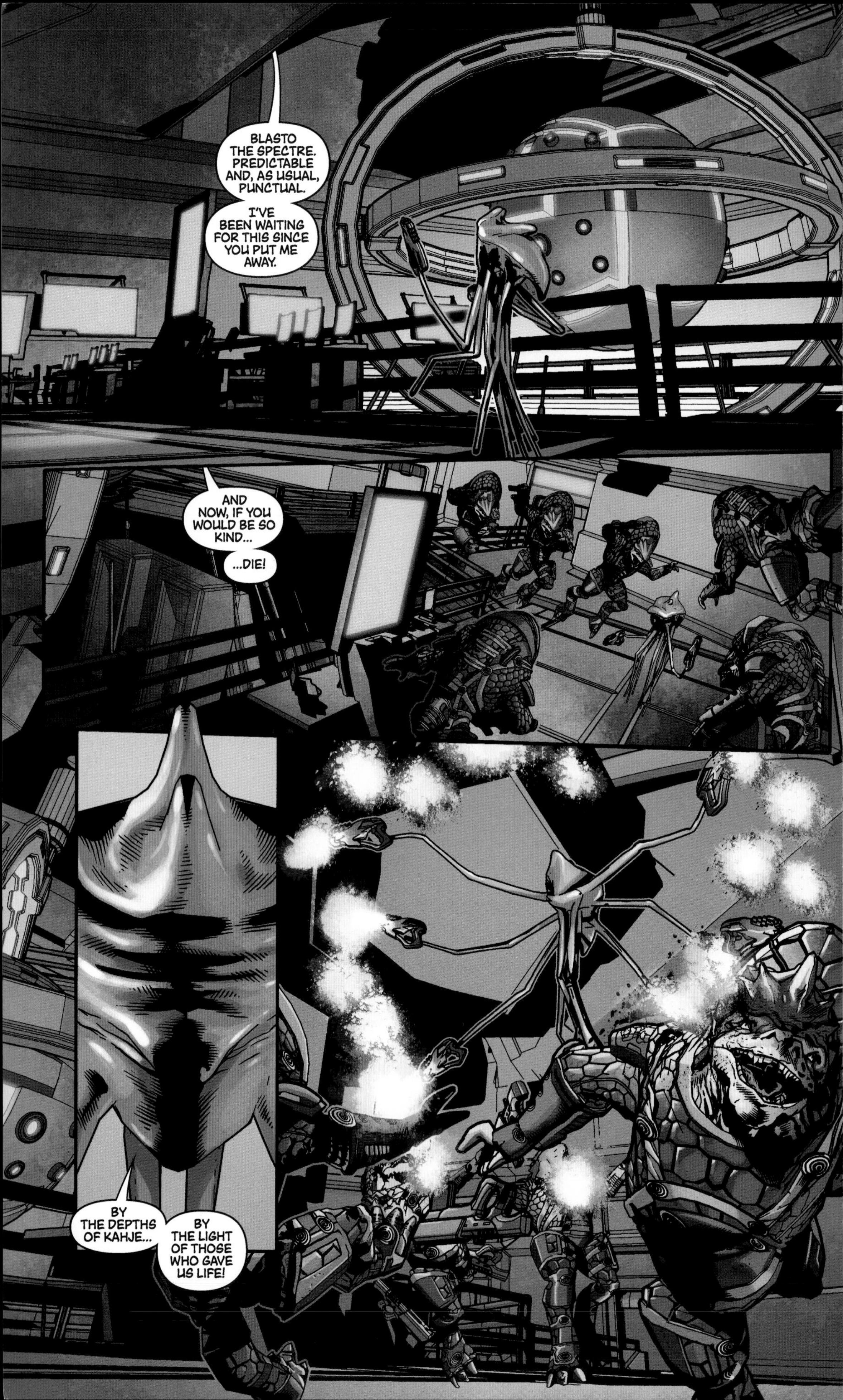
BLASTO THE SPECTRE. PREDICTABLE AND, AS USUAL, PUNCTUAL.
I'VE BEEN WAITING FOR THIS SINCE YOU PUT ME AWAY.
AND NOW, IF YOU WOULD BE SO KIND...
...DIE!
BY THE DEPTHS OF KAHJE...
BY THE LIGHT OF THOSE WHO GAVE US LIFE!

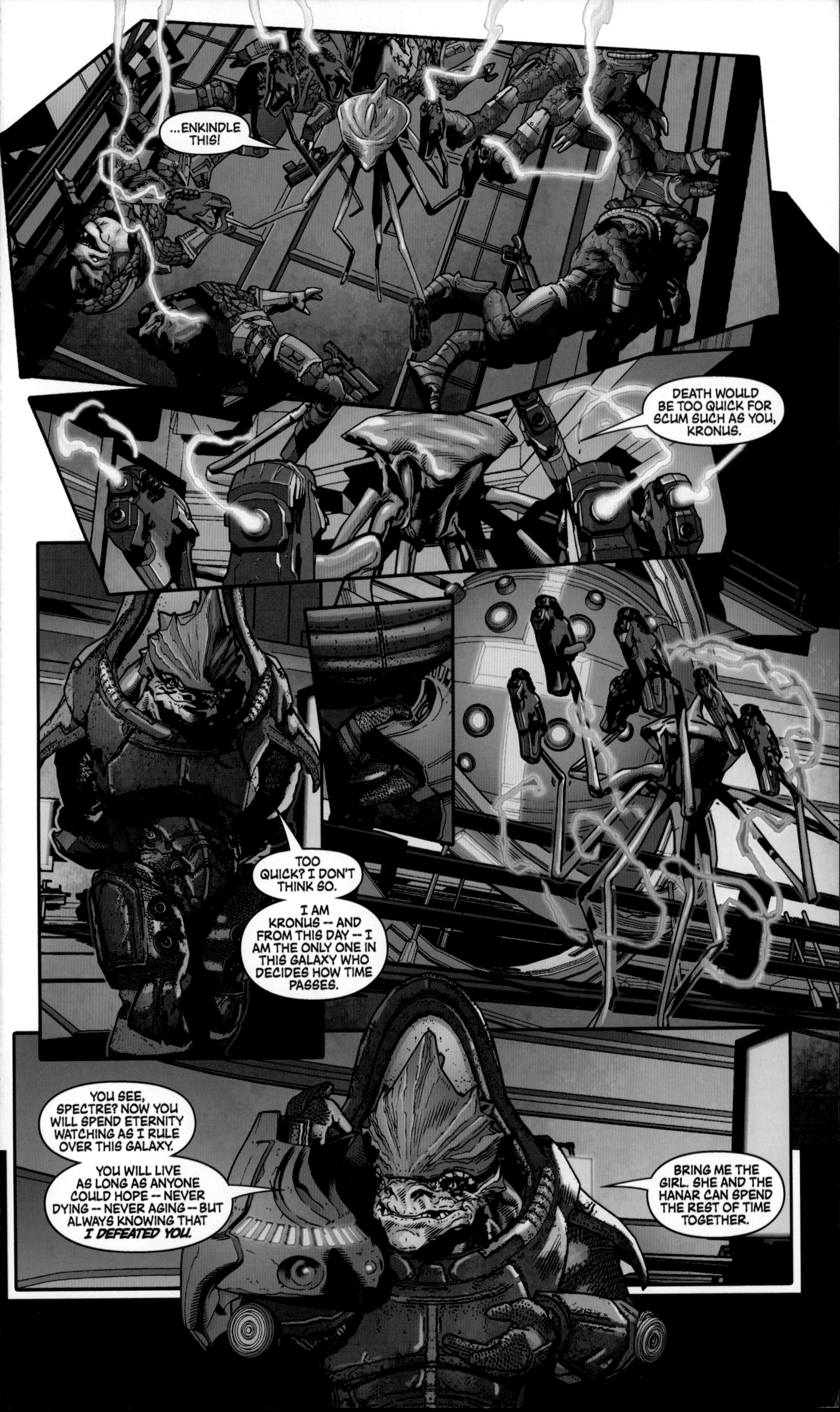
...ENKINDLE THIS!
DEATH WOULD BE TOO QUICK FOR SCUM SUCH AS YOU, KRONUS.
TOO QUICK? I DON'T THINK SO.
I AM KRONUS -- AND FROM THIS DAY -- I AM THE ONLY ONE IN THIS GALAXY WHO DECIDES HOW TIME PASSES.
YOU SEE, SPECTRE? NOW YOU WILL SPEND ETERNITY WATCHING AS I RULE OVER THIS GALAXY.
YOU WILL LIVE AS LONG AS ANYONE COULD HOPE -- NEVER DYING -- NEVER AGING -- BUT ALWAYS KNOWING THAT *I DEFEATED YOU.*
BRING ME THE GIRL. SHE AND THE HANAR CAN SPEND THE REST OF TIME TOGETHER.

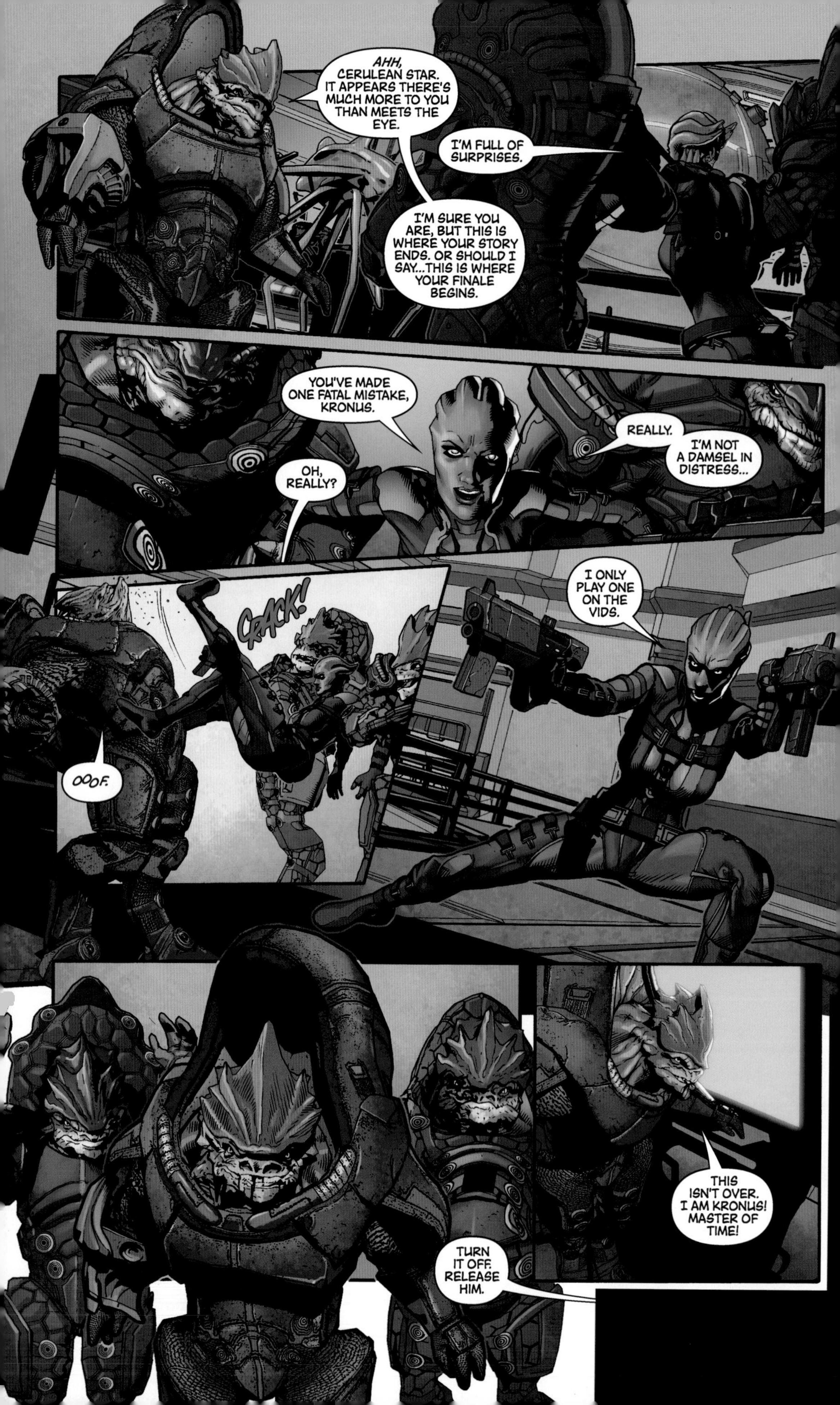
AHH, CERULEAN STAR. IT APPEARS THERE'S MUCH MORE TO YOU THAN MEETS THE EYE.
I'M FULL OF SURPRISES.
I'M SURE YOU ARE, BUT THIS IS WHERE YOUR STORY ENDS. OR SHOULD I SAY...THIS IS WHERE YOUR FINALE BEGINS.
YOU'VE MADE ONE FATAL MISTAKE, KRONUS.
OH, REALLY?
REALLY.
I'M NOT A DAMSEL IN DISTRESS...
CRACK!
OOOF.
I ONLY PLAY ONE ON THE VIDS.
THIS ISN'T OVER. I AM KRONUS! MASTER OF TIME!
TURN IT OFF. RELEASE HIM.

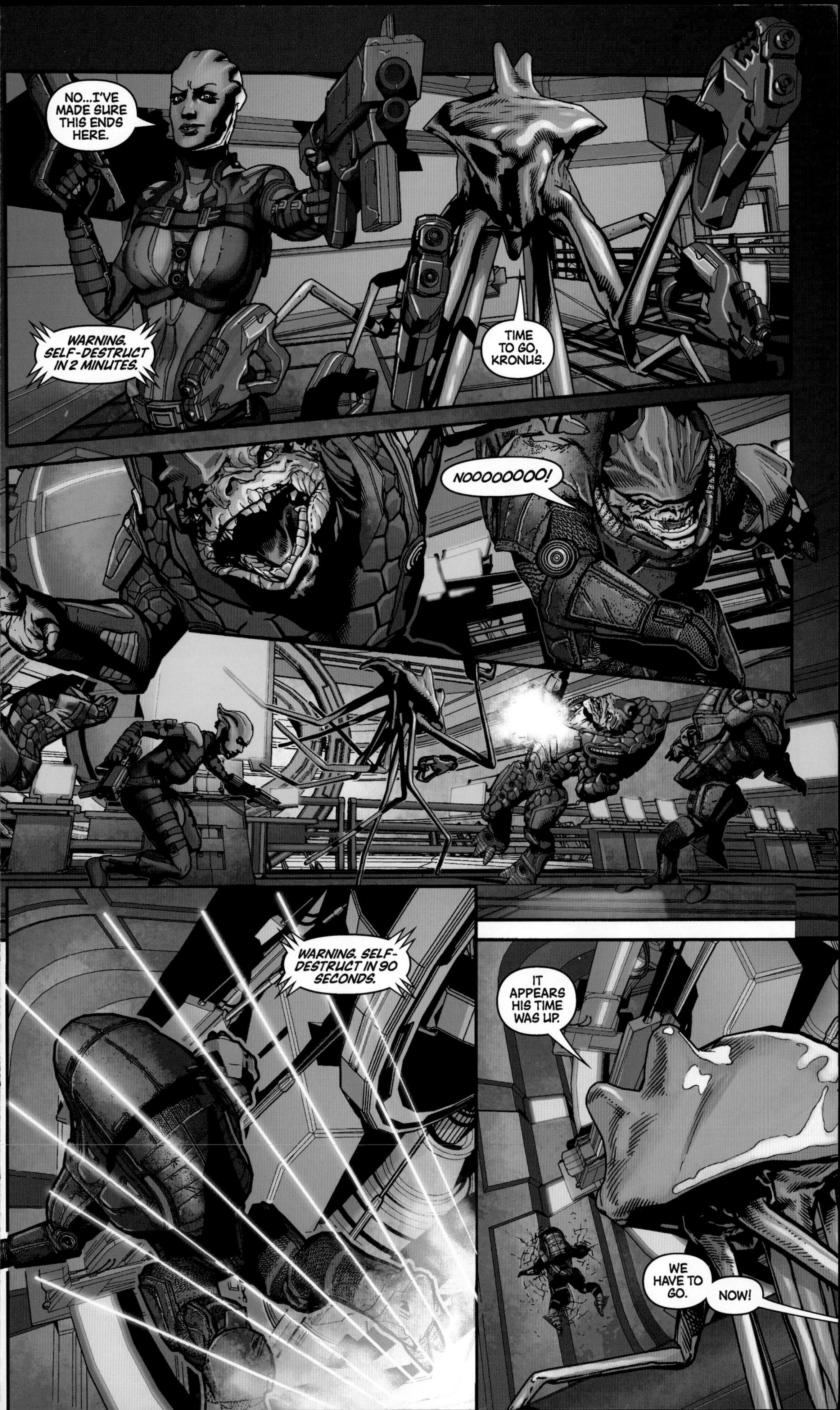
NO...I'VE MADE SURE THIS ENDS HERE.
WARNING. SELF-DESTRUCT IN 2 MINUTES.
TIME TO GO, KRONUS.
NOOOOOOOO!
WARNING. SELF-DESTRUCT IN 90 SECONDS.
IT APPEARS HIS TIME WAS UP.
WE HAVE TO GO.
NOW!

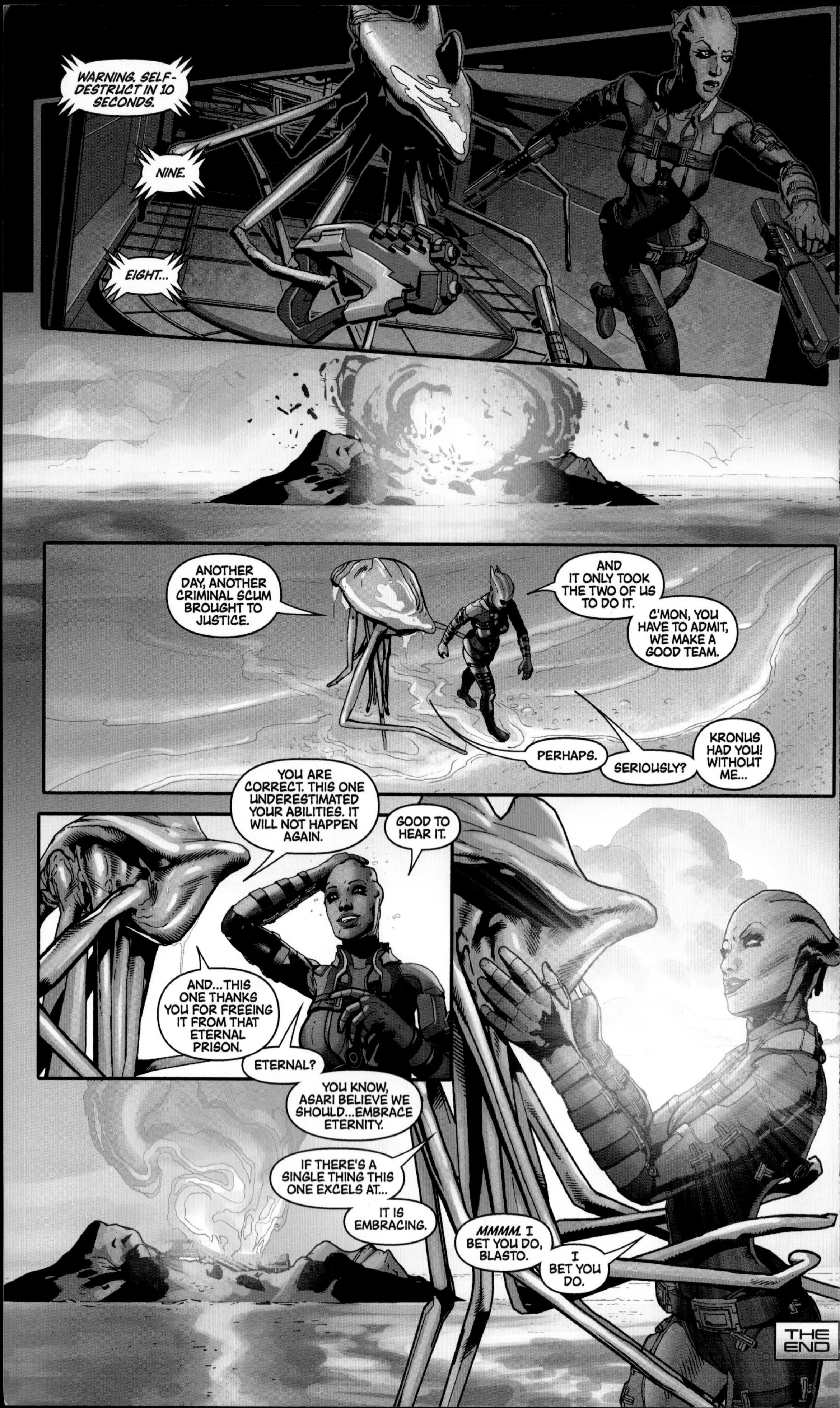
WARNING. SELF-DESTRUCT IN 10 SECONDS.
NINE.
EIGHT...
ANOTHER DAY, ANOTHER CRIMINAL SCUM BROUGHT TO JUSTICE.
AND IT ONLY TOOK THE TWO OF US TO DO IT.
C'MON, YOU HAVE TO ADMIT, WE MAKE A GOOD TEAM.
PERHAPS.
SERIOUSLY?
KRONUS HAD YOU! WITHOUT ME...
YOU ARE CORRECT. THIS ONE UNDERESTIMATED YOUR ABILITIES. IT WILL NOT HAPPEN AGAIN.
GOOD TO HEAR IT.
AND...THIS ONE THANKS YOU FOR FREEING IT FROM THAT ETERNAL PRISON.
ETERNAL?
YOU KNOW, ASARI BELIEVE WE SHOULD...EMBRACE ETERNITY.
IF THERE'S A SINGLE THING THIS ONE EXCELS AT...
IT IS EMBRACING.
MMMM. I BET YOU DO, BLASTO.
I BET YOU DO.
THE END

EXPLORE THE MASS EFFECT UNIVERSE WITH DARK HORSE!

Created in close collaboration with BioWare and the writers and artists of the games, Dark Horse's *Mass Effect* graphic novels and merchandise are essential companions to gaming's deepest universe!

MASS EFFECT: REDEMPTION
ISBN 978-59582-481-3

MASS EFFECT: EVOLUTION
ISBN 978-59582-759-3

MASS EFFECT: INVASION
ISBN 978-59582-867-5

MASS EFFECT: HOMEWORLDS
ISBN 978-1-59582-955-9

$16.99 EACH

SX3 ALLIANCE FIGHTER
ISBN 978-1-61659-296-7 | **$29.99**

ALLIANCE NORMANDY SR-1
ISBN 978-1-61659-368-1 | **$34.99**

TURIAN CRUISER
ISBN 978-1-61659-395-7 | **$34.99**

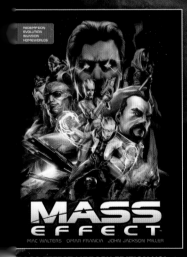 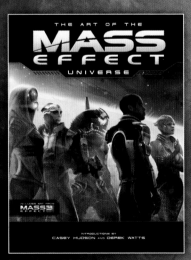 

MASS EFFECT LIBRARY EDITION VOL. 1
ISBN 978-1-61655-111-7 | **$59.99**

ART OF THE MASS EFFECT UNIVERSE
ISBN 978-59582-768-5 | **$39.99**

MASS EFFECT: FOUNDATION VOL. 1
ISBN 978-1-61655-270-1 | **$16.99**

ALSO FROM DARK HORSE AND BIOWARE

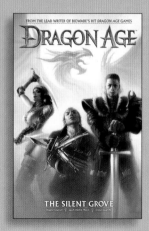

FROM THE LEAD WRITER OF BIOWARE'S HIT DRAGON AGE GAMES
DRAGON AGE
THE SILENT GROVE

DRAGON AGE:
THE SILENT GROVE

David Gaider, Alexander Freed, Chad Hardin

Dragon Age: The Silent Grove is the perfect introduction to BioWare's dark fantasy universe! In this essential, canonical story from David Gaider, lead writer of the games, King Alistair, accompanied only by rogues Isabela and Varric, embarks on a quest deep inside the borders of Antiva—a nation of assassins! Together, they will encounter a prison break, dragons, the mysterious Witch of the Wilds, and one of the greatest secrets in the history of the world!

$14.99 | ISBN 978-1-59582-916-0

FROM THE LEAD WRITER OF BIOWARE'S HIT DRAGON AGE GAMES
DRAGON AGE
THOSE WHO SPEAK

DRAGON AGE:
THOSE WHO SPEAK

David Gaider, Alexander Freed, Chad Hardin

With the pirate Isabela's dark past laid bare, she must resolve to escape the Qunari dungeon or lose herself forever, even as King Alistair must take up arms against an old ally if he is to have any hope of uncovering the fate of his father!

$14.99 | ISBN 978-1-61655-053-0

DRAGON AGE II

$4.99
UPC 7 61568 19140 0

DRAGON AGE II
PLAYING CARDS

The BioWare development team helped Dark Horse design a fantastic deck of *Dragon Age II* playing cards. The detailed artwork captures the look and feel of the game, and the set is a perfect addition to your *Dragon Age* game collection!

DRAGON AGE II EMBROIDERED PATCHES

Chantry, Kirkwall, Qunari, Templars

Collect all four embroidered patches from BioWare's world of *Dragon Age II*. Each patch is beautifully embroidered with the logos representing the Qunari, the Chantry, Kirkwall, and the Templars. Each patch sold separately.

$4.99 | UPC 7 61568 21343 0

$4.99 | UPC 7 61568 21344 7

$4.99 | UPC 7 61568 21345 4

$4.99 | UPC 7 61568 21346 1

DRAGON AGE II
FLEMETH STATUE

$49.99 | UPC 7 61568 19139 4

DRAGON AGE II FLEMETH STATUE

Master sculptor Joe Menna has taken BioWare's game files and painstakingly created a beautiful, detailed facsimile of Flemeth. The game developers worked with Dark Horse every step of the way. Sure to impress any *Dragon Age* fan!